A CAJUN IN FRANCE

A Cajun in France

Journeys to Assimilations

Sidney P. Bellard

Bellard Books

Published by Bellard Books

Print ISBN 978-1-5398-3628-5

Typesetting services by BOOKOW.COM

ACKNOWLEDGMENTS

As a neophyte, I thought that writing a book was a process where the writer would toil in isolation until magically, a book would materialize. Certainly, most writers do toil in isolation, but I quickly learned that the process of bringing a book to fruition requires an army of support. I am especially grateful for the contributions of the following:

My wife Freddie who supported my efforts despite patiently enduring countless hours listening to a language she didn't understand while our French friends and I solved the problems of the world.

Mary Perrin, who meticulously did the final edit and Warren Perrin who did historical verification.

Long time friends Dr. Sam Dauzat, PhD and Dr. Jo Ann Dauzat, PhD who encouraged me to write this book in addition to providing valuable guidance and reading my very rough drafts.

My father, Sidney Bellard, Sr. whose countless stories provided me with detailed depictions of the Cajun sharecropper lifestyle of the early 20th century.

My sisters Verna, Bertha, Linda, and Aunt Hazel who provided me with family history details.

My long-time friend, Sam Bella, who often guided me to positive directions.

The many French friends who treated Freddie and me with kindness and generosity, especially those from Rennes, Strasbourg, Annecy, Apremont, and Caussade.

My cousin, El, and his wife Judy who spent many hours reading and reviewing my early text.

The Northshore Literary Society for providing me with valuable information on the writing process.

Author, O'Neal DeNoux, who gave me many tips on the publishing process.

Marilyn Hebert who gave my book a final, neutral reading before publication.

Finally, our black standard poodle, T-Boy, who kept me company during every word that I wrote as he patiently waited for a treat, a ride in the car, or just a pat on his head.

CONTENTS

PREFACE

Inscription on the Statue of Liberty:

Give me your tired, your poor,
Your huddled masses, yearning to breathe free,
The wretched refuse of your teeming shore,
Send these, the homeless, tempest-tossed to me,
I lift my lamp beside the golden door

Emma Lazarus

THESE words evoke sentimental pride for millions of Americans, as indeed they should. The United States has given opportunity and freedom to untold millions of immigrants from all corners of the world who were in search of political, religious, and economic freedom. It is indisputable that an overwhelming majority of immigrants were relatively quickly assimilated and went on to achieve their dreams. However, before this success in assimilation was achieved, there were dues and initiation fees to be paid, a big one being the language barrier that relegated most of them to the most menial jobs or farming. Nevertheless, they worked hard, and often launched their children into mainstream America.

There were barriers of prejudice to overcome, as many Americans were suspicious of immigrants and often regarded them as inferior. Immigrants regularly became the object of jokes and putdowns as there were Irish jokes, Polish jokes, Italian jokes—name the nationality or ethnic group and without fail, there were jokes and denigrating adjectives custom-made for them.

Sidney "Pierre" Bellard's first language was Cajun French. On his father's side he was first to finish high school and to graduate from a university. His father died at age 91 in 2002 and spoke only a little broken English and could only sign his name. His mother, who died in 1987, spoke even less English. They never achieved assimilation. These facts in themselves are not unusual as there are millions of recent immigrants in the U.S. struggling toward assimilation and a better life. What is unusual is that Pierre's ancestors have been in America since 1632 and in the United States since before there was a United States. They were honest, hard-working Americans. How can a family who had been in the U.S. for over ten generations not have one of its members reach literacy and assimilation until the 1960's? Those who are knowledgeable about Louisiana may know that, unfortunately, this late assimilation is not a rarity. The French-speaking Acadians came to Louisiana with a mistrust of the British who burned their homes in Nova Scotia and forcefully deported and dispersed them. After this, the Acadians wanted to find a sanctuary to propagate their culture in isolation. After three generations or so, they lost memory of the expulsion by the British, but by then many were illiterate French-speaking sharecroppers or subsistence farmers which continued to keep them in isolation from mainstream America. The agrarian economy provided their meager livelihoods, but despite being citizens and having been in Louisiana well before statehood, they had not assimilated into mainstream culture. They lived in a parallel world.

Pierre's journey to literacy and assimilation was not an easy one. There were many obstacles to conquer, including the language barrier, the lack of family educational values, and of course, the feeling of inferiority possessed by many children of similar background because they were different from mainstream Americans. Eventually, he developed two major drives that were antithetical to each other, two drives he did not become fully aware of until the writing of this book. The first was to master the English language and become literate in it, and the second was to achieve literacy in his first language, French. Generally, in his generation, French was often dropped once English was learned because most Cajuns did not want to be reminded of the ridicule and insecurities they felt during childhood. Additionally, speaking French in school, while not prohibited in his life outside of school, was discouraged. But, for Pierre, dropping French was not an option as he would need to communicate with his parents for as long as they lived, therefore being bilingual was a necessity. His quest for French literacy would ultimately lead him to make 17 voyages to France and to develop very special relationships with many French nationals.

Except for Native Americans, everyone in North America or the New World is an immigrant or a descendant of immigrants. It is the author's desire that readers will become more aware of their heritage and respect the difficult transitions their ancestors had to make to achieve the American dream for themselves and their children. Finally, Pierre invites you to discover France and its people through his experiences and impressions, both of which have enriched his life immeasurably.

INTRODUCTION

"A people without the knowledge of their history, origin and culture are like a tree without roots"

Marcus Garvey.

SOME of the earliest Europeans to colonize the North American continent were a small group of 60 French families who arrived in what is present-day Nova Scotia (then Acadie) in the early 17th century. The contest between England and France to colonize North America became a fierce one and a continuation of their centuries of power struggles. The French were concentrated in Canada and the English were mostly located in the Atlantic Seaboard region. The 60 families were composed mostly of families from northwest France, but some came from other regions such as Burgundy and some from other areas. The colonists found in Acadie a hostile environment of very cold winters, poor soils for agriculture, and a large population of Indians. The first tasks were to build a fort to protect the colony and to construct shelters for the families. A food source was necessary which meant agriculture, but they would have starved waiting for harvest. Fortunately, the Indians were friendly and provided them with food and showed them how to survive in their environment by hunting and fishing.

The colonists, who became known as Acadians, quickly discovered that Nova Scotia was composed of sandy, rocky soils punctuated by bogs and forests that were not conducive to successful agriculture. They found the best lands to be along the seacoast, but these were too narrow to produce the food they needed for survival. They reclaimed the land they needed from the sea by building a series of small levees in which gates were installed that would allow water to flow to the sea, but not allow salt water to flow back towards the inhabited land. They brought this method with them from France where they had harvested salt from seawater. Due to the high salt content, the reclaimed land had to lie fallow for several years while the dike system did its job before it would be suitable for agriculture. In the meantime, the newly-recovered land was used as pasture to transition it to agricultural use. As the colony grew, more land was reclaimed, and the Acadians became self-sufficient. Animal stocks of cattle, sheep, pigs, and chickens completed their nutritional needs. They stored extra production of grains in communal depots to share with families who did not produce enough or suffered some catastrophe.

Through hard work and industriousness, the colonists became successful and established villages in present-day Nova Scotia and New Brunswick. A high fecundity rate and successful agricultural operations produced a rapid population growth which doubled every 20 years. They had achieved their dream—freedom from a peasant existence and the onerous French monarchy. They were very content and in control of their destiny. They enjoyed 80 years of this contentment that ended in 1710 with the British conquest of

French Acadie. The Acadians would endure 45 years of British rule during which time they would continue, nevertheless, to prosper. The problem was that the British wanted an unconditional oath of allegiance from the Acadians to the British Crown; however, in 1730, they had been allowed to give a conditional oath exempting them from military service in any future wars against the French. They were very resistant to this new idea of unconditional allegiance.

The French and Indian War (1755–1763), also called the Seven Years' War, would eventually lead to the disruption of the Acadians' paradise. The British colonial officers suspected the Acadians of aiding the French; consequently, in the period from 1755–1764, the Acadians were expelled from Nova Scotia. This expulsion resulted in tragic consequences as over 11,000 Acadians were rounded up, placed on ships (some unseaworthy) and dispersed to the Atlantic seaboard. Virginia refused to receive them and sent their allotment of Acadians to England because they were considered British subjects. The homes of the Acadians were then burned to prevent their return. Some families were separated and at least 2,000 drowned, died of disease, or starved at sea.

After the war, the Acadians tried to resettle in many other places such as the Caribbean, South America, and the Falkland Islands. The Acadians were unhappy no matter where the British deposited them. Those deposited along the Atlantic coast were forced to live among the English colonists who often regarded them as lazy, ignorant, and inferior refugees. The Acadians sent to France were no more pleased as they were already four to five generations removed from France, and because of their taste of independence, were unwilling to deal with the French monarchy and the unfertile soils proffered. The Acadians had become, in essence, francophone North Americans—a whole new ethnicity.

In 1765, a group of 202 Acadian émigrés voluntarily sought refuge in Louisiana which was Spanish-owned at that time due to the Seven Years War. These Acadians were given a good welcome along with land, tools, seed, and animals to initiate their farmsteads. They sent word to relatives in France, England, and the Atlantic coast about the great opportunities in Louisiana. Additionally, the Spanish government recruited Acadian exiles in France and gave them passage to Louisiana. The Acadians felt very fortunate finding themselves in an extremely fertile territory with no need to reclaim land from the sea. Fish and game were abundant everywhere, and those long, cold winters were no more. Most of the inhabitants of Louisiana at that time were French and Creoles with whom the Acadians could communicate. Most importantly, they found a land where they could protect their culture

They adapted to their new home and quickly carved out farmland from wooded and prairie areas. They built settlements where they were in the majority and saw no need to learn another language. Later, with the attainment of statehood at the turn of the 19th century, many English-speaking Americans came to Louisiana. With the Great Expulsion still fresh in their memory, the Acadians were considerably less than enthusiastic about this intrusion. But they prospered, produced large families, and changed little until the 20th century. One thing that did change: they became known as Cajuns instead of Acadians.

While most Cajuns worked small farms, fished, or trapped for a livelihood, some became cattle farmers or entrepreneurs who were able to gain financial success, learn English, and enter mainstream culture. This group produced leaders in the field of politics, education, and business. It was not until the Great Depression's grip was broken by WWII, the enlistment of Cajuns in the military, and the employment of many Cajuns in the oil industry that a large number of Cajuns were able to experience upward mobility and assimilation. Unfortunately, many Cajuns didn't catch that train and remained sharecropper farmers.

How to Read this Book

- Many good, avid readers often go to Chapter I to start reading a book. This book is best understood and appreciated by reading the preface, the historical orientation, and the prologue first. These really help to prepare the reader for what is to come in the book. This is a case where "front matter" really matters.

- This book is a non-fiction memoir, but written to read much like a novel. Additionally, it has a prologue and an epilogue which are usually found in books of fiction. These are also non-fiction, set in France, and serve to further introduce the book and to give it closure.

- Real names were used for family members and close friends. Others were given fictitious names to protect their privacy.

- Finally, unlike most memoirs or autobiographies, which are usually written in 1st person, I chose to write this book in 3rd person. My reason for doing so was that it, in a sense, removed me from myself to provide a measure of objectivity. It was somewhat like I was sitting in a crow's nest watching myself making my journeys. I hope these unorthodox techniques work for you.

PROLOGUE

"Fields of lavender to infinity – seas of blue, indigo, turquoise & green – exquisite wines – dazzling skies – delectable cuisine – hilltop villages – friendly people – strewn with the DNA of antiquity. Who could come here only once?"

SPB

Provence, France 2014

SIDNEY "Pierre" Bellard and his wife, Freddie, were in the midst of a great vacation in their favorite region of France, Provence. That morning, they had just visited Les Baux de Provence, a hilltop village of historic ruins and shopping opportunities along with breathtaking views of the gray-green olive groves and vineyards below. Leaving Les Baux, they then stopped nearby to do some wine tasting at a winery called "Mas de la Dame" where they tasted and bought a few bottles of its excellent wine. Being hungry from the energy expended walking up and down the steep, cobbled streets of the perched village, they drove a few miles to St. Remy for lunch.

They found Saint-Remy-de-Provence to be an interesting town

and had time to explore a little before lunch. They saw where Nostradamus, famous seer, apothecary, astrological consultant and translator was born in 1503. They learned about another of St. Remy's famous former citizens, Vincent Van Gogh, a Dutch painter who spent one year in an asylum there in 1889-1890. While in the asylum, he painted 142 paintings, including "Starry Night." As they continued ambling through the streets, they noticed several artists working on painting buildings and street scenes. Pierre mentioned to Freddie, "Strange, we have visited many towns where famous artists painted in the past, and we often saw aspiring artists painting in the streets. Do you think they believe the spirit of Van Gogh and the others are still lurking here and will perhaps seize their psyche enabling them to paint masterpieces?"

"Oh, you're crazy."

"I wasn't before we got here; perhaps Van Gogh's insanity spirit also hovers over this town."

They chuckled and decided it was time to eat. Fortunately, restaurants are never scarce in French towns, but the most difficult task is to choose one which would have something each would enjoy. For Pierre, it was easy, as his Cajun heritage prepared him well for French cuisine. On the other hand, Freddie, who was of Scotch/Irish/German origins and reared in a large city in Alabama, had a difficult time with it despite having been in France several times. Pierre had vowed to himself that he would stretch her culinary horizons, but he had not been successful. She almost always had a hot goat cheese salad. Well, that was a little progress, as French goat cheese is somewhat non-pedestrian and even mildly exotic. Pierre had goat cheese salads several times and enjoyed them very much, but there were so many other dishes to enjoy.

They found a suitable restaurant and sat, as always, at an outdoor table, this time under an umbrella under a sycamore tree (a plane tree in France). The waiter was quite busy setting up tables, but that was not a problem as they were on vacation and had all the time in the world. Besides, noon and lunch were time to rest at midday, like the French did. Their table, if they so desired, was theirs until the restaurant closed at 2:00 P.M., and they would not be rushed to make the table available for other customers.

They observed their little environment and took in the sights of the huge omnipresent plane trees which always evoked childhood memories for Pierre, who as a young boy had the compulsion to climb every tree within his reach. He remembered how smooth the sycamore limbs were after the tree had shed its outer bark as well as the hard round balls with stems attached which came in handy to whack someone in the head—usually a classmate or his younger sister. The beautiful, large, star-shaped yellow-green leaves provided, in early spring the color of life which excommunicated the dead, brown and gray colors of winter for a glorious nine months. It caused a veritable resurrection of his spirit.

They never tired of observing the quaint architecture that abounded in every corner of France. In Provence, it was normal to see plain stone structures decorated with rainbow colored flowers, vines, shutters—some of fresh, bright colors and others aged, faded, crackled—and romantic. Often, the provincial sun and shadows collaborated to work their magic by granting golden glowing tones and charm to structures that were only mundane moments before. Finally, the blanket of antiquity put on its finishing touches which made them irresistible to tourists of all nationalities.

Finally, this was an excellent time to people-watch as everyone in town was out and about searching for lunch during the two-hour break. Pierre often wondered if people watched them. He could imagine them saying, "Don't look now, but see that couple over there? They look strange—look at the way they hold their forks— they must be Americans." The surrounding tables were beginning to fill up quickly with people from the local stores and businesses. Some were obviously having business lunches while others were tourists just like they and others were friends enjoying each other's company.

As they were discussing their environment, the waiter came up to take their order. He heard them speaking English, and he imme- diately knew they were American. He addressed them in halting English. Pierre, who spoke excellent French, relieved the waiter by giving his and Freddie's orders in French. Naturally, the waiter was happy not to have to struggle with his limited English to get in his order.

As they waited for their order and people watched, Pierre said, "Did you notice that practically every restaurant we go to has no or few people there when we first arrive, and then hordes of people appear? Do you think we should get compensated for bringing in customers, or, at least, get a free meal?"

"No silly, we didn't bring anybody in; it's just that we're always early."

"Oh well, it was a good idea while it lasted," he murmured.

Of course, they knew better, they just enjoyed being silly.

The waiter came with their orders, and the dishes were gorgeously done, and ample. Pierre's garlic-roasted leg of lamb with sauce came with potatoes and ratatouille decorated with colorful bits of veggies and spices. Freddie's hot goat cheese salad (surprise) was beautifully done with slices of egg, ham, olives, copious amounts of lettuce, walnuts, onions, salad dressing, and, of course real, pungent, goat cheese rounds fried in oil for a crunchy coating. The good news for Pierre was that Freddie never could finish one of these salads, and he would get to finish it. The bad news was that she had usually eaten all the goat cheese. One day, Pierre thought, he would convert her to be a universal scavenger that he was so she could have more opportunities for gastronomical pleasures. Good luck on that.

They enjoyed their lunch as they washed it down with a half-liter pitcher of the house red wine. The waiter came by and asked if they would like dessert. Though the dessert list was tempting, as usual, they declined because they seldom did desserts unless the meal happened to be light and in France, that seldom happened. Pierre told the waiter, "No dessert, but I would like an espresso coffee (called *un petit noir* in Paris)." Small it was, about two thimbles of coffee, but very strong, flavorful, and satisfying. One drank it tiny sips at a time and followed with a bit of the chocolate or almond provided with the coffee. It was a wonderful way to stretch lunch.

With the espresso ritual completed, it was now time for *l'addition* —the check. Pierre motioned for the waiter who came right over with his credit card machine and the check. Pierre gave his credit card, and the waiter processed it. *Le Garçon* gave him the portion to be signed, and Pierre completed the transaction with his signature. Then it happened again; the waiter asked the question that so many other waiters and other French citizens had asked him during the many times he had been in France, "Monsieur, what is your nationality? How did you learn to speak French so well?" Pierre and Freddie looked at each other with an understanding look which meant, "Here we go again." They had often discussed (in jest) that perhaps he should have a printout explaining why he was so fluent in French, especially for an American, and simply give a copy to those interested. Of course, he could never do that as he enjoyed sharing conversations with the French and took every opportunity to do so. He saw this as an opportunity to enhance his language skills. Once again, he gave his canned, mini story of why he spoke French. He told them that he was Cajun and from Louisiana (this rang a bell because French television has done many documentaries on the Cajuns of Louisiana), and had learned French as a first language and later learned English in school, and as an adult had spent a lot of time in France. This response usually satisfied the interested without taking too much of their time; after all, they were working, and Pierre and Freddie were ready to move on to the next destination. Besides, Freddie had heard this story so often that she understood it even though she spoke and understood very little French.

But this particular time was different; Pierre realized more fully that a lot more factors were involved in explaining his ability to speak French other than the ones he gave the waiter. He thought about how his life had been so unusual, especially for an American citizen. After all, wasn't it unusual for a person whose French ancestors had come to America beginning in 1632 to still speak French as a first language? Though unusual, Pierre was not alone in that category as approximately half of his high school graduating class spoke, at least some French, and throughout the rest of Southwest Louisiana, there were a huge number of French speakers in the 1960's. However, the most common experience for most of the millions of other immigrants who came to America was to lose their native language within one or two generations. Finally, Pierre wanted to explore and understand the factors that led him to choose his life's course.

As they left the restaurant, he mentioned to Freddie that it was time to start writing the book they had spoken about over the years. She thought it was a good idea, and that he should do it. Pierre had no illusions about being a Pulitzer Prize winner or making any best seller list; he merely wanted to share his experiences with others who may have similar ones or whose ancestors went through the assimilation process in America.

Part I

Assimilating into Cajun and American Cultures

CHAPTER 1
A SERENDIPITOUS VOYAGE

"We can be happy without knowledge of our ancestral roots, but our sense of self will be diminished"

SPB

B EFORE coming to Louisiana in 1769 at age 30, Antoine Bellard, Pierre's first ancestor in Louisiana, was in Baltimore, Maryland. It is not definitively known how long he had been there or where he had been previously. There is evidence that his father was born in Picardy, France. Some sources indicate that Antoine was Acadian, and some genealogists believe that to be so. Other genealogists indicate that there is no evidence of Antoine ever being in Acadie. There are some indications that Antoine may have been in Canada, near Montreal. It is known that he, at age 22, had married Marie Trahan, an Acadian, in Baltimore and a later census showed he had a son named Etienne-Simon, aged two. Many Acadians had been deposited in Maryland during the Acadian expulsions from Nova Scotia by the English. They were not happy there. Antoine, his wife and child, six other Acadian families, several non-Acadian passengers departed for New Orleans from Port

Tobacco, Maryland on January 5, 1769, on the British ship, *Britannia*.

On February 21, 1769, they reached the coast of Louisiana, but the captain of the ship, because of heavy fog or incompetence, missed the mouth of the Mississippi. Heavy winds drove the ship westward until they landed on what is now the Texas coast which was a Spanish possession. The Acadians probably felt relieved because Spain had been very receptive to the Acadians in Louisiana. The crew, hoping to find assistance, went ashore and found a Spanish officer who instead of being their salvation jailed the crew and passengers. It is probable that the Spanish were suspicious because the crew and ship were British, Spain's mortal enemies.

During their six months incarceration, the unfortunate crew and passengers were forced to work as semi-slaves on the fort and nearby ranches. In the first days of September, a Spanish officer arrived and gave orders to send the prisoners to Natchitoches in present-day North Louisiana. As the *Britannia* had been stripped down by the Spanish and the Indians, she was no longer seaworthy; consequently, they would have to make an overland journey to Natchitoches. On September 11, the Acadians, other passengers, and the English crew began an arduous 420-mile trek to Natchitoches and arrived in late October. One can only imagine the hardships suffered by the men, women, and children traversing a wilderness of forests, rivers, wild animals, Indians, and insects.

Governor Alejandro O'Reilly sent the Acadians to Natchitoches because they knew how to cultivate rye and wheat. The Natchitoches settlers welcomed Antoine Bellard and the Acadian families and provided them with animals, supplies and food. The Acadians, however, were not happy in Natchitoches because they wanted to be with their relatives in South Louisiana. Going there was easier than their previous journey because they could get there by going down the Red and Mississippi Rivers. Antoine and his family lived a short time at St. Gabriel on the Mississippi River and later crossed the Atchafalaya Basin to establish themselves in the Opelousas District in the 1770's. Antoine fought under Col. Bernardo de Galvez against the British during the American Revolution, qualifying his descendants to join the Daughters of the American Revolution (DAR) or Sons of the American Revolution (SAR). Some of Antoine's grandsons moved to the nearby Church Point area in present-day Acadia Parish in Southwest Louisiana, now in the heart of Acadiana, a 22-parish area designated by the Louisiana State Legislature in 1971. This is where Pierre's parents were born and reared.

Chapter 2
The Journey Begins, A Father's Stories

"What we remember from childhood, we remember forever –
permanent ghosts stamped, inked, imprinted, eternally seen."

Cynthia Ozick

MANY of Pierre's earliest memories are those of the many stories and family experiences his father related to him throughout his life. It was quite natural for his father, an illiterate, to have developed a strong oral tradition as it was the only method he could impart information to preserve family history. Being loquacious, his father was a good story teller, and Pierre was a good listener, no matter how many times he heard the same stories. His father even told a story from Aesop's Fables, "The Ant and Grasshopper." He didn't know if his father remembered this story from the few times he went to school as a child (the fables were an important part of the curriculum in the early 20th century) or perhaps he had picked it up from another storyteller at a later date.

One thing Pierre knew for sure, his father emulated that ant for a lifetime. He could remember when he was perhaps three or four years old, his father would bring hickory nuts he had gathered from the woods where he often worked. They would sit near the cast iron wood stove and his father would place a piece of firewood upright on the floor to crack the nuts on with a hammer. With its thick shell, there was little nourishment in the hickory nut, but the nut was rich with flavor, as were the stories he told. So they ate and talked. The stories, detailed depictions of the minute details of the sharecropper lifestyle, continued throughout his life, and Pierre listened until his father passed away. He wrote some of the stories down to preserve them and perhaps to submit them for publication some day, but he never seemed able to get around to it.

Un Bal de Maison

J'ai été au bal hier au soir,
Je va returner encore à soir,
Si l'occasion se presente,
Je va retourner demain soir.

("I was at the dance last night, I'm going back tonight, If the occasion presents itself, I'll return tomorrow night"). Cajun lyrics by Ira LeJeune, translated by Ann Allen Savoy.

His father often mentioned and told stories of the house dances (*les bals de maison*), some of the most important events in a young Cajun's life. It was one of the few occasions at that time for young people to meet each other. Adults were also known to participate in these dances.

It was an unusually hot, steamy Saturday morning in May near the town of Church Point, Louisiana. Pierre's father, then a seventeen-year-old Cajun sharecropper's son, was busy hoeing cotton with a hoe whose hickory handle was worn smooth by years of use and whose blade, once five inches high, was now worn and over-sharpened to a crescent-shaped, two-inch blade. He was barefooted, but the soles of his dust-covered feet were already toughened to the point where he did not feel the sticks and clods of dirt under his feet. He wore old pants and a long sleeve shirt, and on his head was a sweat-stained, wide-brimmed straw hat to protect his milk-white skin, a skin he was proud of and protected because it drew compliments from young ladies. He inherited this extra fair skin from his mother who was so fair as a baby she was named Blanche —French for white. To further protect the integrity of his fair skin, he had his mother sew in a strip of cloth under the hat brim to give his neck additional protection from the burning sun.

Many young Cajun men did not have to work on Saturdays, but his father, Noah, squat and powerful, was a determined, hard worker driven by the fear that if he did not produce enough, the landowner would utter these most frightening words," J'ai besoin ma place" ("I need my property"). These words meant that the landowner would lease his land to another sharecropper, relative, or to whomever, and he would have to find another place to farm. Finding another place to work could be difficult, and often, prairie farms did not have enough trees for firewood. Firewood was a necessity as it was the only fuel available for cooking, heating, and cleaning. Sometimes, the landowner reserved the firewood for his personal needs. Additionally, some landlords would limit the amount of land they would permit the sharecropper to use for vegetables in order to maximize cash-crop acreage of cotton, potatoes, and corn. So the family worked hard, sometimes seven days a week, and gave one-third of their production to the landowner. This lifestyle was quite normal to them, as it well should have been, because their ancestors had lived this way since the 1600's in France. The share-croppers were resigned to their condition, which unknown to them, would get worse due to the Great Depression, an era they would never understand.

His two younger brothers were behind him about 50 yards, and he cast an occasional gaze their way to inspect their work and to see if they were indeed working at all. The two youngsters were more interested in play than work, and twice that morning he had to drop his hoe to break up a dirt-clod fight. He admired and envied their playfulness because being the first born in a large family, he seldom had the luxury of play. Ever since he was seven years old, he had had to plow behind a mule; tasks most young boys didn't and couldn't do until they were much older. Though he was happy that his younger brothers had the luxury of play, he had to admit having them in the cotton field was more of a hindrance than a help.

He heard a roaring sound coming from the sky; it was one of those airplanes he had heard about—it had double wings and a single motor. He wondered how that thing could stay up in the air as the wings did not flap like birds' wings did. He had never seen one on the ground and only rarely in the air. Though he would live to be 91 years old, he would never understand the principles of flight. He remembered the old people saying, "You know, there are people in those things."

Having hoed cotton since he was seven years old, it was now an automatic process that consisted of cutting the grass and thinning the cotton by leaving two stalks on each side of the hoe blade. While working, he had a great deal of time to be absorbed in his thoughts that were driven by a lifetime of poverty and isolation. He did not feel that he was especially chosen for a life of pain and suffering, as everyone he knew led the same life, and that was just the way it was. He had rarely traveled more than a few miles from home, and wherever he went, it was by horse, buggy, or on foot. No one in his extended family had a car as only relatively successful people could aspire to own one of the occasional Model A and T's like those they had seen in town.

He did recall the journey he had taken to Texas by train when he was around six years old. His mother's relatives had, like many Cajuns at that time, migrated to East Texas in search of jobs and land. He remembered his excitement when his mother announced the upcoming trip. They spoke about it constantly, and he conjured up images in his mind how wonderful and beautiful it would be. He imagined, with his six-year-old mind, that it would be a place of beauty, full of bright lights, and nothing like the farm and the small town he knew.

The day finally arrived, and they boarded the train in the nearby town of Church Point. His mother paid the fare which to her was exorbitant, and it took up a good portion of the little money she had saved for the trip. But, like for most Cajuns, it was important to her to visit her relatives. His father did not make the trip as it would have been too expensive and he had work to do. Additionally, he had to stay with the younger children.

All boarded and seated, they were quickly on their way to paradise. He was amazed at how fast he was traveling, much faster than his horse could run at full speed, and the click-clack noise from the iron wheels hitting the spaces between the rails made it seem even faster. He was excited. He kept his nose pressed to the window as he watched the countryside go by in a blur. Finally, they reached their destination and disembarked. He looked around and asked his mother where they were. "Well, we have arrived, we're in Texas," She said. He looked around again and suddenly he was enveloped by a wave of disappointment as he realized it was no different than Louisiana. He said something in French approximately equivalent to, "Aw shucks." It would be a long time before he would get on a train again.

His education was very limited, as he had attended school only a few times after fall harvest and sometimes in the winter before spring plowing and planting began. He had made it up to fourth grade, but he still spoke only Cajun French, and all he would ever be able to write in his life was his name. His limited English skills and sporadic school attendance made academic success very unlikely, and he felt that education was possible only for those *"Americains"* and others who spoke better English, but not for him, and all of his relatives and friends were just like him. Because of their isolation from mainstream culture for so long, these Cajuns felt that their condition was completely normal.

His world may have been small, but one thing he did know was that he could not wait to go to the *"bal de maison,"* or house dance. Families took turns sponsoring house dances to provide the neighborhood adolescents an opportunity to meet and dance with members of the opposite sex. He had gone to one last week, and it was so wonderful to hold and dance with the girls. The dance was the only contact he would have with females. He could not wait for noon so he could knock off from work and go home to get ready for it. The host family had invited him and his neighboring friends and relatives to attend it the week before.

By the time he got home, he was starving, as his breakfast of milk and cornbread was long gone. He would have preferred eggs for breakfast, but eggs were used to barter for coffee, sugar, and sometimes soap or money. His lunch was substantial: perhaps rice and gravy, meat, beans, and if he was lucky, some leftover gumbo. He ate voraciously to relieve the hunger pangs and to finish up so he could rest some before getting ready for the dance.

At last, it was time to get ready. He drew some water from the shallow well, carried it into the house, and poured it into a large, galvanized washtub. He always used only a couple of inches of water in the tub as it would be too laborious to haul a tubful of water into his house. He then did a quick wash and dried himself. He put on some deodorant and got clothes together: suit pants, white shirt, socks, and a bow tie which was the normal attire young men of that era wore to the dances. Even in those days, young Cajun men and adolescents had a prescribed dress code. He carefully combed his hair straight back, without a hair out of place; he could not leave anything to chance as this was the most exciting event of his life.

The sun was about to set; it was time to leave. As he went to the barnyard, he carefully avoided stepping in the omnipresent animal dung; to do so would render him less than a romantic figure at the dance. He quickly currycombed his horse and hitched it to his buggy as he thought about the real possibility of one or more of the million fleas jumping on his freshly washed body. As he finished hitching up his horse, he felt very fortunate to have a buggy as most of his friends and cousins didn't have one. In that era and area, a young man with a buggy was considered quite desirable by the young ladies.

He climbed into the buggy and began the short trip on a dirt road to the dance. Memories of when his first cousin taught him to dance when he was 16 flashed through his mind. He wondered who would be at the dance and what band was going to play. These bands were small and consisted of an accordion player, a guitar player, a fiddle player, and a triangle player. Sometimes there was only an accordion or fiddle player for the dance. He especially liked Alex Simoneaux on the accordion. He wondered what girls were going to show up, and just thinking about it quickened his testosterone-driven pulse.

In a short time, he could see his destination about a quarter mile up the road. It was a typical farmhouse of the area—unpainted cypress, tin roof, and very modest. He knew the place well; it was his friend's house. House dances were for the young; participants were usually 16 to 20 years of age. The adolescents took turns begging their parents to host a dance. Only the invited were expected to attend. Uninvited guests could cause trouble, especially if boys from other more distant farms danced with the local girls. As he got closer to the house, he could see the horses and buggies tied near the house, and he could see the animals that belonged to people he knew. The sound of musicians tuning their instruments caught his ear. The urge to dance was overwhelming to him. It would not be long now!

After tying up his horse, he walked to the porch and greeted friends and relatives as he looked around to see which girls showed up. He recognized several, some who were at the dance last week. Some of the boys were drinking moonshine whiskey and gin in the shadows and were already laughing loudly. The girls did not drink, and drinking was not allowed in the house. Even though it was early, the house and yard were already crowded with adolescents and parents. The young ladies seldom came to these dances without being escorted by one or both parents.

The dance was about to begin, so he stepped into the house. Young men were helping to clear the largest room for the dance by placing the sparse furniture in the other rooms. Even so, there was not a great deal of room for dancing. Flickering kerosene lamps called *"les lampes à coal oil"* by the Cajuns barely illuminated the dance room and the rest of the house. The walls were bare boards and free of decoration except for an occasional religious picture, an oval framed picture of an old relative, or perhaps palms from Palm Sunday shaped like a cross (*les rameaux*). As there were no palms available in the area, large magnolia tree leaves were used as palms. Traditionally, in times of stormy weather, Cajuns prayed and burned these blessed palms for protection from harm. Some of the parents, mostly men, were in another room playing cards, usually poker. *Bourée*, the well-known Cajun card game, would not become popular in that area until later. The musicians were set up in the corner of the room, and some of the mothers were sitting near the wall to be in a position to watch their daughters dance.

They would keep a watchful eye out for improper dancing, such as dancing too close. "Too bad these mothers didn't stay home," he thought.

He paid his 15 cents admission, money that would be used to pay the musicians. Even though times were hard, he always had the money to dance. Some were not as fortunate and had to wait outside until 11:30 when the collection stopped. At 11:30 they could come in and dance the half hour until midnight for free. He remembered one occasion when a hat was passed around after the dance to collect money for the musicians, and the musicians went home with very little money. Now, the money was collected as soon as the dancers entered the door.

The music began and soon the room was a whirlwind of activity complete with whirling bodies and the movement of people in and out of the house. Understandably, the noise level was quite high with the wailing of the accordion, the stomping feet, the laughter of the drinkers and screams of the younger children who ran in and out of the house playing games. In total, there were about 45 to 50 bodies milling in and out of the house; consequently, the temperature began to rise quite rapidly on that Saturday evening in May, and bodies began to perspire. As the open windows provided less than adequate circulation, it was obvious that not all used deodorant.

The dance was now in full swing, and every young man was seeking to dance with the girl of his choice. The musicians alternated slow and fast numbers, and the dancers did the waltz and the two-step respectively. What a good time he had dancing with his cousins and young ladies! He had waited for this moment all week. As he danced, he began to give some thought as to which girl he would walk or ride home. Then, all of a sudden, a commotion broke out outside, and everyone ran out to see what was going on! Fights were common at these dances and sometimes the consequences were serious because knives and sometimes guns were involved. Jealousy, uninvited young men, and alcohol were the most common causes of these fights. He ran outside to see what was going on. He hoped it was not too serious because a fight with injury could end the dance, and he would have to wait a whole week to dance with the girls again. Two young men were fighting, and the chaperones were in the process of breaking them up as there were no police or constables at these dances. The cause of the fight was that one young man told another that he had a big nose and was ugly—more than enough reason for a disagreement between two drinking adolescents who wanted to save face in front of their friends.

Luckily, peace was restored, and everyone resumed what they were doing before the fracas broke out. Things could have been a lot worse as he remembered someone in a past dance putting dried horse dung in the punch bowl. Arguments broke out, and the dance ended early. "How stupid," he thought. "Just two dances for 15 cents—not a good deal."

The dance continued, and soon it was 11:30. The dance floor got more crowded all of a sudden as the group of young men who could not afford to pay the 15 cent fee entered. They could now dance for free till midnight. There was also only one-half hour left for him to select the young lady he would walk home that night. He quickly glanced around the dance floor to survey his choices and saw the full-bodied brunette he had danced with several times that night. He wondered if he had made enough of an impression on her that she would accept his request to walk her home. What he wanted was to sweep her into his buggy and ride far away to fulfill his fantasies. But that was not possible because first of all, she probably would not accept, and secondly, her mother was right there watching every move she and all the boys in her presence made. Of one thing he was certain, he would have to make his move quickly before someone beat him to it. He could not take a chance by waiting for the last dance because that might be too late.

His pulse quickened as he saw her alone, now was the time to make the move. In the blink of an eye, he was next to her asking for the next dance, a waltz. He preferred waltzes to two-steps because he could hold his partners close (well, as close as the mother would allow) and feel the warmth of their bodies; what a feeling that warmth was—it was a hell of a lot better than hoeing cotton in the hot sun. Not only that, he could talk to them while dancing, and that was important.

The waltz started, and they were soon gliding across the floor among the other waltzing bodies as her mother cast a glowering look at him. It seemed that she suspected the intentions of any young man who came within ten feet of her daughter. To make matters worse, he felt she knew his real intentions. He steered her to the corner farthest from her mother to ask her the pressing question. Small talk was in order, and he asked her how she enjoyed the dance, how she liked the band and which was her favorite song. Enough small talk, he summoned up his courage and asked if he could walk her home. To his delight, she accepted, but the walk would be a short one as she lived only about a quarter mile away on the next farm.

Midnight arrived, and the dance ended. The sponsor announced the location and time of the next dance, and the dancers and parents quickly dispersed in all directions. All left as they had come—on foot, on horses, in buggies and wagons. The host family was busy replacing the furniture they had moved for the dance, and quickly sweeping the floor. Trailing voices could be heard as they distanced themselves from the house. The musicians collected their money and were headed home for a much-needed night's sleep. After all, playing music was not lucrative enough to make a living, so they had full-time jobs like everyone else. As he walked to the young lady to ask her if she was ready to leave, he saw next to her: her mother, a little sister, a big brother, and her grandfather. All of a sudden, he realized things were not happening as he had planned. Was this what he had waited for all last week? Sure, he knew his real fantasy was just that—a fantasy, but at the very least, he expected a nice, romantic walk with a pretty girl—perhaps even a good night kiss!

So the party of six started their quarter mile walk on the headland at the edge of the field. They went by twos: the young man and his date, the mother and grandfather, and the brother and sister. He felt that the mother held up the lantern not so much to see the path as to watch him. Never before, he thought, had a young couple been watched so closely by so many. He felt like eight eyes were piercing holes into their backs. He tried to start polite conversation to lighten the mood of the lugubrious voyeurs, and perhaps if they started talking, he might be able to have some private words with his date. The effort was for naught as they continued walking towards their destination blanketed in suspicious silence.

After some contemplation, he decided to take a chance and place his hand lightly on the young lady's lower back. Furtively and unsteadily, his hand extended out to reach her waist, and he fully expected a lantern to come crashing down on his head. Nothing happened. So far, so good, he thought as he walked stiffly and clumsily up the headland. Soon, his arm and hand were aching from the awkward position and his tenseness, but he did not dare to lower his arm as the young lady might interpret that motion as him having lost interest in her.

After what seemed like an eternity, the morose group reached the front porch of the young lady's house. The mother, grandfather, brother and sister went into the house. At last, he thought, they were alone. He stood in front of her and could see her beautiful face in the moonlight. How pretty she was, he thought. If he had understood genetics, he would have said that she defied the laws of genetics. She smelled so good; her perfume reminded him of the aromas he had experienced in his grandmother's flower garden. His testosterone, having been stifled by a quarter mile of fear and anxiety, was beginning to surge again. They had a little conversation about the dance, and he thought this was the time to get a kiss. She was looking up at him as he slowly lowered his head to meet her lips. At that moment, he was in another world, completely oblivious to anything but the two bodies on the porch. The moment he had been waiting for had finally arrived; he was mere inches from her soft, full lips. Life was good! Suddenly, from another world, came a shrill, shocking, shattering voice, "JOSEPHINE, IT'S TIME FOR YOU TO COME IN!"

His intimate world of two shattered as if struck by a bolt of summer lightning. His consciousness began to expand enough to encompass the door that framed the image of Josephine's mother—an image that reminded him of Mardi Gras masks he had seen. Once again, he tasted disappointment as Josephine said good night and reluctantly slipped into the house. The mask-like figure, to compound his injury, told him in a demeaning voice, "It's time for you to go home!" He quickly got back to his horse and buggy and directed the horse to home. What a night he thought. He said to himself, "I should have seen that her whole family was there. I should have known that something was wrong when she was still available so late in the dance. I should have asked the other guys about her. I should, I should, I should. Well, it's too late now." He moped as he made his way home. Then he remembered something; his cousin told him that the next dance would be at his house. His spirits began to lift at the thought of the next dance. There was something to look forward to again. Things had to get better; they could not get any worse.

Courir de Mardi Gras 1930

Capitaine, Capitaine, voyage ton flag,
Allons c'ez l'autre voisin,
Demander la charité pour nous-autres,
Vous venez nous rejoinder,
Vous autre vous venez nous rejoindre,
Oui au gombo se soir.

"(Captain, Captain, fly your flag, Let's go to the other neighbor, to ask for charity for you all, come join us, You all come join us, Yes, at the gumbo tonight)." Traditional Cajun Mardi Gras song lyrics translated by Ann Allen Savoy.

Mardi Gras was a very important event for the Cajuns on the prairies as it provided relief from the dreary weather and came at a time when they had less urgent work on the farm. This Mardi Gras is not to be confused with the huge New Orleans Mardi Gras or even the small-town, Southwest Louisiana Cajun Mardi Gras. His father told him stories of a Mardi Gras which consisted of the inhabitants from an area of small farms populated with relatives and neighbors. It was a boisterous interlude for the whole community as it provided an opportunity to visit, tell stories, eat prodigiously, and dance.

Pierre's father remembered the winter of 1929-30 as having been relatively pleasant and mild in Acadia Parish, Louisiana. Most farmsteads had crock jars with an ample supply of salted pork slabs put away from last fall, and the smokehouses still contained sausage, intensely smoked meats called *tasso*, and *andouille*, which was pork intestines slipped inside one another, seasoned, and heavily smoked. Additionally, many crates of potatoes were stored in the barn. Seasoned firewood cut last fall was neatly stacked near the farmhouses. Besides the daily barnyard chores and animal care, he and the other young men would get a reprieve from the usual hard work until the main spring plowing.

With time on their hands, the young men waited with great anticipation for the *"Courir le Mardi Gras"* (the running the Mardi

Gras) which would be a pleasant diversion from the hard, monotonous farm life most prairie Cajuns experienced. Mardi Gras in Acadia Parish was nothing like the popular Mardi Gras traditions of New Orleans and smaller cities of Louisiana which consisted of large, organized Mardi Gras clubs, or "krewes" sponsoring parades of huge, elaborate floats. In Southwest Louisiana, it was a rural tradition of the common people whose parades consisted of horsemen stampeding through the countryside begging for ingredients to make a community feast of gumbo for the ensuing Mardi Gras dance. This tradition, originating in Medieval France, was brought to Louisiana by the earliest French settlers and modified by the Cajuns.

Running the Mardi Gras was a young man's activity. Most runners were single men between 16 to 20 years of age. In a few instances, young married men would also participate. All runners were expert horsemen and were expected to have a horse in order to participate. Each little community had its own Mardi Gras, and these traditions were carried on into the 21st century.

The young men got together before Mardi gras and elected Pierre's father to be "*Le Capitaine*," or captain, of the running. The Capitaine was chosen based on his maturity. As the oldest of a family of eight children (five boys and three girls), his calm demeanor and sense of responsibility made him a solid choice. Additionally, he was 19 years old and therefore, had the respect of the younger boys. It was rather unusual, him being single at almost 20 years of age— it was not unusual for young men to marry at age 16 or 17. Girls often married as young as fifteen and sixteen. Finally, his having a horse and buggy, necessary to carry all the goodies the runners collected, cinched his election.

The Capitaine had many responsibilities such as going ahead of the runners to ask permission from the farmers to grant entrance of the Mardi Gras onto their property. Usually, they were happy to make a small donation of gumbo ingredients or money because they would get to share the huge gumbo and other treats that night. Sometimes, however, some families did not participate due to very limited resources or perhaps a recent death in the family. It was the Capitaine's responsibility to collect all donations and take them to the dance site that night. He was also responsible for the group's behavior, not only during the running but also at the subsequent dance.

All runners had to be masked and costumed since the main objective was to mask the whole body. Costumes were usually handmade from a material with bold, bright stripes. Sometimes old oversized shirts and trousers were patched with colorful squares and circles. The long pointed caps, shaped like the stereotypical dunce's hat, were called *capuchons* and fashioned from stiff cardboard covered with bright, geometric designs and topped with tassels and or balls. The origin of it can be traced back to the Middle Ages when the peasants wore them to make fun of the mortarboard hats worn by university graduates—it being the opposite of the flat, academic hat. The only part of the costume the runners had to purchase were the masks that resembled grotesque faces with long noses, large ears or mouths, or other misshapen features. Costumes were saved to be used again the next year and eventually handed down to a younger member of the family.

The much-anticipated time to run finally arrived. It was 7:00 AM, the Monday before Mardi Gras, and he could smell smoke from the fireplaces and wood-burning stoves that permeated the cool morning air. Roosters, announcing the morning, could be heard from the neighboring farms all across the prairie. He heard hoof-beats in the distance getting louder and louder as they approached his father's farm. These were the riders making their way to collect him for the run. Twenty-five to thirty young, laughing riders filling the air with Gallic sounds came in, pulling their horses to an abrupt halt. The Capitaine gathered the young riders to review the rules of conduct and the route they would take for the run. With a thunderous sound, colorfully-costumed runners began their raucous journey over the drab, wintry prairie in search of the ingredients for the community gumbo.

Pierre's father, unmasked and sans costume, drove his horse and buggy about 200 feet ahead of the runners as they traveled down dirt and graveled roads in search of goodies from relatives, friends, and neighbors. He stopped to ask the farmer's permission to receive the Mardi Gras and to collect items for the gumbo. The most desirable item was *"une petite poule grasse"* (a fat little chicken) which was the main ingredient for a Cajun gumbo. Other farmers gave heavily-smoked sausage, flour, seasonings and sometimes a small sum of money. After the farmer agreed to receive the runners, the Capitaine motioned to the runners to advance.

It was like pushing a switch that simultaneously ignited every single runner and horse to immediate action. What a sight it was to see and hear a thunderous herd of horses, a blur of stripes, pointed hats and grotesque masks rushing to the farm. Within seconds, the farmer's front yard was invaded with this strange collection of panting horses, bright colors, and clownish creatures who jumped off their horses to begin dancing and singing. From the front porch and yard, the farmer, his wife, a stair-step collection of a large group of children, a menagerie of skinny, sometimes mangy, always flea bitten dogs watched what must have been to them the greatest free show on earth. The discordant singing and uncoordinated dancing of the runners, the crying of the younger children, the barking of the agitated dogs, and the gleeful laughter of the throng violated the serenity of the countryside.

If the farmer was amused enough and gave the fat little chicken, the runners had to catch it. Confusion reigned as the runners made a mad, desperate dash for the fleeing, frightened chicken. The chase took them under houses, fences, horses, and often through the omnipresent cow and horse dung that gave additional color to the already colorful costumes. The hapless, hopeless, and helpless chicken was finally surrounded, captured, and kept alive for the next day's gumbo.

This process was repeated over and over most of the morning until the Captaine's buggy was virtually a cornucopia of raw materials for the community gumbo. With the money collected, the Capitaine bought cookies, candy, whiskey, and gin for the upcoming dance.

The Mardi Gras day dance was when the rest of the community joined the celebration. The dance was held in a home, usually not a large one. The scant furniture was removed from the largest room to make room for dancing. Despite this lack of space, over one hundred Cajuns, arriving on horseback, buggies, wagons, and foot, jammed into the house and overflowed into the yard. As one could imagine, it was a joyous, noisy affair with gaggle of Cajuns drinking, dancing, and celebrating. Many children were running around playing games, eating candy, and sometimes falling asleep wherever they could find available space. Because there was no electricity, musical instruments were not amplified, which meant that only the wail of the accordion could be heard above the cacophony. Despite the noise and confusion, mothers kept a close eye on their daughters. The runners, the only costumed and masked celebrants, had special dances called in their honor. A touch of the Capitaine's buggy whip on a runner's shoulder or arm was a reminder to behave in an orderly fashion.

By late evening, huge appetites had been built up by the running, dancing, and drinking. It was time for gumbo, that magical concoction that truly satisfies the Cajuns' bodies and souls. The gumbo was made early that day in a huge, cast iron pot over a wood fire with the ingredients collected by the runners. Every family had a similar huge cast iron pot that served to render lard, cook cracklings, make soap, boil dirty clothes for cleaning, and make huge gumbos. It took teamwork to make gumbo for one hundred hungry Cajuns, as no Cajun was satisfied with only one large bowl of gumbo and rice. The women did most of the cooking, and much of Monday was spent concocting this elixir for the soul. Some slaughtered, plucked, cleaned, and cut up the chickens. Others made a gargantuan amount of *roux*—a very labor intensive job. They prepared a huge amount of rice. Still others cut up the onions, garlic, and other seasonings. Finally, a few (usually women) cooked the gumbo.

The signal was given—time to eat! The ladies quickly served large bowls of gumbo and rice to those waiting in line. There were obviously not enough chairs for all to sit to eat; the elders got the first choice for chairs. When seats ran out, people stood, sat on steps or the ground to eat. As there were no disposable utensils or enough dishes or space to serve everyone at the same time, the revelers took turns eating, and the ladies washed dishes for the next group. As it was not unusual for men and boys, and even some women, to eat three or four bowls of gumbo, the huge pot was empty by the end of the dance.

By midnight, the festivities came to an end. The house was cleaned and put back in its original shape. There was a ton of dishes and pots to wash. The runners had had a full, wonderful, and exhausting two days. The women were exhausted, too, as they had worked hard all day to prepare food for the multitudes. It was time to start Lent and return to their life of hard work and limited pleasures. However, if a young runner was lucky, he might win the pleasure of escorting a young lady back home.

CHAPTER 3
AGE 3 – 6,
WHEN THE TREES CREATED THE WIND

"The past is never dead. It's not even past."

William Faulkner

For some reason, Pierre had always had an unusual memory that allowed him to remember vividly events from as early as the age of three and vague memories from even earlier. For much of his life, he thought it was quite normal—until he learned that most of his acquaintances remembered nothing or very little of their early childhood and primary school years. Pierre remembered all of his teachers from first grade through high school and specific events and conversations with fellow students in first grade—such as where he sat, who was next to him, questions his teachers asked him, feelings, and so on. He had no idea why he could do this. One thing he knew for sure, it was not because of any great intellectual ability. He always regarded himself as a "middle of the pack" student for most of his academic career.

After spending most of his life as an educator, Pierre felt that students knew where they ranked among their peers whether it concerned strength, speed, endurance, or academics. They just knew. If only he could have kept this type of memory in adult life, things would have been much easier for him. He often thought that because of his unusual childhood, school was such a novel experience that it burned events into his memory. Certainly, as a child whose primary language was Cajun French with extremely limited English, school must have been a memorable place for him.

He was born the third child of four children to a Cajun couple just outside of a small town on the bayou in Southwest Louisiana. His parents spoke practically no English, were illiterate, were born to sharecroppers, had sharecropped, and spent the best years of their lives struggling to survive the Great Depression. Furthermore, his great-grandfather and great-great grandfather were sharecroppers. Additionally, his ancestors in 16th and 17th century France were farm laborers. This ancestry was not unusual as there were thousands of other Cajuns in Southwest Louisiana with similar ones. There were also many black families who were sharecroppers. Indeed, many of the people in rural North Louisiana and other southern states, which were predominately of Scotch/Irish origins, had similar experiences.

The house on the dusty, dirt and gravel road he first knew was small, perhaps 18 X 25 feet, had no running water, no gas, no electricity and, of course, no bathroom. There were three tiny rooms which served multiple functions. The left half of the first was a bedroom with two beds and the right half served as a living room. In this living room was the only intrusion of modernity—a brown radio powered by a huge red and blue battery. The rest of the house was divided into two rooms—the right was a kitchen with a cast iron wood stove, a kerosene stove, a cypress table, chairs, and a small screened cabinet for dishes and pans. The left was a small bedroom with a closet. The floors were pine boards that like the walls, allowed daylight to peek through in certain spots. The roof was of cypress shingles that often leaked, and the inside walls were wide, red cypress boards covered with black felt paper that helped keep out the wind. The black felt paper also absorbed the feeble light emanating from the kerosene lanterns; his older sisters had a hard time seeing well enough to read and do homework. The exterior of the house had clapboards that at one time had been white as evidenced by the flaky, chalky, crackled paint left behind in irregular patterns. In front of the house was a porch that the family used heavily when seeking relief from the summer heat. This house, even when brand new a long time ago, was a shack and went downhill from there.

About 50 feet from the house was a huge hackberry tree near the road that provided welcome shade for play and for the many pedestrians, black and white, who walked up and down the bayou road. He had watched this tree and others bend in the wind and deduced that the moving trees caused the wind to blow. That made sense to him because when the wind stopped blowing, the trees stopped bending. There was an outhouse and a cistern outside, along with a shallow well that produced reddish water due to iron minerals. They carried additional water from the bayou. Baths were in a large galvanized tub with carried water—there was no full body submersion, and they sometimes used the water twice. The family did not feel particularly unfortunate, as in one of their previous houses, they had to suspend quilts above the beds to escape the wind-driven snow pushed through cracks in the roof.

Despite being below norms for the period and town, the home was the first one his family owned. During WWII, his father left the sharecropper life and began working for a contractor doing oil field work. That career change would have a most profound effect on Pierre's life in the future. His father's lack of education and skills condemned him to one of the hardest, dirtiest, and lowest paying jobs in the oilfields—building board roads for drilling locations, but the job liberated him from the tyranny of nature and landowners. The pay was not much, but it was steady, and through his parents' frugality, they saved enough money to buy the house and a 100 by 175 foot lot. His parents would never buy anything until they could pay for it in cash.

When Pierre was two years and nine months old, his youngest sister, Linda, was born, and he has vivid memories of this event since his sister was born at home. Like his two older sisters who were also born at home, she was delivered by a black midwife. This midwife was different from the ones who delivered his older sisters in that she was a *traiteuse*. A traiteuse was a woman who healed people through prayer and herbs. They treated ailments such as burns, sunburn, sprained ankles, headaches, etc. The African American and white community highly respected this traiteuse and many often called upon her for advice as well as regular treatments. Pierre's grandmother and an aunt were also traiteuses and would later treat him for sunburn and a sprained ankle.

The day Linda was born, Pierre was aware that this was not a usual day; for one thing there was this strange woman in the house, and he was not allowed to go to the front bedroom/living room where there was something apparently very interesting going on. Then the strangest thing happened. He noticed that one of his older sisters appeared to be "cooking" small pieces of cloth in a cast iron skillet. He knew then that was not natural. Many years later, he found out they were sterilizing pieces of the cloth to bandage his little sister's navel. This birth was important to him as the two little siblings would spend 15 years growing up together. Of course, there would be arguments, rivalries, and jealousies, but they both benefited. Within five years, his older sisters, Verna, and Bertha would be married and gone from the house.

At age three his family experienced a watershed event—they got city water. Thoughts of water in the house with sinks, lavatories, and indoor toilets are to be banished, for the reality was that a single pipe brought city water to about 20 feet from their house, which was not a disappointment to them—it was life changing! At last, they had safe, chlorinated water to replace the water from the polluted well, the contaminated cistern, and the bayou. This singular isolated water pipe eliminated countless hours of backbreaking labor, saved hours of time each day and spared them from countless episodes of amoebic attacks. With a water hose, his mother could have water next to the tubs behind the house to wash clothes.

And age four brought enlightenment—they got electricity for the first time in their lives. Pierre remembered when Aunt Hazel's husband, Uncle Robert, came to wire the house. Of course, Pierre was all eyes as this was so unusual, not that he understood that they would soon have electricity, but that the activities were so bizarre. His uncle Robert was walking everywhere in the house and the attic with gray wire in his hand. There was excitement in the house as the whole family was there waiting in anticipation, except for his youngest sister Linda who was only a year old.

At last, all the wires were run, a few receptacles put in and bare light bulbs with string pulls were attached to the low ceiling. Everyone was in the living room anxiously waiting for the moment. When the circuit box was switched on and the string pull pulled, there was an explosion of light never seen before in this small dark house. That light bulb was so bright. It was not that they had not seen a light bulb before as practically everyone in town had them; it was just the thrill of seeing this light bulb in such an unlikely place—their house. It was like a sunrise in their house neutralizing the darkness and gloom of the black, felt-covered walls.

Soon after that electrifying episode, his father bought a Frigidaire refrigerator for the kitchen. It seemed like progress was coming in bunches. Not long ago a refrigerator was just a dream—one not likely to happen. But here it was, plugged in and ready to go. The delivery man explained to his father and mother how to operate the appliance. He explained to them that ice could be made by putting water in little trays and placing them in the small freezer section. After the man left, his father quickly prepared ice trays and placed them in the freezer. He waited about ten minutes and checked the ice trays and found just water in the trays. Slightly perplexed, he waited another 20 minutes and checked again—no ice. Now he was perturbed and issued forth a plethora of Cajun profanities. He checked a few more times before going to bed—still no ice.

Being the eternal pessimist, his father was certain he had been cheated. The next morning, he woke up and went straight to the refrigerator and found the ice trays completely frozen. He was like the kid who had been trying to catch Santa Claus only to find Santa had come and left presents after he had finally fallen asleep. Now they would no longer have to depend on the red ice truck that brought a block of ice twice a week which they had stored in a cooler on the porch. Pierre remembered the man carrying the ice with tongs, and even remembered the dividing lines between blocks of ice which he found out much later were caused by the freezing coils. The lines were not of clear ice, but of a snow-like consistency with a different taste.

The years of three to six were very consequential for him as they would be for any child. Psychologists and educators believe these are the most formative years of a person's life. His father bought his first automobile, a 1936 Ford, which was already about 12 years old when they got it, but it was exciting for Pierre and his family. They could now visit relatives, even ones in Acadia Parish, 25 miles from home. His favorite place in the car was always standing up on the drive shaft hump behind the front seat for a better view which provided stimuli for prompting a million questions from him.

His parents often told him he asked too many questions.

Pierre had about 30 cousins around his age, and he looked forward to every visit. He felt the trip of 25 miles was tediously long and the 75-mile trip to Lake Charles to visit his father's sister, Mamie, took forever. Most of the visits, however, were just a few miles from home to his father's parents and siblings. And that was a good thing because the car often stalled, and his older sisters and mother had to push it to start it up again.

No matter where they visited, French was the language used. They seldom came in contact with English-speaking people. Why would they visit anyone who didn't speak their language? Even in the stores, there was always someone who spoke French to wait on them. On the radio, there were many stations with French-language news, Cajun music, and weather. At church, there was always the French-speaking priest from Canada, who gave sermons in French and English. They were practically living in a parallel world.

Visits to his grandparents, Noah and Blanche, were interesting. His grandparents had moved near his little town on the bayou in 1931 in search of better farmland and the availability of wood for heat and cooking. They had loaded a horse-drawn wagon with their few possessions and six children and left early in the morning for the little town. It was a slow, laborious journey of 25 miles that took all day. In contrast to the prairie lands they left in Acadia Parish, their rental property contained unlimited wood. One only had to go out and cut it. They sharecropped on three different farms from 1931 to 1945, and they were finally able to buy a small farm with the help of the money they received from their 3rd son Isaac's checks for military service. Finally, they would no longer have to move to search for farmland to sharecrop anymore. They were then 55 years old.

When he visited his grandparents, he remembers his grandfather, Noah, whose ancestors came from Picardy, France, as being very loquacious and humorous. He was always barefooted in the house, exposing feet with extremely high arches and bunions. He loved to tell jokes and make fun of people by mocking and mimicking them. He could be funny, but was also remembered for the severe rope beatings he gave to his five sons. His diet was unusual in that he hated vegetables and preferred pork with skin and fat left intact. The pork gravy soaking his rice was essentially melted fat. He cut up his pork to have an equal mixture of skin, fat and meat for each bite he took along with the rice. Stranger still for Pierre was that he ate with a knife only. "How could he do that without cutting his mouth?" he wondered. Despite this seemingly unhealthy diet, he lived to be 94 years old and worked actively until the age of 92.

His grandmother, Blanche, was also interesting. She was one of 19 children whose ancestors came from the Champagne region of France in the 18th century. She was the matriarch of the family and besides making all the decisions, she made it her business to keep up with the whole family's business! When Hazel announced to her that she had a boyfriend, a man she would later marry, she asked for his name. Giving her mother his non-Cajun name, she responded derisively, "He's an *Americain* isn't he?" He was, and Robert would be the first non-Cajun to marry into Pierre's paternal family. He was also the one who wired his house for electricity and the one who would later contribute to Pierre's reading progress. Thankfully, his grandmother did not contest her daughter's choice. She had rejected an earlier boyfriend because she didn't like the appearance of the nape of his neck. Pierre still wonders what that neck looked like.

When his grandparents retired from farming, they left the farm and built a neat little house in town next to bayou Teche about one mile away. Though the house had an indoor bathroom and plumbing, his grandfather kept the outhouse on the edge of the bayou bank that was about ten feet above the water line. Due to erosion, the outhouse became perched precariously on the very edge of the bank.

His children were constantly concerned about his safety as he refused to stop using it. They could just see their partially clothed father locked up in his outhouse with pants at his ankles floating down the bayou screaming for help. Eventually, they tore it down before it tumbled into the bayou water.

Pierre also remembered his great-grandfather, Charles, very well. He recalls him being in poor health, slim, rather dark-complexioned, tall and white-haired. He was a retired sharecropper and known to be a hard worker well into his 80's. When Pierre was around five years old, his family made a visit to see his great-grandfather. As usual, there was a huge family lunch with great amounts of food. Pierre especially liked the chicken fricassee and helped himself to all the drumsticks he could eat. On the third drumstick, he just could not finish it and left more than half of it. At home the following week when he was hungry, he thought to himself that he should have finished that drumstick! His great-grandfather lived to be 87 years old.

Among Pierre's most vivid memories were the occasions when his parents took Verna and Bertha to "the dance." In Cajun culture, the dance had always been important no matter how poverty-stricken they were. It was often the only opportunity young people had to socialize with the opposite sex. There were few marriages where the couple did not meet at a dance. Even his father, who did very few frivolous things, brought his daughters to the dance—that was just the proper thing to do. Besides, the girls did not have to pay to dance—only the boys did.

The dancehall was a large building located next to the bayou about a mile from home. Of course, his sisters waited with great anticipation to dance and meet the boys. Bertha and her black girlfriend often practiced dancing together. The dance was one of their few pleasures, and they loved it. The family, all six of them, got in the old Ford and drove the mile to the dancehall. The first thing one saw upon entering the hall was an unpainted, four-foot tall wooden fence corralling the dance floor. The dance floor had been sprinkled with a sawdust-like material to facilitate dancing. The parents and non-dancers stood behind the fence to watch the dancers. At the left end of the dance floor was the bandstand where the musicians were tuning their instruments. The discordant cacophony of the fiddle, steel guitar, accordion, bass guitar, and lead guitar sounded like a music room filled with musically challenged students taking their first lessons.

The dancers, parents, and anybody who just wanted to be there filled the old wooden building. There were some tables next to the floor for dancers to sit and have refreshments, such as alcohol if they were old enough and their parents would allow it, or Cokes or Seven-Ups if not. Of course, not all the dancers were adolescents as there were people of all ages participating. Old men and women were even in there dancing up a storm. It was not uncommon to see frail, elderly men or women who normally had a hard time walking become quite mobile and energetic once they got on the dance floor. They then walked back to their seats limping as soon as the dance was over.

Pierre, about five years old at the time, noted that most of the men were holding cans of some sort—to him anyone over 15 was a man. The cans were metal with a conical top from which the men and boys drank can after can of the mysterious liquid inside. He learned much later that they were drinking beer. Other men had various sorts of mixed drinks. Then the Cajun musicians cranked up their instruments and began to make sounds completely unlike those they made when tuning their instruments. The music was loud due the amplifiers driving the instruments, and the people had to shout to be heard. Together, the music and people created a raucous, deafening sound. The dance floor began to fill with dancers, mostly girls who danced with each other until a few brave boys worked up enough courage or drank enough beer to ask them to dance. When the young men stepped on the dance floor, the floor walker would approach them to collect 50 cents and staple a ticket on their shirt collar. Fifty cents was a sizable fee at that time, so some young men would try to steer their partner away from the floor walker while turning his shoulder to hide his shirt collar. Eventually, every young man had to pay the piper.

The musicians performed very differently from modern Cajun musicians. The musicians who played the accordion, steel guitar, drums, and fiddle usually played sitting down while only the guitar player usually played standing up. One thing all players had in common was that they played with stoic expressions and practically no body movement—quite different from what one would see 35 years later. Most of the musicians had other jobs, some of them farmers, most were under educated, and only the love of music drove them to perform. Of course, the extra money they received was a very important supplement to their meager incomes.

Some of the musicians who played at the dance hall on the bayou were some of the best known in Cajun music, notably Ira LeJeune, perhaps the best-known Cajun musician at that time.

Pierre stood with his mom and dad behind the fence. His mother probably thought how fortunate the dancers were to have such a nice, large dance floor complete with electric lights to dance on. She probably recalled how she had to go to house dances where the dance floor was in a small, dim room. Peering through the fence boards, Pierre could see the activities going on. He saw his grand-mother standing across the dance floor behind the fence looking at the dancers. She was watching her youngest daughter, who was just a little older than his sisters, dance. Of course, he didn't know why she was watching, just that she was. Later, he would find out she was watching who she was dancing with, and how close they were dancing—after all, the boy a girl danced with could become a son-in-law. One could not be too careful.

Later in the night, the action continued at an even more frenetic pace. The noise increased in proportion to the liquor consumed. People were moving about everywhere. There were bourée games going on at the end of the dance floor opposite the bandstand. His father often played cards there to pass the time while waiting for the girls. There were waiters scurrying around frantically to meet the copious alcohol needs of the dancers and watchers. Even outside, there were clusters of people visiting with friends, getting fresh air (cigarette smoke was always thick in these dance halls) and perhaps just escaping the noise for a while. To Pierre, everything was be-ginning to be uninteresting. It was way past his bedtime, and he was getting sleepy, restless and grumpy. His mother took him to the car and put him in the back seat to sleep. He still remembers, before drifting off, the sound of dozens of feet crunching in the graveled parking area as people constantly walked back and forth.

Around age five, events began to change Pierre's life. His oldest sister, Verna, married and left the household. His memories of this wedding are vague. It did mean, however, that he would get to share the second bedroom with his second sister. For him, that was a big improvement. That bedroom was a little cooler than the rest of the house due to a faint breeze that sometimes lost its way and accidentally came in. Even with the breeze, it was still hot, and the moss-filled mattress was hot under his body, much like lying down on an electric blanket in summer. Additionally, he got to sleep with his second sister, Bertha, who was like a second mother to him. Later, she would jokingly claim that the reason she has arthritic hips is because she carried him on them when he was a baby. The little English he knew at this time, he learned from her. He remembers her teaching him the Lord's Prayer in English. It was rote memorization as he did not fully understand the words. Words learned in a vacuum mean very little.

Pierre became more aware of the roles his parents played. His father was up before daybreak to go to work in the oilfields. Before he was awake, his father had already left, and sometimes he came back home after Pierre had gone to bed. His job had no benefits, no retirement and he was earning minimum hourly wages—less than a dollar an hour at that time, and the work was hard and dirty. Often, trees had to be cleared to construct the board roads he built leading to the drilling platforms. Trees were cut with crosscut saws as there were no power saws or chain saws. After felling the trees, the trunks were shortened with crosscut saws and the branches were chopped up with axes and burned. Sometimes the locations were in marshland which made the process even more difficult. Louisiana's climate of high heat and humidity added to the difficulty level of the work. Winters were often cold and icy which presented other challenges to outdoor work. Those who did this work had no other choices—they did it because they had to. They usually had no skills and no education and were often sharecroppers trying to make extra money to supplement their meager income. All they had to offer was their labor.

When his father was not working at his day job, he would work the family garden with basic tools—spade, rake, and hoe. The garden was very important because it provided food that they did not have to buy. Additionally, because of his farming heritage, he was just programmed to grow things. He produced an abundance of corn, potatoes, tomatoes, snap beans, butter beans, peas of several types, mustard greens, turnips, bell peppers, hot peppers, okra, cucumbers, lettuce and sometimes watermelons, cantaloupes, beets, and radishes. He gave his excess production to relatives and friends. He would continue to work his garden until he was into his 90's.

Because of his limited time from work, his father was no longer an avid hunter, but he did do some squirrel and rabbit hunting that provided some dietary variety as well as appreciated delicacies. Squirrels were pot-roasted in a cast iron pot with smoked sausage or sometimes used in gumbo. Every little bone was picked clean, and the skull split to extract the little brain—a special treat. Rabbits were also usually pot-roasted with smoked sausage to produce a gravy to serve over rice. On some occasions, especially after a snow (which seemed to happen more often then), he went out to shoot black birds that bunched up into dense flocks. One blast from his 12-gauge shotgun could produce up to 50 birds. These were plucked, cleaned, and prepared to make a bird gumbo along with smoked sausage. The birds, composed mostly of breast meat, were completely consumed except for the bones. They consumed even the head, with brain intact, and neck. The little neck provided a convenient handle to pop the head into the mouth to be squished to release the flavorful little brain. For the price of one shotgun shell, a whole family could be fed. However, not only fed; gumbo was not just food for physical nourishment but nourishment for the soul. When family and friends ate gumbo together, the sense of community was complete as everyone regarded it as a favorite meal. They made gumbos most often during the winter months to escape the kitchen heat. When the women served gumbo during the first cold snap, it was an auspicious time for company and for family bonding. The house was warm and cozy; it was truly "soul food."

Pierre's mother had also been a hard worker since she was a child. Because she was needed on the farm to help her sharecropper father do farm work and help her mother with the household work, her schooling was limited. She had eight siblings, and the older ones had to take care of the younger ones. As a result, she went up to the fourth grade, and due to missing so much school and dropping out after fourth grade, she forgot the little she had learned. His mother had often told him her teachers said that she learned very quickly and could do very well if only she would attend school regularly. Unfortunately, that was not to happen. At age 18, she lost her mother and father to cancer. She and her older sisters helped take care of the younger ones until she married in 1931.

In many respects, the women's lot in this rural culture was more difficult than that of the men. As the wives of farmers, they often had to do farm labor equal to that of their husbands, and then leave the field before noon to fix lunch for the rest of the workers. Then, she would go back to the fields and continue working. In addition there were the household chores to do. Cooking a chicken involved catching, killing, and cleaning the chicken before the cooking began. Finally, they were completely dependent on their husband, and divorce was rare due in part to their lack of skills to support themselves and their children.

As a child of five to six years, Pierre remembers the massive work she had to do with so little. Her washing was done in the rear of the house using two large wash tubs and a washboard. One tub was used for scrubbing the clothes on a washboard with home-made soap. The other tub was used to rinse the clothes. Before they got city water two years before, his sisters would laboriously walk to the bayou with buckets to bring back water—a distance of 200 feet round trip—and many trips were needed to fill the tubs. Now with city water, the task was much easier. After washing, the clothes were hand wrung and carried to the clothes-line to dry. This process was for normal clothes. His dad's work clothes which were often soaked with sweat, drill mud, oil, creosote and various other contaminates required hauling water to a large cast iron kettle for boiling. Wood was gathered and placed under the kettle. Pierre's job was to gather wood chips to start the fire. When the water reached boiling point, home-made soap was dissolved in the water. Dirty clothes were then boiled and swirled in the water with a paddle. Then the clothes were hauled back to the rinse tub for rinsing before a trip to the clothesline for drying.

The total labor needed to wash a batch of clothing was staggering. Tasks such as hauling the water, heating the water, wringing the clothes by hand, carrying heavy wet clothes to the clothesline, and emptying large tubs of water constituted a level of labor beyond the imagination of anyone who has not done laundry this way. They were in the middle of the 20th century, not colonial days. Electric washing machines had been available since the 1920's. Mechanical-roller clothes wringers were available, but his parents would never spend their limited money on such luxuries. Also, his parents were always the last to purchase any of the then-modern conveniences, even if they could afford them. The Great Depression and poverty had conditioned them to save every penny possible and to buy only the most essential items. Except for the automobile they had, they were essentially living an 18th/19th century life in the twentieth century.

Then there was the house work. The floor, though of plain pine boards, needed constant attention. The continuous hauling of firewood into the house for the wood stove always dropped chips, dust, and sometimes insects that necessitated endless sweeping. She mopped the floor with soap and water to clean most of the dirt and used pieces of soft red brick to scrub the heavy stains. Soft red brick was also used to clean rusted and oil-caked cast iron pots and pans. The first step in ironing clothes was to heat cast iron irons on a wood or kerosene stove. Dusting was a never ending chore due to automobiles and trucks stirring up huge clouds of impenetrable dust which found its way through the open windows of the little house. Pierre could feel the grit as he walked barefooted on the floor. Moreover, there were the garden chores to be done. There was the constant hoeing to remove grass and aerate the soil. Planting and harvesting, and most tedious, the constant shelling of beans and peas was a continuous process. Canning tomatoes, figs, and pears was time-consuming hard work and most uncomfortable in the heat of the kitchen. No wonder his mother had no patience with laziness. If someone slept late, anything past 6AM, she would shout, "Get your butt (*ton derrière*) out of bed before it takes root to the mattress!" Pierre would forever be an early riser!

Finally, due to his father being away most of the time at work, his mother was the enforcer of rules in the family. She was also the one who saw that the Catholic faith, which was by far the most common religion among the Cajuns, was observed by the family. They went to church regularly and received all the sacraments on a timely basis. Pierre remembers the many times when a severe thunder and lightning storm occurred, how his mother pulled out Magnolia tree leaves that the priest had blessed on the most recent Palm Sunday, the Sunday before Easter. She burned the leaves as everyone recited the rosary in hopes of escaping being struck by lightning—a procedure she performed for the remainder of the storms he would spend with his family.

When the crisis was over his father often told a story of a large family who, like them, had burned the leaves and prayed the rosary to escape danger. The family commenced praying and the father, who was only halfway into his rosary, observed that his eldest son was not praying. He asked, "Why are you not saying the rosary?"

The boy replied, "I'm already finished, Pop."

"Well goddamn, you getting to be a real son of a bitch on that rosary."

His father never mentioned that house being struck by lightning.

Linda, 10 months, and Pierre, 4 years old

Linda & Pierre, five & eight years old

CHAPTER 4
GRADES 1 – 3,
PARALLEL WORLDS COLLIDE

"The direction in which education starts a man will determine his future life."

Plato, *The Republic*

AROUND age six, Pierre's limited little world would expand relatively exponentially. Until now, he had come in contact only with his immediate family and other relatives. But soon, he would discover that other world. He would start school. Crossing into this new world would be a challenge—one had to speak English there. This meant that much of what he had learned during his first six years was now unacceptable in this new world. It was as if someone had told him, "Now Pierre, we are going to press your little reset button now so we can program you for your new world."

After dressing in his freshly-pressed short pants and cotton shirt, his sister Bertha, brought him to school that first day, and what an eye opener that would be. There were a lot more children at school than at family gatherings with his many cousins. He felt very shy and stayed close to his sister. Some of the children were like him and spoke mostly Cajun French. Some were Cajuns who had mastered English fairly well, and of course, there were the non-Cajuns who spoke English well. Pierre met a little boy who spoke English and French fairly well who helped him get around to do the necessary things first graders needed to do.

Even the adults at the school were unusual to Pierre—they all spoke only English and they dressed funny. The men wore clothing he had never seen his father wear. The ladies were even stranger with their colorful dresses, differently-styled hair, and flowery perfumes. One thing they all had in common was that they were always making them do things, strange things like working with a paste that gave the whole classroom a peculiar scent, a scent he would be immersed in for the next four years.

Then, the instruction began. His teacher was a short, rotund little woman who was of Cajun descent. That would be a good thing for Pierre. Students sat in rows in wooden desk units fixed inline to the floor. Each desk had an indention at the top to keep pencils from rolling off, as well as holes on the top right of the desk to hold ink bottles. He sat in the third desk, second row. He remembers when the boy in the back of him, whose name was Danny, pinched him. When he turned around, he saw a boy twice his size glaring at him. He just turned around and faced the front. But the pincher would later become a lifelong friend. Then the teacher passed out papers with images to color with crayons. He had never done this before and could not color within the lines. In later life, if he were to become an artist, his style would have to be abstract/impressionism.

He recalls borrowing colors from a girl across from him on the third row. His pack had only about five or six colors; her box had at least a dozen. At that time, he didn't understand that the more affluent kids usually had more colors in their boxes.

His reading lessons had a very inauspicious beginning. Of course, his limited English skills did not help. There were no special programs to help students bridge that gap such as "English as a Second Language" that would be ubiquitous in most modern schools. The method of teaching reading was sight reading as opposed to phonics. Students started learning the alphabet and then the smallest of words and then on to larger words. His most memorable reading interaction occurred when his teacher placed a word card in the slot board and called on students who raised their hands to pronounce the word. Pierre knew very few words, only a few two letter words, one of which was "is." When the word "is" came up, his little arm shot up like a rocket and threatened a rotator cup injury from waving so enthusiastically. His teacher, knowing that it was one of the few words he knew, mercifully called on him. Then he felt good —he had done something good! A couple of days later during the reading class, the word "is" came up again. Again threatening a shoulder dislocation, his little arm shot up to get to pronounce "his" word. His teacher, ignoring him, looked around the room and called on another student. He was devastated by the betrayal he felt—she had given his word to someone else!

But it was not all bad. He had recess and lunch—these he could do well. He enjoyed playing outside with his classmates. This consisted of just running randomly around chasing each other. Of course, there were wrestling matches and the occasional fight. He could see the older boys playing marbles on smooth packed dirt. The older girls were jumping rope while singing rhyming songs. When recess was over, his horizons were broadened when he went to the restroom. He saw that there were white troughs to urinate in—a first for him. Then there were little rooms with white chairs to sit on to do their other business, and when they pushed on the little bar, their business was washed away to some unknown place. At home, his "business" stayed put for a long time.

The cafeteria was another new experience. He had never eaten anywhere but at home or at the homes of relatives. Eating in restaurants was not done—too expensive. The cost was five cents for lunch which included a small glass jar of milk sealed with a pressed-in cardboard seal. He found the food good as it was much like at home but also got to eat things that he never had at home. Some kids complained about the food, and those who complained were often those who got less at home. He remembers waiting in line to be served and talking to his friends as they moved up. What he remembers most vividly was the scent of the cafeteria, not a bad scent, or a great one, just memorable. It would be the same scent he would experience in school cafeterias for the next 65 years.

By some miracle, he passed to the second grade, probably just barely. Like many of his friends, he received no help at home with his homework. His parents, who knew it was important to go to school, could not help him—they could not read. There were no books in the house—why would anyone have books if one does not read? He has no recollections of ever doing schoolwork at home.

One of his out-of-school experiences at this time included one of the occasions when his mother made a quilt. His mother would save every scrap of cloth from worn-out or outgrown clothing, and remnants of fabric from completed sewing projects. She would then cut out squares, little by little, from the material and sew them together to make the cover of the quilt. Sometimes the reverse of the quilt was also made of this patchwork, but often the reverse of the quilt was just a plain sheet. When she had enough material sewn together, it was time to construct the quilt. First, she would tell family members and neighbors that she would begin making the quilt on a certain day, and they would come to help. This custom was a remnant of the Acadian tradition of giving a helping hand (*donner un coup de main*)—like the barn raising tradition of early Americans. They hung a quilting square from the ceiling in the kitchen—which took up most of the kitchen space. They then stretched the bottom side of the quilt fabric on the frame and placed a layer of cotton batting on it. Finally, they placed the top side, the most attractive one, on top of the cotton. Then the tedious work of hand-quilting began. His mother and her helpers sat around the quilt frame to quilt and have much conversation and coffee. Pierre and his little sister enjoyed playing on the floor under the quilt as the ladies sewed. To them, it felt as cozy as a tent. Pierre enjoyed the additional pleasure of listening to the ladies' conversations.

Quilts had always been an important item in Cajun households and particularly in their household where the temperature outside during winter was often the same as the temperature inside. His father did not believe in leaving anything burning inside the house at night, even when they got gas heaters later. His fear was that the gas might get turned off at night and come back on to asphyxiate the whole family. So, they slept with layers of quilts and blankets to ward off subfreezing temperatures. The weight of the quilts and blankets made it difficult to turn around in bed. Additionally, they wore knit caps to keep their heads warm. Getting up in the mornings was a chilling experience—not fun.

When he thought of second grade, the first image in his mind was his teacher, whom he felt was not as nice as his first-grade teacher. She was what one would consider today the stereotypical teacher of the 50's—old, wore glasses, no makeup, single, gray clothes, and gray hair rolled into a bun on top of her head. And she was mean. She was known to strike students' open hands with a ruler. Her process was to hold the four fingers to keep the palm exposed, and with a strength belying her age, deliver several painful whacks to the palm.

His most vivid memory of her was a talk she gave to the students during the school year. At that time, there was construction going on to build the school gymnasium that was being framed with steel beams located perhaps 60 to 70 feet away from the classroom. As they listened attentively, she began, "Now class, I have a very important announcement to make. There is and will be construction to build our new gym during the school year. During recess, you are not to go near the work site because it is very dangerous and you could get hurt very badly, or even get killed. Most importantly, the men are doing a lot of welding that makes a bright blue flame that you are not to watch because you could be blinded." At that moment, 25 little heads and necks swiveled left in complete synchronization to watch the bright blue lights. Had "The Exorcist" been filming in the area at that time, there would have been 25 viable candidates for the lead role. So much for grave warnings.

Oh, and no one went blind; the blue lights must have been a little too far away.

By second grade, most kids were resigned to the fact that they must go to school and stay there all day. There was one exception. One little boy, for some reason, was not doing well academically or behaviorally. He would ask the teacher to go to the bathroom, and when granted permission, he went home which was over one-half mile away. As most parents had no telephones, there was no way to check with the parents. The principal searched everywhere around the school; his search was fruitless. Then the classroom door opened and in ran the missing boy, followed by his father beating the tar out of him with his belt. Unfortunately, this would not be the last time he would go back home, and he would quit school long before his graduation. Problem children, often labeled as stubborn, lazy, or dumb, did not have special education classes available to them.

Each day, lunch money was collected from the students. At five cents each, multiplied by 25 children that made a total of $1.50 to give 25 students lunch. Each day, a student was selected to count the lunch money. No doubt this was done to reinforce newly taught math skills. The teacher asked, "Who wants to count the lunch money today?" He raised his hand along with several other students, and the teacher chose Pierre. He walked to the table on which lay a small pile of change, mostly nickels, and perhaps a quarter or two. He commenced counting, "One, two, three, four, five …" The teacher erupted, "Go sit down! You don't know how to count money! Tommy, come here and count this money." Tommy proceeded, "Five, ten, fifteen, and twenty …" Of course, Pierre felt embarrassed. He would not volunteer to count money again, certainly not in second grade.

Though his math skills were not exemplary, he did do fairly well in reading. He read about a boy and girl, Dick and Jane, who lived on Cherry Street. It was interesting and fed his natural curiosity, but he didn't know any kids like that. They had a bike and a red wagon to play with, and their parents were nothing like his. It was like reading about people from far away—much farther away than Lake Charles. He still had to color things, and still couldn't stay within the lines.

As a second grader, recess was different as many of the boys his age would now play marbles and the girls would jump rope or play hopscotch. He took an interest in marbles. There were two types of marble games—the one using a big circle of four to six feet called "Boss," and one with a small circle of about six to eight inches in diameter called *mouri* which is Cajun French for dead. Games were played for "funs" or "keeps." The younger players usually played for "funs" while the older boys usually played for "keeps." The boys decided what they would play for, or how many marbles each player would place in the center of the ring. They played for onesies, twosies, or threesies—the number of marbles each would place in the ring. The better players usually wanted to play for higher stakes so they could win more. Of course, the weaker players wanted to play for less to minimize their losses.

The game began by "lagging"—seeing in what order players would shoot determined by how close one could get to a line with a thrown marble. There were often serious debates as to who was closer to

A Cajun in France

the line. With the shooting order established, it was time to play marbles. The first shooter would shoot his "taw" (prized shooter marble) from the edge of the large circle drawn on the grassless, packed soil. The object was to hit one or more marbles and knock them outside the ring. These marbles became his. His next shot would be from wherever his taw stopped. The goal was to keep his taw as close as possible to the marbles. A good shooter had the possibility of knocking all the marbles out of the ring and end the game before anyone else got a shot. But if he missed, the next person in line got the next shot. Also, if a person's taw stayed in the ring after a miss, the next person could shoot his taw out of the ring and collect all the marbles the taw's owner previously shot out of the ring.

In the small circle game (*mouri*) they again would set the stakes and lag marbles for shooting order. The goal was to hit marbles out of the small circle without the taw stopping in the circle. If a taw stopped in the circle, the shooter was "dead" and out of the game.

When the bell rang during the marble game, two things could happen. The players could divide the marbles left in the ring. The most common scenario was that someone would yell "razoo!!" which was the signal for every player to rake in as many marbles as possible. Then the marble players, distinguished by their dirty knuckles and knees, and all the other students, ran to the classroom to avoid tardiness. They took their seats and were metaphorically light-years away from being ready to learn anything. They were more concerned about finding out who won and who lost, and most importantly, if they had won or lost. Some boys, Pierre included, kept their hands in their pockets to count their wins or losses. Invariably, a pocketful of marbles was dumped on the floor and bounced and rolled in all directions. Of course the teacher, being less than pleased with this disturbance, confiscated all the marbles and punished the guilty with no recess and lines to write.

After continuous problems with the old Ford car, his father decided to buy another vehicle. Like in most Cajun families, the husband was the one to make this decision. He probably did discuss it with his wife, but his was the final word. He went to town to shop and came back with a brand new 1950 Ford pickup truck. The family was excited about a brand new vehicle as no one in their family had ever had one before. It would be nice not to have to get out and push that old car again. As usual, his father paid cash—a total of $1,600. At $1.00 an hour wages, it took a long time to save that amount of money. Now they could go visiting. Pierre and his little sister would sit in the truck bed during good weather. That was exciting. Of course, when all five got in the front seat, it was a bit crowded, but no one complained.

The most memorable event for Pierre that year was the marriage of his second sister, Bertha. His sister had been dating her boyfriend, Charles, for about a year, and Pierre had many recollections of that courtship. His parents would not allow unescorted dates so they could see each other at the dance or he could visit her at home. His parents were not overjoyed for Bertha to have a "gentleman caller." Parents of daughters in his family were often suspicious of young men's motives, perhaps because they remembered what they wanted to do at that age. Often, mothers did not look at their daughter's wedding as a joyous occasion because they felt that after marriage, their daughter would have the same hard lives they had.

When his sister was expecting her boyfriend to come to visit her at home, she would place two metal lawn chairs on the porch close to each other. Pierre found this amusing and teased her about it. He and his little sister were a genuine nuisance to them during those visits since they were constantly there bugging them. Just their presence was an antidote to romance. His future brother-in-law and sister were probably thinking of finding some humane method to make them disappear. Pierre incessantly asked questions, and when Bertha told him he asked too many questions, he responded, "How am going to learn anything if I don't ask questions?" Certainly, they thought that he should go somewhere else to learn something. On one occasion, he told his future brother-in-law, "Mom says you're a little fart." She actually had said that! Pierre did not know enough to fathom the embarrassment and pain the couple felt. His untimely remark certainly was not a vote of confidence for the prospective groom. He would also make Linda ask the young man for a nickel, and he would give her one. Despite their less than cupid-like behavior, Cupid's heat-seeking arrow found its mark, and romance did blossom for Bertha and Charles on that front porch. The wedding date was set for spring.

The wedding day finally arrived and started with a great deal of excitement. There was the getting-ready part such as cooking food and baking cakes for the reception. Though Pierre did not like cake, he loved to taste the cake batter before they messed it up by baking it. He loved his job of scrapping and eating the small remains of batter from the bowls. When his mother wasn't looking, he would sometimes furtively dip his finger in the batter and lick it clean. Then there was the other getting-ready part—getting dressed in his best clothes and putting on shoes. Going to the church, seeing his sister in a long white dress, and most important of all, seeing all the relatives and friends who had come to the wedding was puzzling to Pierre. He did not recollect any of the actual wedding ceremonies.

They held the reception in their little house, and there were people in its every corner and spilling out into the yard. The women spread out the cakes and food prepared that morning and he took advantage of this veritable feast. Then the fun ended for him. Pierre was sitting in his little rocking chair in the living room. People were milling all around him going in and out of the house and greeting the bride and groom, when one of his older cousins teasingly told him, "Your sister is going to leave you and never come back again." This revelation hit him like the proverbial ton of bricks as he didn't fully understand this marriage thing. In his mind, she would still be here when the wedding was over, and her boyfriend would go back home just like before because she was the one who had always taken care of him. Then he reacted by crying like a baby. People came up to him and asked what was wrong and he tearfully replied, "She is leaving me and will never come back." It took the efforts of many to console him and convince him that his sister would come back often to visit.

By the skin of his teeth, he started third grade with his classmates. It had to be another miracle as he knew his grades were not good. He recalled seeing red marks on his report card. He didn't care about his report card grades—he didn't understand the concept of grades. It was like something inevitable and out of his control.

School was a place his parents sent him every day and where he had to stay and be told what to do while waiting for recess, lunch, and 3:30. He now imagines that the teachers and the principal got together to decide what to do with him—should he pass or should he be held back? Perhaps someone reluctantly said, "Let's promote him, and if he doesn't do any better next year, we'll hold him back then." Uncharacteristically, for a poor student, he had perfect attendance most years.

His third-grade teacher was a pleasant non-Cajun woman (*une Americaine*). In Cajun culture, being an "Americain" had nothing to do with nationality. Americans were simply English speakers and not Cajuns. He had pleasant recollections of third grade mainly because of the many interesting activities he experienced. One activity was the little projects they made relevant to seasons, holidays, and events. He was fascinated with the kites that he had seen older children fly around town. It was magical the way these kites could fly up so high in the sky. The spring project required each student to make a kite with colored construction paper. Pierre's kite was green with a white paper tail. All of the students' kites were hung in a corner of the room, making that area a concentration of that omnipresent paste smell. He remembers being proud of seeing his kite among his classmates' kites. He also remembered his disappointment that these kites could not fly. Perhaps one day he would have one. The chances of his parents buying him one were as likely as a kite breaking off its string and flying to the moon. He knew they would never spend ten cents on a kite.

Another new activity he enjoyed was spatter painting. The students cut out shapes of birds or animals. He chose an owl. They pinned forms to white paper and sprayed with a sprayer that looked just like his parents insect sprayer. When the students removed the form, there was a perfect white image of his bird on the paper. More magic! How does she think of all these things? Then the class would color their birds and animals with appropriate colors.

The most exciting of all events was when they had chorus once a week. The chorus teacher, who was also the band teacher, was unique to him. She was tall, had gray, well-coiffed hair, and what a captivating scent she had when she floated into the room. Having two older sisters, Pierre knew about perfume, but this was unlike anything his sisters had. The scent stayed in the room even after she left. Her makeup was obvious to him as she wore dark red lipstick and a lot of powder on her face. In addition to necklaces, she wore the most colorful dresses he had ever seen: he particularly liked the bright red one. When she made her charismatic entrance into the classroom, she was welcomed with applause and yays. Santa and Peter Rabbit ho-hoing and hopping through the door couldn't have pleased them more. She began by teaching the words to a song, usually a Steven Foster song. Pierre remembers the class singing "Old Folks at Home," "Jeannie with the Light Brown Hair," "Camptown Races," and "Oh! Susanna." She was different from all the other teachers—so energetic and exciting. Then, disappointingly, she would go away and not come back until the next week.

On the home front, Pierre made progress. As he was fascinated with the bayou nearby, he had always wanted to go near it and fish in it. He had been able to go there with his older sisters, and sometimes with his father for fishing, but his mother forbade him from going there alone. The bayou was very deep, and she was afraid he would fall in and drown. Now that he was older, he was allowed to go fishing alone, but only in front of the house. He had fished before with his dad and had already caught his first fish —a small catfish. Now he was grown up enough to fish on his own. His fishing excursions were a very simple affair. He would dig up some earthworms near the bitter pecan tree across the road in front of his house. He would then make his fishing pole from the branch of a tree. The string was cotton, recycled wrapping string. His father always had some fish hooks around. He then got all his "gear" together and headed for the bayou. He never made huge catches, but he usually caught a few perch. He kept everything he caught and his mother cooked it. Pierre had begun a hobby he would enjoy for a long time.

While fishing, he observed a wide variety of things. He saw the fresh water clams in the mud at the edge of the water. He saw the tracks they made as they slowly moved in the mud over it. Sometimes he caught some of the clams and made fish bait from the soft, white flesh. He saw snakes in the water and coiled on limbs just above the water. The snakes reminded him of the time he had gone fishing with his father in a slough about a quarter mile up the bayou from his house. The slough was a small tributary off the main bayou and lined with moss-laden cypress trees. The water was not deep, but it teemed with an abundant supply of fish, crawfish, and frogs which attracted battalions of snakes. Pierre was too small to fish there, so he sat on the bank and watched his father walk into the water to reach a deeper fishing spot. He had rubber boots on which reached to his knees, and he walked out until there was only about an inch of his boots above the water. He then cast his line out to catch anything that would bite—mostly catfish. When he caught a fish, he threw it on the bank for Pierre to put in a bucket. All of a sudden, Pierre noticed 15 or 20 snakes in the slough, many of which were swimming in all directions. Then some were swimming toward his dad. He warned his dad about the snakes, but he did not respond. Pierre was getting nervous as he had been taught to stay clear of snakes. Then, the snakes were swimming all around his dad and between his boots. Pierre was now almost petrified with the thought that the snakes might jump up and bite his dad. His father continued fishing unperturbedly while he caught all he fish he wanted. On the way back home, he asked his father, "Why were you not afraid of those snakes."

His father replied," Those were water snakes, they are not poisonous."

His snake memories were interrupted by a *pop pop putt pop pop putt pop* sound from far down the bayou. He knew what the sound was. The old man who owned the property next to them was returning from a moss gathering expedition in his boat. The putt putt sound slowly got louder as the slow moving boat crept towards him. After ten minutes or so, he had a full view of the boat, man, and motor, all three of which were relics from the past composing a veritable floating museum. The old man, standing in his moss-laden boat, was thin, wiry, and deeply suntanned from many years on the water. He wore a formerly white sleeveless undershirt that now exhibited variegated shades of brown from the stains of sweat, dirt, and grease from the motor. He knew the man spoke only French, but strangely, he had never spoken to him despite seeing him nearby for years. The man never stopped long enough for Pierre to approach him. The ancient, cast-iron, inboard engine had one cylinder, a flywheel, and a water jacket for cooling. These engines were popular in the early 1900's and seemed to hang around forever. They had just enough power to propel a boat into motion but not fast enough to create a wake. The boat, made of cypress, was flat bottomed, about five feet wide and 16 feet long. It was kept afloat by pouring melted tar in its bottom each spring to seal the leaks.

By the 1950's, moss gathering was already an occupation of the past. At the turn of the 20th century, moss was widely used as stuffing for mattresses, chairs, and furniture. Pierre's mattress was moss-stuffed, and he would sleep on it until he left home for college. While a moss mattress was comfortable enough initially, it quickly packed down into a hard sleeping surface with a huge indention where one slept. In the 1950's, only a few people still picked moss. Sometimes kids or extremely poor families would gather moss for the little money it provided. The old man, however, had a little moss operation. He would collect moss from the trees overhanging the bayou by twisting a long, forked, tree branch into the moss and pulling it down into his boat. He would spread the green moss along the bayou bank in front of his property. When the winter and spring rains came, the rising waters of the bayou covered the moss for much of the time. By summer, the moss had made a transformation. The soft, gray outer layer had decomposed, leaving the black, wiry core of the moss exposed. The moss gatherer was now ready to sell the cured moss to one of the few remaining moss gins for very little money.

Pierre realized it was time to pick up his little fish string and go home, only about 100 feet away. He loved being near the bayou, even though he didn't always catch fish. He also wanted to learn how to swim. He knew some of his cousins who lived up the bayou swam all the time, and some were younger than he. He recalled one time when he visited them, the whole family, including his Uncle Leonce, was in the bayou. They were having so much fun laughing and giggling as they swam. He envied them. When they finished swimming, they got a bar of Ivory soap and washed up in the bayou. That was so much better than bathing in a couple of inches of second-hand water in a tub. He thought, "I have to learn how to swim." It would not be simple because his mother forbade him to get in the bayou. But how else would he ever learn to swim?

He started his walk home, but he had to be careful because the ground along the bayou was littered with thorns which could cause serious injury. He hardly ever had shoes on, except in winter when he got his annual pair. By early spring, the soles were worn out and detached, and his father would cut off the detached sole and placed cardboard into the shoes for a couple of weeks of extra wear. From being barefooted most of the year, the soles of his feet had developed a leather-like layer of skin, enough protection for stickers, but not enough to thwart thorns that could be several inches long. If a thorn lodged in his foot, he simply pulled it out and continued on his way. Often the penetrating thorn broke off in his foot and had to be extracted by his sister or mother with a needle. If the thorn could not be extracted with a needle, it was later removed when infection and pus brought the thorn to the surface.

Chapter 5,
Grades 4 – 6,
Expanding World

"Youth is the best time to be rich, and the best time to be poor."

Euripides

At age nine, Pierre was prepared to go to fourth grade. It was time to buy school clothes for him and his sister to start the new school year. Most of their clothing came from the Sears and Roebuck catalog and sometimes from the Montgomery Ward catalog which they looked forward to receiving by mail annually. His older sisters would have to place the orders because his mother couldn't write. When the clothes came in, they were too big at first as they were ordered a size larger to compensate for growth. They would wear these clothes until they were threadbare or worn-out. The best part of the process was the catalog itself. It was truly a wish book to them as he and his sister could only admire the many things they would never have. The models looked so pretty or handsome and were always happy. They wondered where a world like this existed. It was nothing like the world they knew. His father liked looking at the female models and asked his wife if he ordered the dress, would the model come with it? She didn't think that was funny.

His teacher was soft-spoken and nice. She had white hair and a plain face that looked a lot like Gilbert Stuart's portrait of George Washington. This year would turn out to be eventful, not so much in the classroom as he still had not bought into this "school thing." It was just something "they" made him do, and his mind wandered in class even though he was looking right at his teacher. Thoughts of marbles, climbing trees, recess, lunch, and other kids presented a formidable barrier to the teacher's instructions. He did not understand the concept of homework or study. He liked some subjects, but not enough to make good grades in them. His English was improving, but it was still heavily accented and would be for a long time—like forever. Anyone not from South Louisiana would have had a hard time understanding him. He did go to school every day, but once he got home, school was a faint, distant memory. He did learn an important concept—watched clocks don't move. Every classroom had a clock on the wall and the magical time was 3:30 —end of school! He was certain that the closer the minute hand moved toward 3:30, the slower it moved.

A positive was that his reading improved significantly, but his progress was not completely due to his teacher's instruction. He discovered comic books. Of course, he could not buy any as he never had spending money. His parents gave him a nickel a day to pay for school lunch. Then, during a visit to his aunt's house in Acadia Parish, he was reading a comic book he picked up from a table when his older cousin, Rita, asked him if he wanted some of her old comic books. He couldn't believe it; he had never seen so many comic books in his life when she handed him 25 of them. He took his comic books home, and for the first time since his older sisters left home, there were books in the house. Well, to be precise, there had been occasional schoolbooks in the house which he brought home from school, but those didn't count.

Within a short time, he read all his comic books. What now? Pierre learned from his friends that he could swap comic books with other boys who read them. Soon, he had a network of people with whom he traded. When they visited each other, the books were placed on the floor or the porch for each to review the other's stack. Each selected ones they had not read. Subsequently, he almost always had fresh ones to read without buying any. He does not remember ever purchasing a comic book. Characters like Nancy and Sluggo, Tubby, Archie, Veronica, Jughead, Superman, Plastic Man, Dick Tracy, Casper the Friendly Ghost, Sad Sack, Little Lulu, and Mutt & Jeff are still engraved in his memory. These "books" played an important role in Pierre's reading progress.

His family made a memorable family visit to his aunt's house in Port Arthur, Texas that year. It would be one of the very few times they made an overnight visit. His mother had two sisters and some nephews who had moved to East Texas in the towns of Orange, Beaumont, and Port Arthur. These were refinery towns where many Cajuns went to seek employment and a better life. A phone book in these East Texas towns read much like the one in Lafayette, Louisiana.

Very early in the morning, the family of five, three adults and two children, squeezed into the small pickup's cab. This was no small task as Pierre had to sit on Bertha's lap, and his youngest sister had to sit on his mother's lap. With his father's propensity for not stopping en route, this would be considerably less than a pleasant trip. The trip to Port Arthur required crossing a narrow, steep, high-rise bridge in Lake Charles. From a distance, the bridge appeared to be almost vertical, and his mother was extremely fearful of the impending crossing. As they approached the apex of the bridge, she nervously said, "Y'all hold on!" Pierre could not understand how holding on inside the truck would make them any safer. Years later he and his sisters still chuckle at this.

After a successful bridge crossing, they reached his aunt's house, a very nice home with all the modern conveniences of the time. Something magical happened to people who moved west of Cajun country to East Texas! His aunt gave them a warm reception followed by a wonderful lunch. Late in the afternoon, they were given a tour of the Port Arthur area. He found this very interesting, especially when they visited a pier that extended out into a lake. He had never seen so much water before, even more than his bayou. Even more interesting were the flaming lights that created an eerie, orange glow in the sky over the water as far as their eyes could see. These were gas flares that were used to burn off natural gas which, at that time, was considered a nuisance to the process of extracting oil. Who could guess how much natural gas was wasted in this way, to say nothing of all the natural gas wasted in countless other oil fields in Texas and Louisiana.

Later that evening, he and his sister were in the garage perusing all the interesting objects stored on the walls. The garage itself was even interesting as it was connected to the house, something they had never seen before. Then their aunt's husband came in and asked them if they would each like one of the inner tubes that they had seen hanging on the wall. They couldn't believe their ears! Ten pounds of Easter candy could not have made them any happier. One of their few toys was a heavy tire that they rolled on the gravel road as they followed behind it pushing with frequent, heavy hand strokes. Pierre had tried before to repair discarded inner tubes, but all he had to work with was roofing pitch that was totally ineffective as the air just blew through the soft pitch. Now, they were about to receive new tubes which, with a few light taps of the hand, would float lightly over the rocks and gravel on the road. Life was good!

Perhaps the pivotal event of his fourth grade year was the spring flood that inundated much of his town and most of the homes along the bayou. Heavy rains for several days over a large area was the cause of the flooding. Several days before the high waters came, the family visited his grandparents, and several other family members were there. It was raining and they knew flooding was imminent as the bayous were rising rapidly, and they speculated as to what would happen. Someone mentioned that this could be as bad as the flood of 1927, the worst flood to occur in Louisiana within their memories. Pierre, who always enjoyed listening to adults talk, listened intently to every word. In his mind, he envisioned a blanket of raindrop-pocked water flooding the bayou over everything he knew as the current carried loose boats, limbs, and trash out of sight. Maybe they would have to swim to save their lives, but he couldn't swim. The adults talked on and on, but there were no encouraging words.

As predicted, the waters continued to rise—it had reached the road and yard. The house was on blocks only about 20 inches from the ground; the bayou would soon be in the house. They would have to move as soon as possible. They decided to move to his uncle's home in Church Point, La. They packed some necessities into the Ford pickup. Before leaving, they elevated the refrigerator and a few other items. There was not much time. Bertha was living with them then until his brother-in-law would return from the army. So his father, mother, and Bertha sat in the front of the pickup and he and Linda, who was six years old, rode in the truck bed along with clothing, utensils, and other necessities they would need. His mother's relatives received them graciously. They enjoyed a good dinner, and, naturally, the flood was the main topic. They also discussed how much higher in elevation Church Point was than the little town on the bayou. Pierre envisioned being on a mountain compared to where his house was.

After a couple of days in Church Point, it was evident that the flood waters would be there for a long time. They would have to find a long-term solution for housing. His father located a rental house in a nearby town with higher elevation. They repacked the pickup, said goodbyes to the relatives, and drove the 15 miles to their new home. The house was small and green and one of three identical rentals next to each other. The rental house was about the same size as his own house. It was not a lot better than the house they owned, but at least it was not going to flood. It had two small bedrooms, a kitchen, and a small living room. Outside the back of the house was an outhouse with a flush toilet that Pierre liked much more than the outhouse at home. It was a rather strange neighborhood as right across the street there were some large, nice homes.

His mother and sister immediately began to clean the house, which was filthy. Later they would find out it was more than filthy; there were bedbugs in the house. Pierre would not learn this until many years later when his sister told him. After the cleaning and placing of their few possessions, life began in their new home where they would live for three weeks. Their neighbors in one of the other rentals, whom they knew well, were from their hometown. They had three children around his and Linda's age. They would spend a lot of time together. His father would continue going to work each day in the oilfields which were not flooded.

One of the unpleasant events was the mandatory typhoid shot everyone had to take, which was standard procedure anytime there was widespread flooding. The nurse gave the shot in the deltoid muscle with a very small needle. Immediately, there was a burning sensation that subsided rather quickly, and the children continued their normal activities the rest of the day. The next day, things got worse as they awoke with stiff, painful arms and shoulders. The pain was a dull, aching pain rather than a burn. They could not elevate their arms due to the pain and stiffness. Doing what kids do, they enjoyed hitting the painful shoulder of their friends with their good arm. Thankfully, the pain subsided in a few days.

Pierre soon began to explore his new neighborhood, which was very different from his at the little town on the bayou. For one thing, it was much larger, and the houses were much closer together. He visited the people across the street in the nice white clapboard house. There was a girl there about his age and other children. The people spoke only English, and he was aware that they were different from him, his family and friends. They dressed better and always wore shoes. He did not understand that they were from a much higher social stratum than he. The yard had nice things like swings and other fun things, but the most exciting thing they had was a bicycle. He did not have a bike nor did he know how to ride one, and he would not have one until he would be around forty years old.

One day, he asked the girl if he could ride her bike. She said, "Sure, go ahead." He had never ridden a bike before except for his little sister's tricycle, and he was somewhat jealous of her because he had never had a tricycle when he was her age. One of his friends from home who knew how to ride a bike had told him, "Riding a bike is easy; all you have to do is wiggle the handlebars." Pierre got on the bike, luckily in the yard and not on the street. He pushed the pedals, but could not stay up without putting a foot down to avoid a fall. Then, he remembered his friend's advice and began wiggling the handlebars vigorously from side to side. He was able to stay up on the bike, but he was zigzagging all over the yard without control. Pierre had a very inauspicious initiation into the world of cycling. After a few more tries, he realized he was "wiggling" the handlebars too vigorously and improved rapidly by being more subtle with the "wiggling."

He soon got enough confidence to ride on the street. Later, he would often borrow the bike to take long rides and come back home perspiring. He loved feeling the wind in his hair, the speed he could attain, and the distance he could travel in a short time. He often visited a construction site where a new school was being built to see the materials and the day-to-day progress. He was saddened, however, to know he would not anytime soon own a bicycle. It was just not something for which his parents would spend money.

Unfortunately, not all of his experiences were as pleasant as riding the bike or playing with his friends. At one point, he was playing across the street with the neighborhood children having a good time swinging on the swing—there were so many things to play with here. Then, one of the children's fathers came over and heard Pierre talking with his playmates. The man called to another man across the yard and shouted, "Come see, we have a little 'coonass' here." Pierre did not know what "coonass" meant or if he had ever even heard the word before, but by the tone of the man's voice and the derisive laughter of the two men, he knew it was not good. He knew what the French/Cajun word "*ecraser*" meant—literally, to smash but used figuratively to mean "put down or make fun of"— that's just how he felt. The four other Cajun children in the group were younger than Pierre; therefore, they did not note the slur. He continued playing with his friends, but he was no longer having fun. For the first time, he had an intimation that he was not like a lot of the other children.

After three weeks, the flood waters finally receded, and they would soon have to go home to see what the situation was like and to get the house cleaned up and ready to move back in. They did not know what they would find. Certainly, his parents would have an idea as they had seen floods before. The trip home took about 20 minutes. They approached the house from the rear because the bayou road was still impassable. The bayou, with its strong current, was still over its regular banks, but just up to the road. The house and yard were above water. Pierre and Linda sat on the rise behind the house while his mother, father, and Bertha walked to the house. His sister had morbid fears that the house would be full of snakes seeking shelter from the flood. They approached the house and saw the yard covered with sun-baked brown muddy sediment that was beginning to crackle from the sun. Layers of mud suffocated all of the spring's green grass. The smell of dead vegetation was pervasive, but not new to them as the bayou flooded its banks and produced that smell almost every spring. They walked into the house, and to his sister's relief, there were no legions of snakes at the ready to pounce on them. Perhaps the snakes found better habitation somewhere else. The same type mud covered the floors, only not crackled. The walls were still water soaked. The linoleum rug that once gave a relief of bright colors to the dismal, dark interior of the little house was ruined. Pierre remembered when his father bought the rug—it was a big event. When the rug was unrolled, a cornucopia of bright, geometric figures met their gaze. Colors like this had never invaded this house before. It didn't match anything else in the house, it was like painting ten clown suits in a Montana winter landscape, but no one noticed that. Martha Stewart, had she been there, would not have approved, but the rug helped to keep some of the cold winter wind from entering through the cracks in the floors, and the smooth surface was so much easier to sweep and keep clean.

In the living room the large black armoire was collapsed into a pile of rubble in the mud. The water and moisture had dissolved all the glue that had held it together. Only the two thick mirrors were salvageable. They would attach them to the walls later. The armoire was the only decent piece of furniture they had ever owned, and they would never own one more beautiful. Pierre was saddened to see its demise as he remembered this was where his parents hid the Christmas presents until "Santa" brought them for Christmas morning. Since some of their presents were apples and oranges, the scent of the apples was not difficult for him to sniff out through the armoire's doors. Apples were a holiday gift, not daily fare in his family.

The laborious task of cleaning began. They took the trash and rubble outside to burn it. Then, with spades and hoes, they removed the mud from the floors. Thanks to the city water and a hose, they could wash away the remaining mud. They left the house to dry for a few days and drove back to the rental house.

The last three days in the rental passed about as fast as a toothache. The axiom, "No matter how humble, there's no place like home," was so applicable here. His dad went to work as usual, and his mother and sister packed and got ready to move back home. Pierre was still busy playing with his friends. Finally, the day came to load up the pickup once again—this time to go home. They felt like it had been such a long time since they had been home. There was so much work still to do and things to be bought to replace lost items. Fortunately, the refrigerator survived as his father had elevated it before the flood. They bought a cedar chifferobe to replace the black armoire. It had a nice scent but didn't replace the armoire as it was small and square with no mirrors. His family got no assistance from the Red Cross because his father had a job. They knew families who purposefully destroyed their furniture to receive aid. His father would be resentful of the Red Cross for the rest of his life. Nevertheless, they got everything in place and regained a modicum of functionality. Pierre had lost three weeks of school. He apparently didn't miss anything.

Despite having had electricity for four years, there was still no ventilation in the house except for a small fan that cooled one person if that person sat no more than five feet in front of it. The summer after the flood seemed to be hotter than normal, especially the nights when sleep was almost impossible. Perhaps, losing the vegetation around the house after the flood made it hotter. The humidity, heat, and body temperature made their mattresses feel like an electric blanket on a high setting. His father would often get up in the middle of the night to sit in a tub of water to cool off by splashing tepid water on his body. Sometimes his father would lie down on the relatively cool linoleum rug. His brothers had window fans and told him how effective they were at night. As usual, his father was always the last to get those "modern conveniences."

After suffering enough, his father finally made the decision to buy that window fan and bought one just like his brother had. His brother came in to help him install the fan in the living room window. That night, with great anticipation, he turned the fan on and went to bed for the night. The efficaciousness of the new fan underwhelmed everyone in the house. It was a little better for the people in the living room/bedroom, but Pierre and his sister felt no difference at all. Of course his father, the king of pessimism, assumed he had wasted his money on a useless contraption. He spoke to his brother Leonce about his disappointment with the fan, and his brother came in to look at it. He quickly noticed that it was on the wrong setting. The fan was reversible and could pull air into the house, as it had done the night before, or pull air from inside the house to outside. With the windows raised about eight inches around the house, the air was pulled into the house with some velocity. That night, with the fan properly set, a cool stream of night air rushed into the house, and the difference was miraculous. In the morning it was almost chilly—what a luxury!

Despite the flood, a good thing happened that year. He and Linda got to see a lot of movies, only they didn't know them as movies as they called them "picture shows." It was a strange paradox that a family who would not pay a nickel for a cold drink would pay fifty-five cents for one adult and two children to see a movie. His mother did not attend these movies. For some reason, his father loved cowboy movies and took Pierre and his little sister to see them on Friday nights. Bertha, who lived with them for two years while her husband was in Germany with the Army, took them to the movies each Wednesday night. Wow! Two movies a week! It was Nirvana in a very unlikely place for two kids who lived in a shack, hardly ever had a cold drink, and had only one pair of shoes per year. Most other kids in similar circumstances never got to see a picture show at all.

The brick paper-clad box-like movie theater was about two-thirds of a mile up the bayou. The obligatory posters arrayed across the front of the building announced the present and coming attractions. Upon entry one saw to the left the admissions booth and, to the right, a small concession area where one could purchase popcorn and drinks. Needless to say, Pierre and his sister never got to eat popcorn or drink cokes on Friday nights, but his sister sometimes bought them popcorn on Wednesday nights. Inside the theater was a sloping floor with the big screen at the end. The theater occasionally hosted special appearances on the stage in front of the screen. At the rear of the theater was a balcony where the blacks sat to watch the movies, and when they got up to go downstairs, their silhouettes were projected on the screen. At the rear of the balcony was the huge projector that magically shot those wonderful moving images to the screen. Electricity arcing between two carbon rods provided the intense light necessary to project images. Pierre knew this because he saw the remnants of the copper-coated carbon rods in the trash pile behind the building, and someone told him what they were.

For ten cents admission, a movie was the best deal since the Louisiana Purchase! For one tenth of a dollar, five courses of entertainment were served. First were the Cartoons with the Looney Tunes characters such as Bugs Bunny, Sylvester, Tweedy, Yosemite Sam, Donald Duck, and a host of others. There was the Newsreel, which gave the viewers dramatic news and images far removed from the little world on the bayou. The Continuing Series were fun and frustrating as they kept viewers on edge by an exciting episode reaching a climactic moment only to end with, "Continued Next Week." It did keep the attendance up. Then there was the Preview of Coming Attractions. The actual Movie was the final course. Wednesday nights were often comedies like Bud Abbot and Lou Costello. In one memorable one, Bud and Lou found a series of dead bodies in closets. Pierre had nightmares that night. Other Wednesday movie genres were the romantic comedies and love stories. Those, he didn't enjoy as much as he was not yet "romantic". The Friday night movies were mostly westerns or jungle movies starring Tarzan or Jungle Jim. Some of his western heroes were Roy Rogers, Lash LaRue, Whip Wilson, Johnny Mack Brown, The Lone Ranger, Rex Allen and, of course, Gene Autry. Most of these movies were very similar—an injustice was done by a bad guy or guys and the hero caught up with them and either killed them or brought them to justice. It seemed like these movies always ended on the same hill on which the hero caught with up with the last and worst bad guy after a long chase on horseback before jumping on the villain to knock him to the ground. They then rolled together down the hill where the hero knocked out the bad guy with a well-placed punch. The posse would then arrive to take the bad guy away to jail. As this was going on, every kid in the theater, including those lying down on the stage, cheered and clapped for the hero.

What an eventful year—from the flood to movies twice a week and the discovery of comic books. Even the flood had some benefits as he probably learned more than he would have had he not missed those three weeks of school. His brother-in-law finished his time in the Army and came back home after a two-year absence. He and Bertha were so happy to see each other again. They embraced on the same porch of their courtship. Pierre did not get to sleep with his sister anymore. He understood why—well, sort of.

Pierre passed to the fifth grade, a grade in which he began to understand the humanity of teachers. His teacher was a young and rather attractive woman, the first time he had a young teacher, and he found that a welcome change. After being in her class for a few weeks, she walked into the room with a scent of cigarettes trailing behind her. No one in his family smoked, but he knew other people who did. Of one thing he was certain; this was his first teacher, to his knowledge, who smoked. He did not regard this as a negative, on the contrary; it made her more human, more reachable, more like a regular person. After all, he wasn't even sure if teachers went to the bathroom. He also learned about the teacher's lounge and the clouds of cigarette smoke which streamed out the door. Apparently, many other teachers smoked too. He had a school boy crush on her and imagined what it would be like to smoke a cigarette. Last year, during the flood he and his friend smoked some dried vines. When he was younger, kids and sometimes he had candy cigarettes that looked like a piece of new chalk with a red tip. As an adult, he wondered if this candy cigarette contributed to people becoming habitual smokers. Despite this, he never became a smoker.

Another new awareness was Pierre's first encounter with French nationals which occurred during this school year. A Cajun serviceman married a French woman, and the family of husband, wife, mother-in-law, father-in-law, daughter, and son moved near his grandfather's house. Pierre was intrigued by this unusual family—he still has a vivid memory of each family member's face. He felt there was a vague connection between his family and theirs, but he did not know enough to know why. Many others were equally intrigued. The daughter, Madeleine, was in second grade with Linda, and he would later often hear her mention her. Pierre also heard his grandparents talking about this French family. While visiting his grandfather, Pierre often saw Madeleine's grandfather walk past the house to pick mushrooms in the woods. Pierre and some of the other natives of the little town found this unusual since mushrooms were not part of the Cajun diet at that time. They did know that some mushrooms were poisonous and wondered how the Frenchman identified the non-poisonous ones. Linda is still friends with her former French classmate who later graduated from USL and a French university and now resides in Cairo, Egypt.

As fifth graders, they were allowed to have P.E. and recess in the rear of the school near the football field, bleachers, and pine trees. Pierre and his friends would climb the trees during recess. Pine trees had to be climbed carefully because their branches would often break away from the trunk. In his many tree climbing experiences, he had often had a limb break under his weight, but he never fell, because he knew that he must always have a good hand grip on a limb as he stepped on another limb. When the bell rang, they looked like monkeys dropping out of the trees to get to class on time. A heap of banana peelings on the ground would have completed this picture. When not climbing trees, they were all over and under the bleachers and jumping down from the top seats, usually to fulfill a "dare." If a "dare" did not get someone to jump, then a "double dare" and a "triple dare" would follow. If one still did not jump, then he was called "chicken" which usually triggered a jump. Somehow, except for a few sprained ankles, there were no serious injuries.

For physical education classes, an organized game of baseball was often played. The teacher selected two captains to choose team members. Of course, the best players were chosen first, next best was next and so on. Team captains usually chose Pierre second or third to last. He had never played any organized sports as sports were not encouraged in his family. They saw sports as wasted energy best used for something more important, like working. Even so, now and then, he got lucky and hit or caught a ball. Some of his classmates were already showing signs of being good athletes. It was amazing to him how they could catch the longest fly ball on the run, every time. One classmate, who was a Cleveland Indians fan, was already doing that in third grade. Pierre did not understand the concept of professional baseball at that time.

He watched with interest the high school athletes train for their sports near the home bleachers. Some were doing the broad jump, some the hop-skip and jump, and some the high jump using the straddle technique. Pole vaulters used a stiff, bamboo pole. Others were running track—both speed and endurance training. To Pierre, they were doing things he could never aspire to do. It was like they had a predetermined, special ability he would never have. To a fifth grader, these athletes looked so big, even though weight training had not yet come to his school community.

In the classroom, he began to observe that certain students made better grades than others. Usually, students who spoke English as a first language made better grades than those who spoke French as a first language. Of course, there were exceptions as one francophone girl made very good grades, and some others did as well. He was rapidly developing the attitude that making good grades was not for someone like him; it was something only others could do. It never occurred to him to study more. How could one do more of something he had never done, seen, or understood? Most damaging was that there was no one at home who could guide the educational process. His parents believed if he went to school every day, everything was fine, and the school would take care of it all. They never once visited the school except when he graduated from eighth and twelfth grades. In class, he was not a problem kid; he had friends and was not an unhappy child. His grades were not great, but due to his relatively good reading skills, he was getting by in all subjects except math, which he failed most years. He liked history for some reason, perhaps due to the stories his father told him about past family history. When he was in American History class learning about the Seven Years War between England and France over control of America, he wanted the French soldiers to win. He identified more with them than the English soldiers.

He never shared this with anyone in his class; it was just the way he felt. The French did not win the war, and Pierre did not understand at that time that this was the reason his ancestors were deported from Nova Scotia in the 18th century and that he would have to learn English well to have an opportunity to participate in the American Dream.

Life at home was still almost the same. Linda was in the second grade and doing very well in school, much better than he did in second grade—she could count money. His father, due to his perseverance, hard work, and dependability, got a promotion. He got to be foreman of the work crews, which meant that he got paid twenty-five cents per hour more than minimum wage. Physically, he was spared some of the laborious work, but managing a crew of workmen was no small chore. The work was hard, and the workers would complain and sometimes quit the job during the day. Often, men would not show up for work leaving the crew shorthanded. As foreman, he had to figure out the jobs and show the men how to do it. He would spend the rest of his working life in this position with the same contractor. Larger companies had offered him much more pay with some good benefits to work for them, but he was too insecure to make that move due to his lack of basic literacy skills. Sadly, he missed great opportunities to make life better for himself and his family.

They still visited relatives on both sides of Pierre's family. His mother's family was about twenty-five miles away in Church Point, Acadia Parish, which was much more francophone than his little town. She had three brothers and one sister there. That was a day trip they took when his father was off on the weekend. There were many cousins his age there, and he enjoyed those visits. In his family, relatives were not given advanced notice before visits. The visitors just showed up. They did not consider this gauche. Besides, they had no phones and most could not write a letter. He remembers his mother looking out the window as she was washing dishes and seeing relatives driving up for a visit. She dropped everything she was doing and pulled out something to cook for lunch. The same thing was done for his family when they arrived for the day.

He and his Church Point cousins spoke mostly French to each other. They rambled about looking for turtles in the gullies, or they would go exploring around town. During one visit, they played in an empty warehouse where they met Aaron, who was handicapped. He seemed normal and was healthy, but he could only speak a little and was difficult to understand. Pierre knew a boy living near his house who had the same type handicap. They played with him as if he were normal. Other times he and his cousins would go to the grounds of a large estate consisting of a mansion and large yard with trees, shrubs, swimming pool, and huge clumps of tall bamboo. They loved to climb the bamboo, hold on to three or four stems, and rock back and forth. They never saw the owners, and no one ever told them to leave. The owners must have known they were there. Perhaps they just wanted to give poor kids an opportunity to have a little fun.

His father had four brothers and two sisters who lived nearby as well as his mother and father. Since all of Pierre's uncles and aunts had children, he never ran out of playmates. They usually made visits to relatives after his father came home from work. After cleanup and dinner, Pierre and his family drove the short distance to visit a selected family. During the visit, the children would run around outside, often to chase fireflies which were abundant at that time. Sometimes, they would play in the flea-infested barn. For some reason, the fleas seemed to prefer Pierre. On one occasion, he had been bitten so often that he looked like he had the measles all over his body. His cousins were virtually flea-free. Pierre later deduced that the fleas appreciated fresh blood. The adults would sit and talk on the porch in the summer and inside in winter. They usually griped and complained about things or people (a very Cajun thing to do) or exchanged gossip and told jokes. These visits lasted only a short time because his father had to get up early to go to work the next day.

As mentioned earlier, there were then now four inhabitants in their little house, but that was not completely correct. After those family visits, the family returned home after dark. When his mother pulled the light string to flood the house with light, another one hundred (at least) inhabitants scurried about in all directions to escape the light—roaches! Such was the normal welcome they got each time they came in after dark. Pierre didn't realize that the roaches were doing the same thing after they went to bed at night. He should have known as there were many occasions when a large roach landed on his face during the night. He would grab it, throw it across the room and go back to sleep. His mother quickly grabbed the pump and began to chase the roaches while frantically pumping the spray pump. The insecticides of that time had no residual killing power. One had to drown a roach with it to kill it, and as that was happening, the rest of the insects ran back to the safety of all the spaces and cracks in the walls. Pierre wondered later if other roaches slowed down when his mother concentrated on one roach, something like when a lion grabbed a gazelle, the other gazelles felt safe and stopped running.

To be even more precise, the insects and family were not the only inhabitants of the house as there was an indefinite number of rodents who checked in for a definite stay. During the night, Pierre could hear gnawing sounds in the closet area of his bedroom. An examination of the closet revealed gnawed holes that mice used to invade the house. His father set mousetraps the following night, and later the dull thud of the trap clamping down was heard. Somehow, it was a rewarding sound as it indicated the invaders were getting their just rewards for invading human space. The adage, "if you see one mouse, there are usually others," was true this time as more mice were trapped the following nights. One night the mousetrap snapped again, and Pierre heard the usual thud of the tripped trap followed by the sounds of the trapped rodent running off with the mousetrap and then quiet. The next morning the trap was found empty. All of this took place about 8 feet from Pierre's bed which did not particularly perturb him. His father knew what happened and set a larger rattrap out the next night. During the night, a huge thud sounded when the powerful spring of the Victor trap sprung. The rat did not run off this time; it was instant execution. The rodent problem was solved—for now.

Sometimes, perhaps once every couple years, they would go to Lake Charles to visit his father's oldest sister, Mamie, who had married a man of German ancestry, but of Cajun culture. The Cajun culture enveloped many Germans, and as a result, they had lost their German language and culture generations ago. He was a veteran of the U.S. Navy, and he and Mamie had lived a short time in

Florida after his discharge from the military. Then, like many Cajuns at that time, they moved to Lake Charles for employment in one of the many petroleum and chemical refineries there. These refineries helped huge numbers of Cajuns achieve full assimilation into American society. The jobs offered unbelievable pay, benefits, and retirement. One can only imagine how a person of farming, or sharecropping background felt upon landing such a job. It was a very transformative experience.

They left early in the morning for such a trip. This time, his aunt had a phone, and his dad's second brother Isaac called her to let them know they would visit. With all four packed into the small pickup's cab, the journey felt a lot longer than it was. To exacerbate matters, his father did not believe in rest stops because, as when he was working, when he started something, he wanted to get it done. Additionally, stopping for a drink or snack was just not done in his family because his father considered this a waste of money.

When they got there, his aunt Mamie greeted them at the door. Her husband was still sleeping because he did shift work. Pierre had never heard of shift work, and it was a strange concept to him. In his world, everyone who worked did so in the daytime and slept at night. He had two male first cousins there close to his age. They were unlike his other first cousins who lived closer to home in that they only spoke English. Their parents purposefully did not teach them French because, like many other Cajuns, they believed speaking French would present obstacles to their children's success. Additionally, they did not want their children to experience the stigma they had experienced as French speakers. Their oldest would go to great lengths to learn French later in life.

Their house always amazed him. They had many modern conveniences that no one else in his family had. They even had a television. The bathroom was clean and colorful, and on the wall of the bathroom was a little glass case containing a small corncob. A little sign underneath read, "In case of emergency, break glass." Pierre could relate to that one. They had a nice car, and he thought they were rich. He could not even dream that he would ever live in a home like that with all those things. To him, as he was, was forever. He had no clue about the possibility of change.

By now, Santa brought only utilitarian things like clothing, fruit, and one time a very good-looking pair of cowboy boots that was incongruous with the rest his clothing, especially when he wore short pants. They were tan with wine-colored toes and heel. One of his friends at school offered to tell everyone in school how pretty his boots were if Pierre would give him ten cents. First of all, Pierre didn't have ten cents, and secondly, he recognized the scam. No telling what his friend would end up doing for a living. He did do a lot of gambling; perhaps he could work his scams in that environment.

His parents, marked by poverty and the Great Depression, could not see any wisdom in spending money on non-essentials at Christmas. When they did get gifts, his sister received a doll and doll clothing, and he got a cap pistol and a few rolls of caps. When he popped the last cap, there would be no more. One good thing in his eyes was that his family had the tradition of Santa coming on New Year's Eve as well as on Christmas Eve. The New Year's Eve Santa left utilitarian items like clothing, fruit, and sometimes candy. They preferred the Christmas Santa. By the time they each got to fourth grade, toys were discontinued even though they had not been naughty. When he and his sister returned to school after the holidays, to avoid embarrassment, they would make up long lists of gifts to recite when the teacher asked the class what they got for Christmas.

If there was a perceived toy deficit at Christmas, there was certainly never a food deficit. There was never a shortage of food at any other time either. Christmas meals consisted of copious amounts of roast pork and beef stuffed with garlic and red and black peppers with wonderful gravy to give flavor to and soak the omnipresent rice. Sometimes gumbo was made to add a little variety. Side dishes of vegetables, such as corn, butterbeans, or green beans completed the meal. The whole family would be there, and each one ate like it was their last meal. Everyone had two or more servings while exclaiming how good it all was. There was usually a cake for dessert, but everyone would be too stuffed to eat it just after the meal, so the tradition was to wait a couple of hours to have coffee and dessert while exchanging conversation. Not surprisingly, the topic was mostly about food, like what they ate yesterday, what they would fix tomorrow, or describing how they cooked a certain dish. Needless to say, food was an endlessly interesting topic for this Cajun family.

Since Santa didn't bring them very much anymore, Pierre made most of his playthings. He made slingshots of strips of rubber cut from discarded inner tubes. The strips had to be cut very carefully in one continuous motion with scissors to avoid breakage when stretched. Sometimes, he was lucky enough to get a piece of a red rubber tube. These tubes had been out of production for many years, but the natural red rubber had superior elasticity. Some black rubber tubes had better elasticity than others. Sometimes he made slingshots with two strips of rubber, a pouch, and a forked branch from a tree. These were the most accurate, but most of his slingshots were a single strip of rubber with a pouch and no handle. He could shoot these slingshots with great accuracy. He must have broken thousands of bottles in his early life. He sometimes lined them up as targets at a nearby junk pile, and other times he would toss them in the bayou so they would sink when he hit them. He hunted birds and sometimes got lucky and killed a few. Sometimes, he and his buddies would play "war" with the slingshots which left welts on their bodies. He made bows and arrows and spears. He would make "tractors" by using an empty, notched spool of thread, a small twig or popsicle stick, a thin strip of rubber or rubber band, and a piece of colored crayon for lubrication. When wound up, it would propel itself.

Perhaps the most exciting toys he made he made were stilts. These were a challenge because his father had none of the necessary tools or hardware except a hammer, recycled nails, and a dull saw. He used his father's old oak tomato poles. The stilts were very simple, only a block of wood for a footrest attached to a pole. A strip of rubber was attached from the pole to the edge of the footrest to keep the feet in place. The challenge was to nail the footrest to the hard oak pole. The recycled nails would usually bend before penetrating deep enough to secure the footrest. For each nail that he could drive properly, there were three partially driven, smashed, spaghetti-like ones against the wood, and often the wood would split. With a drill and screws, this would have been such an easy project, but it would be a long time before he would even know these things existed. He did, however, finally manage to make a pair of stilts for himself and his sister. The first pair he built made them about a foot taller than they were, and they got to be very proficient in walking with them. They could climb up and descend steps with them as well as cross the cattle guard nearby. Soon, he got bored with those particular stilts and made another pair that made him three feet taller. Linda teased him by telling their mother he was going down the bayou on his stilts to visit his girlfriend. He was incensed because first of all, as a fifth grader, he didn't like girls at all, and secondly, the girl she mentioned was much less than cute. That was some appreciation for a brother who had given her stilts and taught her to use them. What an ingrate!

In the spring of his fifth year, he made his first "kite"—well sort of. He noted the construction of the store-bought kites of his friends, so he got two narrow strips of wood and tied them together in the shape of a cross. Then he tied a string around the perimeter of the cross. Next, he got a large brown paper bag and cut the paper about an inch wider than the stringed cross. There was no glue or paste in the house, so he stirred water and flour together to form a paste. He folded the outer edges of the kite-shaped brown paper around the string and glued it down with the paste. He let it dry overnight. He was proud of his work as it looked like a real kite. Of course, it did not have the bright colors and designs of a store-bought kite, but it would have to do. He collected some pieces of string saved from store-wrapped packages and tied them together to make a long kite string. He looked in his mother's scrap material bag and ripped some lengths of fabric to make a tail. He tied them together and couldn't wait to try it out.

He went into the open field near his house for the launch. The sky was gray and threatening rain, but the wind was good. He had seen his friends run with the kites to get them airborne, so he began running and released some string as he ran. After running a little distance, the kite flew up into the air. After his short happy life as a kite flyer, his kite made a series of small rapid circles and dove erratically to the ground in a Japanese Kamikaze fashion. He ran to his kite and found it ruined beyond repair. That was the end of his kite building career.

One of Pierre's close friends, Robin, was the grandson of his next door neighbors. They spent a lot of time together whenever he came to visit his grandparents. They would fish together and explore up and down the bayou. One day, his friend came to his grandmother's house on his brand new bicycle. This bike was not just any bicycle; it was the top of the line Schwinn with chromed fenders, large whitewall tires, and springs under the seat. He took a ride on the bike, and it was so different from the bike he learned to ride on last year. The bike rode so smoothly, even on the graveled road. He never even wished he could have a bike like that; it was out of the realm of even his wildest dreams.

He and Robin often hung out along the bayou to fish and explore. They found a fisherman's net tied to a stake on the bank. They pulled the net up and it was empty, but it had a nice rope which they cut in half and shared. The following week, they went to church for confession. They decided that they should confess their less than exemplary behavior. Pierre went into the confessional first and said, "Bless me Father, for I have sinned."

"What sins have you committed?" Father asked.

"I stole a rope."

"Say ten Hail Marys and bring the rope back," The priest responded.

Pierre went to the nearby pew and knelt down to commence his penance. Robin went in next and began his confession which Pierre could hear very clearly. Robin said, "Bless me Father for I have sinned."

"What sins have you committed?"

"I stole a rope."

"You too!"

"Say ten Hail Marys and bring the rope back."

They later took the rope back where they found it.

Final thoughts on fifth grade: He didn't have to color anymore, nor use that paste ever again. That was a good thing.

After a summer at home, he was ready to go back to school. There were no summer camps or vacations for Pierre. He was happy during the first few weeks of summer break, but then he got bored and was ready to go back to school where he could be with his friends and play marbles. It was too bad they had to learn stuff; otherwise school would be OK. He always felt insecure the first days of the new school year. There were so many apprehensions, such as would his friends from last year still be his friends? Or would they ignore him because they had made new friends over the summer? Who would his teacher be? Would the sixth grade be harder than the fifth?

After the usual ritual of purchasing school clothes and a pair of shoes, the school year kicked off. Pierre would not be wearing his new shoes until the first frost. He would go to school barefooted until then. Wearing his freshly pressed shirt and new pants, he went to his assigned teacher. His teacher again had gray hair (perhaps the students gave the teachers that gray hair), was slim and rather tall. She was soft-spoken and friendly; he liked her.

He noticed, in the back of the room, a group of five or six huge boys sitting in the back of the class. To Pierre, who was not yet 12 years old, they looked almost like men. As the year went on, he noticed that they did not often participate in class activities. He did not know at this time that these large boys were waiting to turn 16 so they could drop out of school. Some of the boys were like him in that they started school speaking French; it was their first language. A couple of the boys were mentally challenged, and most of them came from families engaged in sharecropping or farming their family's small plot of land. Several of his older cousins had been in that category. Each classroom had several similar students. They had no chance to succeed academically because they had to miss school often to help with the harvesting of crops in the fall. They came to school more regularly in the winter but then missed more days in the spring for plowing and planting. Before the school year was over, or certainly by the following year, these students would quit school and work full-time on their farms until they turned eighteen. At eighteen, they would be old enough to get employment in the oil fields doing hard manual labor. Pierre also did not realize that if his father had not left the sharecropping life shortly before he was born, he, too, almost certainly would have grown into a big boy in the back of the room waiting to quit school.

The most enjoyable academic activity that year was listening to his teacher read T*he Wizard of Oz* aloud to the class. Each day, she read a few pages of the book after lunch, and the class paid rapt attention. Each day, he looked forward to the continuation of the story. To him, it was a tale from a strange land occupied with even stranger characters having a wonderful adventure while encountering fascinating circumstances. He knew he would never forget those readings. He would later see the movie, but whenever he thought of the *The Wizard of Oz*, his first thoughts were of his sixth grade teacher reading it to the class and the fantastical images which formed in his mind. He was a little sad when the book ended, in the same way he would feel as an adult when a good book ended—like he had lost his best friends.

He remained a rather indifferent student in most of his subjects and was not aware that this was a problem; after all, he had never failed. His attendance was still good, and he enjoyed playing with his friends at recess. By now, he had become one of the best marble players in his class. Too bad no one told him he could never make a living playing marbles, and if they had, it would have made as much of an impression as dropping a pin on a memory foam mattress. He would go to school with a few marbles in his pocket and go back home with a pocket full of marbles that he stored in a one-gallon tin can at home. He had discovered that shooting from his knee was more accurate than shooting from the ground. The irregularity of the ground's surface made it difficult to hit the marbles out of the ring, so he placed his knee on the ground and shot the marble directly from knee to marble to avoid the bumps. He got proficient enough to hit a targeted marble in the pot from four or five feet. He had also noted that good players held their shooter marble between the first joint of the thumb and the tip of the index finger. Players who held their shooters between top thumb fingernail and inside middle joint of the index finger were not usually good marble players. He seldom lost when he played the latter type player. If only he would have given as much thought to his math and grammar classes!

He did, however, learn to do something he had wanted to do for a long time. He learned how to swim despite his mother's constant warnings. If he were to learn how to swim, it would have to be without her consent. Pierre had some black friends from a large, sharecropping family who lived a quarter mile down the bayou. The father of the family was, coincidentally, the son of the *traiteuse* who had delivered his youngest sister. Pierre was closest to the traiteuse's youngest grandson, Tony. They would go out to the slough to search for certain plant roots for his grandmother to use for relieving the pain of teething babies. They found the proper plants and pulled up the roots and took them to his grandmother. Pierre would never learn if these roots were successful for their intended purposes.

On a late spring day, he walked down to visit his friends. When he got to the house, the mother told him all the children were at the slough swimming, the same slough that he and his father were fishing in when the snakes had swarmed out. As he got near the swimming hole, he heard the joyous laughter of boys having a barrel of fun. Then he heard the splashing sounds of them jumping into the water. When he caught sight of them, they had a boat turned over with its bow tied to the bank and its stern out in the water. The boys were having great fun running on the boat and hurling themselves out into the water. One of the older boys yelled, "Pierre, come on in and join us." There was nothing he would have liked to do more, but he didn't know how to swim, and his mother didn't want him in the water unless it was in a tub. Additionally, he thought about all the snakes he had seen in the water, and a half inch of duckweed was covering it. One could see into the water only if the swimmers kept splashing the water, and when the splashing stopped, the duckweed closed in to create a solid green coat on the water.

Pierre responded in a subdued voice, "I don't know how to swim, and there are a lot of snakes in that water."

But another boy proclaimed, "We can teach you how to swim, and everybody knows snakes can't bite you underwater because if they open their mouths underwater, they'll drown."

Not having great confidence in the last statement, he meekly replied, "I don't have anything to swim in."

Another boy said while pointing, "Man, look on that bush, there's a pair of extra short pants there."

Pierre looked and saw a pair of worn out short pants stiffened by the sun on one of the limbs of the bush. He could not say no now because he could not think of any more excuses not to jump in.

He took off his clothes and put on the short pants. He walked into the brown water, and the swimmers gave him a quick lesson on kicking his feet and doing the dog paddle with his arms. The slough was not deep, but there was a hole about 10 feet in diameter. He started in the shallow water and had the security of feeling mud on the bottom with his feet. Then he got to the deeper water; he couldn't touch bottom and began to sink. He kicked and paddled harder and faster but could not quite keep afloat. He had to stand up to keep from swallowing the brown water. He tried again, and he eventually could stay afloat for a little while. It was a lot of fun. The older boys relished swimming underwater and grabbing the legs of the younger swimmers who shrieked with surprise.

When they finished swimming, they took off the short pants and hung them on the bush to dry and use next time. Pierre noticed that with the cessation of activity in the water, the duckweed reclaimed the circle of open water they had created. Then he saw a large snake swimming across the spot where they had been swimming as if it were defiantly reclaiming its territory.

The snakes and duckweed did not deter Pierre from continuing his swimming excursions. As the summer progressed, he quickly improved. On one occasion, he and a couple of his distant cousins met with his black friends to swim in the slough. Unfortunately, while in the water, he cut his foot on a piece of broken bottle. It could well have been a bottle he had broken himself with his slingshot previously. He walked to the bank and saw blood was gushing out of the side of his foot. The thought of infection from the stagnant brown water never entered his mind. One of the black boys went to get his father, the son of the *traiteuse*, to look at the cut. First, he pulled out his pouch of tobacco from which he extracted a pinch for Pierre to press onto the cut to stanch the bleeding. Then they all walked to the father's house to get some kerosene to wash out the wound to prevent infection. After getting his foot wrapped, he limped home to face his mother. He knew she would ask him where and how he cut his foot. He had to think of something, so he told her he cut his foot on the bayou bank up the road by stepping on broken glass. Everyone knew broken bottles were common there. She bought his story, and he got away with another one. His foot healed without any further attention, but the cut left a scar on his right foot which he would carry the rest of his life.

Soon, the slough was no longer fun, so it was time to graduate to the next level — swimming in the bayou. This would be a steep transition as the bayou was much more dangerous, and if caught, the consequences would be much more severe. His mother was a very loving mother, but if she got angry and started beating him, the pain could be excruciating. The water in the bayou was over his head only a few feet from the bank and farther out could be twenty-five to thirty feet, depending on the water level. The better swimmers would dive in and surface in the middle of the bayou. Pierre and other beginning swimmers were more cautious and swam a few feet from the bank and swam back. It felt strange not to feel the bottom at will, but the water was nice and clean and free of duck-weed. At that time, there were no alligators in the bayou or most of the rest of Louisiana either; they had been hunted almost to extinction years ago. That was a good thing since they sometimes swam nude.

Often, when he swam in the bayou, he would swim in his shorts which led to his mother questioning him about the mud stains. She suspected he had been swimming in the bayou, but he denied it, of course. To escape further suspicion, he left a spare pair of shorts near his swimming spot along the bayou. The problem now was that it was very difficult to guide muddy feet through his shorts without leaving evidence. Another solution was to swim naked which he and many of the boys did.

His family experienced, for the first time, one of the modern technologies of the mid-twentieth century – television. Of course, his family wouldn't own one for another twenty years, but this encounter came when his father's oldest brother, Leonce, bought a TV. Little did he know that the family dynamics would be changed forever — not just for his family, but everyone's family. At first, it was very interesting and exciting, especially when his family visited his uncle and family to watch the Gillette Friday Night Fights. There were usually ten to twelve people crammed in the small, dark living room watching the fights on the small black and white screen. As his uncles were known to be bar room brawlers and drinkers, boxing was a very attractive sport to them. He would later remember seeing fighters like Spider Webb, Carmen Basilio, Sugar Ray Robinson, Floyd Patterson, Rocky Marciano and Gene Fulmer. The cheering and rooting for their favorite fighters could probably be heard across the bayou. In addition to the fights, his family especially liked the western features, or anything, it seemed, with violence. Pierre did not turn his head from the violence.

Like mushrooms after a summer rain, these magical picture boxes cropped up throughout Cajun land. Large urban areas had already experienced this phenomenon, ten to fifteen years before. Pierre's family dynamics were suddenly succumbing to drastic changes. Visits to family and friends had always been a strong tradition in Cajun culture, and this tradition maintained and strengthened family ties. With the advent of TV, these family ties began to weaken. When Pierre and his family visited relatives with television, the conversation was sparse as they often left the TV on during the visit. His parents would try to initiate conversation, but they received curt responses. After several more similar experiences, his father said, "It's no use to visit anyone anymore because they don't talk and can't take their eyes off the (expletive) TV." Predictably, the frequency of family visits began to wane, and any visits made were of short duration. Major visits now would take place at weddings, major holidays and funerals.

The invasive tentacles of television even intruded into Pierre's school to inflict embarrassment on him. Most of his classmates had television at home and discussed the programs they had seen the night before. Obviously, he could not take part in those conversations. They often would sing the TV jingles that he didn't know. Popular TV characters were unknown to him, plus allusions and analogies to most things from TV meant nothing to him. Sometimes, a student would make a disparaging remark to him for not having a TV at home. Only his reading and the occasional TV he watched at friends' homes kept him from being completely out of the loop. This TV thing was getting quite pervasive. It took away family visits, embarrassed him at school, and was in the process of closing down movie theaters in many small towns. He was grateful that the movie theatre in his little town had thus far continued to survive despite the onslaught of television.

The Flood of 1953

CHAPTER 6,
GRADES 7 – 8,
AGE OF IRRATIONALITY

"I see no hope for the future of our people if they are depen-
dent on the frivolous youth of today, for certainly all youth
are reckless beyond words."

Hesiod, 800 B.C.

PIERRE entered the seventh grade a very different person from whom he had been only three months previously. His class-mates were also different. The boys combed their hair and were more attentive to their appearances in general. The girls seemed more pleasant; they weren't as aggravating as they had been the previous year. There was no longer as much rivalry between boys and girls—on the contrary, they were attracted to each other. He had no clue what was causing these differences.

His teacher, once again, was an older, gray-haired lady. She was a good teacher, but the students, especially many of the boys, had become rowdy due to their physical and emotional changes. Each time she turned her back to the class to write on the board, pandemonium broke out among the students. Pierre and his fellow clowns threw spitballs and used rubber bands to propel tightly rolled pieces of paper, bobby pins, or paper clips all over the room to strike other students. It was like a war. Unfortunately, this teacher did not have the proverbial "eyes behind her head" to catch them misbehaving—probably because of her age. Once the students concentrated on how to shoot others with projectiles, getting the attention of the opposite sex, plus daydreaming, there was little room left for academic achievement. Despite that, a small minority of students really wanted to learn. Most of the rest of the class did just enough to pass, and many failed. Pierre was in the middle group.

Again, they got a new student in their class, a girl. Not just any girl, but a girl who looked like she belonged in high school. Many of the boys were in "love" for the first time, Pierre included. He and his best friend would follow her all over the school yard praising her attributes to each other as if moonstruck. Unfortunately, this attraction remained secret as they were much too inept and timid to convey their feelings to her. It was probably best that way.

Pierre was still an avid reader and a good speller, but his reading interests changed dramatically. There was a paperback book going around in the class, not a library book or a book recommended by the teacher, but one, he had heard, with racy content unlike any book he had ever read. He just couldn't wait to read it. It was surprising to him how *Peyton Place* found its way to his little town on the bayou and his seventh-grade classroom so soon after its publication. It was not completely clear to him who was the initial owner of the book, but he asked a girl in the class, one of the prettiest and most intelligent, to let him read it when it was available. After a long wait, she finally handed him the book. Despite its recent publication, the book was soiled and had many dog-eared pages to mark the most interesting passages. And interesting was an understatement. Certainly, many students had read only the dog-eared pages to view the most interesting passages, but he read the whole book—after reading the dog-eared pages first. Pierre spent most of his spare moments reading this transformative book. He could read the book at home without having to hide it because his parents couldn't read. The fact that a pretty girl had given him the book to read made it even more interesting—they shared a common experience. He gave no thought to the fact that every reader in the class had shared that same experience. It was amazing how the students could quote passages, especially those from the dog-eared pages, and not be able to quote two lines of poetry for English classes. Pierre was certain of one thing: this book was much more interesting than his comic books.

Perhaps one of the most interesting educational experiences that year was the spring class trip to the state capital in Baton Rouge, about 50 miles away. He had ridden through Baton Rouge only once when a relative was in Charity Hospital in New Orleans. He and his classmates waited impatiently for the trip. The spring date arrived, the teacher loaded the bus, and they were on their way. He remembers the shirt he wore on that day—a white and green plaid short-sleeved shirt. Spirits were high as they sang Fats Domino's "I'm in Love Again" while on route to their destination.

When they arrived at the Capitol grounds, they were amazed by their beauty and the height of the capitol building. Most of his class had never seen anything like this, although a few of the more fortunate ones had done some traveling with their parents. The visit to the interior of the capitol was made interesting by the guide who explained what functions were held in each part of the capitol. They also visited the site of Huey P. Long's assassination and shivered at the sight of the bullet-pocked walls. After lunch, they boarded the bus for the trip back home. Again, they sang their favorite Fats Domino song. Fats was king that day. They had a memorable time. The best part for many of them was not being in school and also spending time with their peers. The educational part was "okay."

By now, most of Pierre's peers had TV at home, but he partially made up that deficiency by spending a lot of time listening to the radio. The first music he ever heard was certainly the Cajun music that his father listened to at every opportunity, at times singing and dancing across the floor with an imaginary partner. Then Pierre also became acquainted with country music and was very fond of Hank Williams. He spent a lot of time sitting on a cow hide-bottomed chair leaned against the wall listening to his favorite stations. Evenings were his favorite times to listen because he could easily tune the AM radio to stations all over the United States. Sometimes, however, he would lose the stations and hear only weird "space sounds." The Grand Ole Opry and The Louisiana Hayride were his favorite programs at that time. On one occasion, he heard a girl he knew from his school introduce herself on The Louisiana Hayride. He thought it was quite a coincidence to hear a girl from his little town introduce herself in a city all the way across the state of Louisiana.

Music was not the only thing he listened to on the radio. Late at night, when reception was best, he tuned in the powerful stations from all over the country. Some of the commercials (perhaps pre-TV infomercials) were amusing to him. One went something like this: "This is Radio Station (plus an assortment of Ks, Ys, Ws or Xs) from Cincinnati, Ohio." Then, a nasal, neighborly voice announced, "Friends, do you suffer from itching in embarrassing places while away from home? Have you tried many remedies that gave you no relief? Well neighbor, suffer no more. There is a remedy for your condition. This cure is Red Star Salve. For only $6.95, that's right folks, only six dollars and ninety-five cents, your embarrassments will be no more. But friends, that's not all. If you act right now, we will send you, in a plain brown wrapper, with your salve, an 8 x 10 color photo of Bo Diddley, suitable for framing." Pierre wondered how many people jumped on that offer.

In the spring, Pierre and his father, one of his uncles, and two of his cousins went on a crawfishing expedition to the Atchafalaya Floodway. They left before daybreak with a pickup truck loaded with the five people, a large seine, several burlap sacks, foot tubs, extra sets of clothing, and some sandwiches. The drive on the gravel roads to the levee where they would fish took about thirty-five minutes if they didn't get a flat tire, which was not an uncommon occurrence.

Upon arrival, they unloaded the fifteen-foot wide two handled seine net. To seine, one person held one of the handles at the edge of the water, and the second person took the other handle out into the deeper water. There was some debate this time as to who would take the second handle out into the water. The seiner who took the outside handle often had to dive into the cool spring-time water to get quickly acclimated to the water temperature. Pierre's uncles and cousins pulled the seine as he himself was not yet strong enough to pull a seine that could get heavy with water resistance and crawfish. They pulled the seine until it felt heavy, and his cousin, the one in the water, brought his end of the net forward around to the bank. There was great anticipation to see what was in the net. The first thing they did was to allow any snakes an opportunity to escape into the water. Then there was a scramble to pick up the crawfish and put them in the foot tubs. Next, they emptied the crawfish into the burlap sacks until they were almost full, but not too packed so that the crustaceans could breathe. They repeated the process until each family had at least one hundred fifty pounds of crawfish to take home. If they were lucky, they would sometimes catch a few fish along with the crawfish. They completed the fishing trip by mid-morning, and they were home in a half hour or so.

Once home the tedious work began for each family. The crawfish had to be either boiled or parboiled to allow peeling for the freezer. Some families just pulled off the tails and put them in the freezer raw, which was much more efficacious for preservation. However, his father and mother insisted on boiling and peeling because there was less tail loss and more of the wonderful crawfish fat was retained. Pierre and his sister found this process so boring despite the fact that they could eat a few tails and suck a few heads for the fat as they peeled. But it was still boring, as even Cajuns can eat only so much crawfish. To escape the tediousness, each would vie for the opportunity to make coffee for their parents. Whoever made the coffee, would make it very slowly. Getting to eat crawfish étouffée, crawfish stew, and crawfish gumbo year round, however, made everything worthwhile.

At the time of these crawfish trips, Pierre did not find it unusual that there were relatively few other people crawfishing. Certainly, the area was so vast that it would have taken huge numbers of fishermen to crowd it. Later, however, he would find out that crawfish was only eaten by Cajuns, blacks, and a few others. Many regarded crawfish and certain fish as "trash fish" unfit for consumption. Who would eat stuff out of the mud? It was as if one would achieve a boost in social status if he or she proclaimed disgust for such things. This situation certainly changed as more and more people, for various reasons, developed a taste for crawfish. The demand increased so much that they were eventually farm-raised to meet demand. The crustaceans became so popular all over the United States that demand caused a steep rise in price. In universities throughout the South, the spring semester was incomplete without a celebratory crawfish boil. Strange how culinary tastes have changed—even some foreigners are now sucking the heads. Unfortunately, prices would eventually go up so much that many Cajuns could no longer afford them. How ironic.

The fall butchering (*la boucherie*) was the year's next opportunity to gather food for the family. This occasion took place after the weather got consistently cool in the fall, usually in November. This was the accustomed time for butchering because cool weather was needed to hang meats and avoid insects. Traditionally, families and neighbors would get together to share in the butchering of pigs. However, for Pierre's family, it was an individual butchering. Like most endeavors in his family, the process for the butchering would start early, just after daybreak. There were many preparatory activities to complete. His father sharpened the knives, his mother washed the outdoor kettle, Pierre gathered firewood, and everyone gathered pots, pans, and utensils.

The actual killing of the pig was not for the faint-hearted. It was not quick and even less humane. For his family, and back through the generations, the killing was dispassionate and necessary for sustenance. The pig, which had been corn-fed for a few weeks before the butchering, was not a large one—a large pig would require more manpower to manage. His father held the pig down as he drove a long butcher knife into its heart. The squealing of the pig was sharp, ear-splitting, and could he heard perhaps a half mile away. The blood gushed into a pan from the knife wound, and it would be used later to make red boudin.

His father placed the pig carcass on a table and poured hot water over it to facilitate hair removal. Pierre's job, in addition to fetching items, was to help scrape and later clean the skin with soap made from last year's pig's fat. Finally, the carcass was rinsed and was ready to be butchered. His father then started eviscerating the animal as his mother held a pan to collect the organs—the heart, liver, spleen, kidneys, and lungs. They placed the stomach and intestines in another large vessel. They hung the carcass to cool overnight to facilitate cutting. His mother would clean the entrails and cut up the organs. They utilized every part of the pig except the hair and the squeal. The stomach or tripe and small intestines would later be cleaned and boiled in seasoned water—a Cajun favorite called *tripe* or *ponce bouilli*. One of the first meals from the butchering would be a mixture of heart, liver, lung, spleen and kidney cooked with onions and seasonings and served on rice called *le bouilli*—a family favorite. The pig's feet were set aside to be boiled in seasoned water within the next few days.

The next day, his father began by splitting the cooled carcass in half. He then separated the hind quarters and the shoulders from each half. He separated the meat from the skull to make hogshead cheese. The tongue, considered a delicacy, was separated and put aside to be roasted later after being stuffed with garlic and spices. Then the brain was removed to be cooked within a few days with onions and seasonings or sometimes with eggs. Some of the skin, fat, and flesh were cut into small pieces to make cracklings (*gratons*).

They still had much work to do. The kettle had to be emptied of the leftover water so it could be used to fry cracklings and render the pork fat for cooking lard and making soap. They sliced the meat into serving portions, wrapped it in waxed paper and stored it in the freezer. They still needed to make the hogshead cheese and *boudin*. Obviously, not all of this work could be done in one day by his family. One can see why butchering was best done by two or more families to share the work.

They placed the pork fat in the kettle for melting. Once the fat was melted and heated to a high temperature, the cracklings were thrown in and fried until crispy. Once they skimmed the cracklings from the oil, the oil could be used later as lard for cooking or making soap. To make lard, they canned the oil in jars to preserve it. The clear, hot oil turned white when cooled and would provide cooking oil for several months. Soap was made by adding lye to the oil and stirred. When the oil solidified, the soap was cut into blocks and used to wash anything.

Very important was the preservation of slab pork with salt. His father placed salt in the bottom of a large crock jar, and alternated slabs of pork and salt until the jar was almost full. The crock jar, covered with a cloth, was then placed in the coolest room or location in the house and used as needed to flavor potatoes, vegetables, and beans. Normally, the salted pork lasted until spring. Next, his mother would make the hogshead cheese and *boudin*. Each required a lot of meat grinding, and Pierre often helped with this while his mother performed other processes. The hogshead cheese was a mixture of coarsely ground meat from the hog's head combined with onions and spices. She then placed the mixture on a plate to congeal. They would have the cheese in the mornings for breakfast. As the fat content was enormous, it was an unlikely breakfast food outside of Cajun families. Boudin was a highly seasoned mixture of ground pork meat and liver, onions, seasonings—especially red pepper—and rice stuffed sausage-like into pork intestines. Most of the boudin was white with a smaller portion being red or black due to the pork blood added to the mixture. It was also considerably less than cholesterol-free, but no one seemed to mind as the word "cholesterol" was unknown to most people.

The Cajun tradition of making boudin and hogshead cheese were two of the most obvious culinary traditions brought from France by the earliest Acadians. Boudin is still found in France today in its white and red form, but minus the rice and hot pepper as those were added in Louisiana due to the readily available rice and spices.

Finally, as was the tradition in most Cajun families, a hogback stew was made within a day or two of the butchering. The stew was very thick due to the addition of dark *roux*, a brown mixture of oil and flour. The heavy stew along with a generous amount of pork fat and strong seasonings made it a very hearty dish not recommended for those with delicate stomachs.

The family was happy when the butchering was finally over. It had been a lot of work added to the workload his parents already carried in their daily lives. His father had to go back to his difficult job, and his mother had mountains of household chores to complete, as well as having to continue processing the pork. Pierre went back to school where, unfortunately, he would get well-rested. The good news for all was the good food they would enjoy during the winter.

Ever since Pierre was in the fourth grade, he would pick cotton on weekends in the fall at his uncles' farms. When the cotton was ready, farmers would hire extra help to get it in as soon as possible. When he first started picking, he was too small to pick very much—perhaps sixty to seventy pounds that would give him a dollar plus a little change per day. He would ration his little bit of money to buy snacks like candy, cold drinks, or popsicles or perhaps a wooden top with a sharp metal point to play with along with his friends. When his money ran out, that was the end of the treats.

Now, he was older, bigger, and faster. He picked cotton for his Uncle Robert, the one who had wired his house for electricity. His uncle would pick him up along with several other boys and men early in the morning to get to the farm. When they got there, his Aunt Hazel had already started preparing the noon meal for all the pickers who were paid two dollars per hundred pounds picked plus the lunch.

The workers, consisting of African Americans and white pickers, were brought to the cotton patch. Each one was given a long canvas sack with a strap that went around the shoulder. Each picker took a row to walk down as he or she picked the cotton on each side. Most adults picked around two hundred pounds per day. A few, like a couple of his cousins, could pick over three hundred pounds per day. The work was less than fun as it was relatively cool in the mornings and wet from the morning dew. Everyone's clothing got damp and reeked from the defoliant used to drop the leaves to hasten the opening of the cotton bolls. Then the sun came out and dried the wet clothing which only increased the scent of the defoliant. Soon, caterpillars came out and crawled over the pickers. His uncle weighed the filled sacks and recorded the amounts next to the pickers' names. Men then dumped the cotton into the trailer. The workers were given some water then went back to work.

Then the high point of the day arrived, which was lunchtime. The pickers were brought to the farmhouse on the trailer or walked if they were close to the house. The food was excellent, plentiful, and satisfying. It consisted of fresh vegetables, meat, beans and gravy, and iced tea. Pierre had his first iced tea here as his family never drank tea. He found it most refreshing. The amount of work his aunt Hazel had to do to prepare this huge meal was unbeliev-able. And then there was the cleanup. For Pierre, there was a short break after lunch that he used to sit in an Adirondack chair on the screened porch to rest, or to read a few pages in one of his uncle's books.

The thirty-minute break went by like a comet in the night. Where was that clock he had in school? In slow motion, the workers got back to the fields. By now the sun was blazing as the workers strapped on the sacks and resumed picking. The work was tedious and boring. Around mid-afternoon one day, one of the young black pickers shouted, "Snake!" That got everyone's attention as cotton-mouths were not rare in cotton patches that were close to a bayou. Then, he shouted to no one in particular, "He's going towards you!" The pickers didn't know who "you" was and everyone bolted in all directions knocking down cotton plants while shedding their sacks of cotton. The announcer of that warning was laughing as if he were insane. The pickers caught on to his mischievous joke and got back to work. His uncle was not happy with the distraction, but he did not want to fire a good cotton picker—they were hard to find.

The process of picking and weighing continued until about five o'clock. Each picker's numbers were totaled and payments made. Pierre usually came out with three dollars and change. He would take his money and put it in his bank, an empty elephant-shaped grape extract bottle with a slotted cap meant to be used as a piggy bank when empty. When he finished the picking season, he had twenty-eight dollars saved up (about $65.00 today). He had never had this much money. He rationed it to make it last as long as possible. He was lucky that his parents did not require him to spend his money on clothes or school supplies like some parents he knew. He would eventually spend it all on goodies at the store across the street from the school.

Pierre was now in eighth grade. This would be his last year in elementary school. At that time in his region's public schools, grades one through eight were elementary and grades nine through twelve were high school. After another summer of swimming, fishing in the bayou, hanging out with friends, reading, and other random activities, he was again ready to go back to school. They repeated the ritual of buying school clothes. Now that he was older, he was allowed to go alone to the local general merchandise store to select his blue jeans. He charged them to his family's account which his father paid off every two weeks when he got paid. There was only one choice in jeans—Tuf Nut. It would take several washings to soften them up and eliminate the new jean's smell. His mother hated to press these jeans because she had problems aligning the leg seams.

He and his classmates had grown considerably in height, some more than others, but had not matured much. They were still in the clutches of early adolescence, an affliction that rendered too many of them practically uneducable—they were a teacher's nightmare. The boys were a motley assortment of croaky-voiced, rooster-necked, and often pimply-faced adolescents confined in a room with a peculiar scent composed of a mixture of denim, Clearasil, sweat, body odor, and the occasional fart partially filtered through someone's jeans. Had he visited there, Antoine de Saint Exupery's Little Prince would have been intrigued, as certainly, there was nothing like this on his little asteroid.

For the first time, he had a male teacher, a short, stout, balding man who used very unorthodox techniques to discipline his male students. He perhaps had taken "Advanced Torture 407" as part of his college graduation requirements to teach eighth-grade boys. He must have aced that class because he had a repertoire of many ingenious methods to inflict pain upon them. If someone talked in the rear of the room, he threw with deadly accuracy, a tightly rolled up, taped magazine at the offender. He must have been a baseball pitcher at one time. He relished pinching the base of the neck muscle of a wrongdoer when he was not paying attention. He lifted boys out of their desks by the bottom lobes of their ears. Often a whack with hand or ruler was administered to miscreants. Girls never seemed to need this type of discipline, but they were given lines to write for the slightest infraction—like crossing their legs. Strangely, no one complained about this teacher's methods as far as Pierre knew; as odd as his punishments were, they were accepted as just. Strangely, his students seemed to like him.

The first month of school was scorchingly hot, and the school, not having air conditioning or fans, was most uncomfortable. The boys had just come in after lunch recess one day sweaty, red-faced, and smelling like goats due to their increasing hormones when one of the students who sat next to the teacher's desk started complaining about the heat. This student sat there not because he was the teacher's pet, but because he caused a lot of problems and the teacher kept him close to keep an eye on him. He griped, "We don't want to do any work because it's too hot!" Some of the other boys chimed in and added similar complaints.

The teacher said, "Oh, y'all are hot?"

"Yes, yes, yes …"

The teacher responded, "OK, I'll cool y'all off."

He calmly reached behind him to the blackboard that was really black and actually made of slate, and with his five, horn-like fingernails, scratched the slate with a huge, slow, arch-like motion. The loud, chilling screech emanating from the board gave everyone in the classroom except the teacher powerful, instant chills.

The teacher, with a completely self-satisfied, calm voice asked, "Is anyone still hot?"

"No! No! No! No!"

No one ever complained about the heat in that class again.

After seven years without heat relief in warm months, a stroke of good fortune occurred. The school or parish purchased a large number of army surplus Hunter ceiling fans, complete with the obligatory olive drab paint. The workmen installed two fans in the classroom and what a difference they made—this was much better than horny nails scraped on the blackboard! The room was now bearable. One would think the eighth-grade boys would have been appreciative. Wrong! Some of the boys, when the teacher was out of the room, threw their books and notebooks into the fan blades which damaged the books and threw one fan out of balance. Thanks to the durability of this Hunter, it managed to keep on functioning. Fans have been hit by worse stuff.

Pierre and one of his buddies, Billy, had another method to keep cool before school started. He left home early enough in the morning to go for a short swim with his buddy who lived on the bayou only about 400 yards from school. How pleasant it was to swim in the bayou with no possibility of his mother catching him in the act. His mother had caught him the past summer after his little sister told their mother that he and a friend were swimming in the bayou about three hundred yards up the road. When he saw his mother up on the bank with a belt in her hand shouting at him, he came close to adding a measure of salinity to the fresh water. She beat his butt with a belt all the way home. But now he could swim with wild abandon as he and his friend plunged into the bayou to see how far they could swim underwater. Once they dove into the water, each swam frantically to gain the greatest distance.

One time, Pierre dove in and went deep into the water where it got cooler and cooler the deeper he went down. The problem was the water was murky with zero visibility and was very disorienting. His breath had just about run out, and he raced up for air. He was much deeper than he thought, and his lungs felt like they were about to burst. He finally broke the surface and sucked in the largest breath ever up to that time in his life. He had learned a lesson—stay in the warm surface water. After that swim, they walked the two blocks back to school just in time for roll call. Observing their wet heads, everyone in class knew what they had been doing. Some of the students made remarks, as they considered it unusual for anyone to swim just before school. The two boys would enjoy these swims until the cool fall air terminated them.

Pierre normally rode the bus to school, but often, he would walk to get there earlier so he could spend more time with his friends or go for a swim. One morning, he got to school early and walked into the gym. The gym was empty except for an upperclassman who was in the process of walking up the bleachers to reach the steel girder that crossed the gym floor. When he reached the girder, he climbed on and walked across it over the gym floor, which was perhaps 30 feet below. He then walked back to the bleachers and quietly left the gym. Pierre, who was always one to climb anything, was impressed. He wanted to duplicate what the older student had done.

He walked to school the next day and went straight to the gym and up the bleachers. He looked at the silver-painted girder and saw that it arched up to its peak in the middle of the basketball court. He got on the girder and began his crossing. The first thirty feet or so didn't seem high as he was still over the bleachers. When he got over the gym floor, it began to look higher and higher as he reached the middle of the gym. For a moment he paused to look down at the floor. It looked so much higher than he thought it would. He had climbed trees much higher than this, but in a tree, there were always tree limbs beneath him which obscured the distance to the ground and provided some security in case of a fall. He didn't think about it very long and continued his walk to the other side of the gym and walked back to the bleachers. As far as he knew, no one had witnessed his act of less than good judgment. He did not tell his parents.

Unfortunately, his academic performance remained the same; if he was just barely passing, that was good enough for him. He was still reading whatever he could put his hands on, but he did the bare minimum in class. He brought no homework home, and if he had some work to hand in, it was usually shoddy and partially done. To him, good grades were for the "smart" students, and he did not consider himself in that category. Additionally, he, like most of his peers, had become afflicted with the "adolescent pox," the period when thirteen and fourteen-year-olds are thrust outside of behavioral norms and into the realm of absurdity. Pierre had no clue about absurdity and hormones, but he certainly was afflicted. He did not want to go anywhere with his parents anymore. His peers had become more important to him than his parents.

He was often moody and resentful. He would not discuss his issues with his family because they did not understand his world. In reality, his parents, who truly did the best they knew how, were generations behind in their mindset and values. Pierre's favorite place to withdraw had always been at the edge of the bayou where he could watch the fish jump as he would think. He had a lot to brood about because he was noting more and more the differences between him and most of his classmates. They seemed to do more and have more than he. Unfortunately, daydreams and wishes brought no solutions.

While most boys kept their hair very short around the ears, Pierre's hair was well over the top of his ears before he got a haircut. Sometimes, classmates would ask derisively, "When are you going to get a haircut?" Unfortunately, he was not the one who determined when he would get a haircut; his father did. His solution to avoid embarrassment was to paste his hair down with Royal Crown Hair Dressing and comb it into a ducktail, not to imitate Elvis, but to keep his hair off his ears. One of the boys in his class shouted, "Hey, look at Pierre's hair, the back of his head looks like the rear of a Mercury outboard motor!" It did.

On the positive side, he did get access to dozens of interesting books. His Uncle Robert had a large collection of books that seemed to Pierre like a small library. His uncle had not finished high school but was an avid reader who could converse on almost any topic. His collection consisted of a series of documented histories of World War II with vivid pictures, plus various novels, nature books on the wildlife of Africa, volumes of Reader's Digest Condensed Books, and other books on diverse topics. When his family visited his aunt and uncle, he spent most of his time sitting on the floor reading the books. His uncle was the only relative they visited who had books in the house. He retained much of the information he read, and his reading level improved due to the availability of these books.

By far the most life-changing event of his life happened that year. His family got a new house. He had heard his parents talking about it, but he didn't think it was going to happen. But lo and behold, dump trucks appeared one morning and began depositing loads of red dirt. The plan was to build a new house behind the old one. Mindful of the flood four years ago, this house would be built on an elevated mound about three feet high and set on two-foot pillars. The new house would be well above the water level of the last flood.

The trucks dumped two hundred loads of dirt which a bulldozer later shaped into a flattop mound. Pierre and Linda were excited and envisioned themselves moving into the new house in the very near future but were disappointed when they learned that the mound would not be ready to build on until the rains helped to pack the newly imported soil. The rains came and after several weeks, construction finally began.

These were exciting times filled with anticipation. Even Pierre temporarily escaped his adolescent "pox" long enough to appreciate the significance of what was happening. The family had always lived in shacks with no running water, bathroom, or other modern facilities common at that time. Not only was this house going to be new, but it would also have running water—hot and cold, three separate bedrooms, a bathroom, a large living room, and a glass porch next to the kitchen making it three times larger than their present house. Pierre did not know where his parents conceived the ideas for the house. Certainly, the builder who drew the plans, as well as Bertha, made some suggestions.

The construction process took what seemed like forever to complete, but it was an interesting experience for Pierre. They first put down the brick and mortar pillars that would support and elevate the house, and then the actual construction began. Each day, it looked more and more like a house. The house was not fancy, but very well built and sturdy. The carpenters, who were all Cajun friends of his father, did very good work. To this day, the house is in good shape and occupied.

Curious Pierre spent as much time as possible on the construction site watching and asking questions. Everyone spoke Cajun French, which worked fine for him. As was the custom in Cajun culture, his mother offered coffee to anyone there during the morning and afternoon break, including the workers. She asked him to take some to the workers. The workers were grateful, and each gave him a five or ten cent tip. Hardly ever having any spending money, he was excited. He soon realized that if he brought them coffee every day, he would eventually have a tidy little sum, but then Linda, who was in fifth grade, wanted to be included in the action, too. Naturally, his mother, who always wanted to be fair, allowed her to take a turn bringing the coffee. He was less than pleased at sharing with her.

After what seemed like years, the house was finally completed. It was an impressive sight standing on the mound with its gray asbestos siding and snow-white asphalt roof shingles. Fittingly, his bedroom was light blue and his sister's was pink. The kitchen, glass porch, living room, and his parents' room were a light green. His father and Bertha did all the painting and the pungent scent of fresh paint permeated the house. What a difference from the unfinished, rough-hewn walls of the old house. Each light had a light fixture instead of just a naked light bulb with a string. Wow! Then there was the bathroom complete with a flush toilet, hot and cold running water, and a bathtub—were they dreaming? The floors were of smooth, sanded and varnished pine boards with no light showing through the cracks.

Obviously, the one who appreciated it the most was his mother. She had shouldered most of the laborious work generated by the lack of conveniences in the old house. No more heating and carrying water for baths, washing, cleaning, and cooking, no more roaches and rodents in the house, no more scrubbing floors with old bricks, and no more chamber pots. When she walked around the finished house, the spacious rooms overwhelmed her as did the relative conveniences and the newness. She felt it was so much more than she needed, almost as if it were pretentious for a woman like herself to have a house like this. She had not ever dared to dream this large.

The family moved their few possessions into the home. There was no purchasing of new furniture, appliances, or other frills to go with the new house. They moved Pierre's metal-framed bed, complete with its saggy moss mattress to his bedroom, and it would be there until well after he left home for the university. His mother and sister filled the cabinets with the same pots, pans, and dishes they had owned forever. Despite the house not having air-conditioning, central heating, television, telephone, carpets, or other normal conveniences of the time, they were as happy as the Beverly Hillbillies when they first moved into their California mansion. Their new home was so much more than they could ever have imagined. Compared to all those sharecropper shacks his parents had lived in, this new house was a mansion, a mansion they had built through financial perseverance, hard work, and doing without so many things for so long. They were forty-seven years old.

The icing on the cake was the fact that they had paid for the house in cash; there would be no monthly notes to be paid for the rest of their lives. The cost of the house was six thousand dollars (equivalent to approximately seventy thousand dollars today). It had been a monumental challenge to save such an enormous amount of money given his father's meager income. It never occurred to Pierre that perhaps this was the reason his haircuts had been so infrequent and that he didn't have all the "things" some of his friends had.

Unfortunately, after only one night in his new home, his father would spend the next several days and nights in the hospital after narrowly escaping death on the job. He and his fellow workers were on a crew boat traveling down the Atchafalaya River to reach the worksite. Among his fellow workers were his brother, Isaac, and his oldest son-in-law's brother. Not long after leaving the boat dock, there was an explosion in the engine compartment. Flames instantly engulfed the boat. The only option for the men was to jump into the river and swim to the bank. This was no guarantee of safety since the river was notorious for its fast current and many of the men had various degrees of burns. Luckily, they had life jackets on when they jumped into the river. Pierre's father and his Uncle Isaac, who both had serious burns on their hands, arms, and face, swam together. The bank was about a hundred and fifty yards away, but the swim was much longer because the current swept them down the river. His uncle, who was burned more severely, came close to giving up, but his father encouraged him to keep trying. All but one of the men got to the bank several hundred yards downstream. The only fatality was the boat captain.

The men were rescued, and the injured ones were taken to the hospital. His uncle, father, and his father's son-in-law's brother were kept near to each other. Pierre, his sisters, mother, and relatives were there to visit as soon as the men were stabilized. When he got into the room where his father was, he was shocked at what he saw. He saw a mummy-like man helpless in bed with yards of bandages on his hands and arms, and a swollen face with no eyebrows or eyelids. How could this be his father? His father was always the man who could do prodigious amounts of work. The two other men had been burned even more severely than his father. Recuperation would be slow.

After his father had recovered some, he and his brother Leonce tore down the old house and used the lumber to build a garage and wash house. His brother did most of the work as he was more skilled in that area, and his father helped out as well as he could. No one shed a tear as they reduced the old house to a pile of lumber that gave no clue as to what it once was. In that pile were the rough-hewn red cypress boards complete with grooves carved out by the generations of roaches who lived and reproduced there. This type of board would become very valuable in the future when they would be used by the well-to-do to line their dens.

The completion of the wash house was appreciated by his mother almost as much as the new house was. Then, she really felt like a queen when they placed the new wringer washing machine in the wash house. It did not have all the features some machines had, but it beat the hell out of a tub and washboard. It had hot and cold water, and would wash and wring clothes, but she still had to carry the clothes to the line to hang for drying; nevertheless, she did not complain.

Next, his parents bought a living room set consisting of a sofa, and two matching chairs. Like most living rooms, it was used very sparingly except when an overflow crowd came in for holidays. As it never wore out, it was the only living room set they ever bought. The sofa still looked like new after his father's death when they liquidated the household.

Not everyone fully appreciated all the modern conveniences of the new house. Pierre's father could not quite get accustomed to using the toilet in the house. Like his own father, he refused to tear down the old outhouse. Up to this point, he had seldom used a flush toilet except when he visited his relatives in Texas and Lake Charles. For all of his 47 years, he did his bodily functions either in an outhouse or a barn or in the woods when he was working. Apparently, he was uncomfortable doing in a house what he had always done outside. He often said that it was strange how people used to eat inside and go to the toilet outside, and now, they often eat outside and go to the toilet inside. It would be several years before his mother could convince him to tear down the old outhouse.

The new house brought about other changes. Before the new house, grass and weeds were kept down only in small areas around the house. The rest of the yard was gardens or tall weeds. Keeping the grass cut in the area around the house with a swing blade had been very laborious. His father would cut it very short and sometimes shaved the ground to control the weeds. When Pierre tried to cut grass with the swing blade, it merely bounced off the weeds.

With the new house and more area to cut, his father finally bought a two and one-half horsepower push lawnmower. They had never used a power lawnmower before, and they were amazed how nice and neat the grass looked—just like the lawns in town. Now they had a new house and a new lawn. It didn't stop there; his father had cleared the brush and thorn trees in front of their house between the bayou and the road. His father had an amazing work ethic. He cut the trees without a chainsaw, chopped them up and burned them on weekends when he was not on the job. And now he wanted to keep this grass cut with the lawnmower, too. It was so pleasant to be able to see the bayou from the house. Later, his father would make another garden on a small part of the cleared area. The soil, enriched by organic matter deposited by the spring high waters was very fertile and produced excellent crops of tomatoes and okra. However, there was a little problem. The nutrias living along the bayou ate most of the produce. Eventually, the garden was abandoned.

With the bayou bank and the yard combined, cutting the grass was a considerable task, and Pierre inherited the job. He did not mind cutting the grass; actually, he rather enjoyed it. He was lazy about doing school work, but not physical work, that is, until he found out his buddies in town received a little money or an allowance for cutting the grass, and their yards were much smaller than his. But his father had a different mindset. His own father, grandfather, and ancestors expected children to work to help support the family. Children were not paid. In the sharecropper world from which they came, the son profited from work only when he was seventeen or eighteen years old when his father let him work an acre or so of land and use the profit to get married or start his sharecropping life. Pierre did his job, but the situation added to his adolescent angst.

Sometimes, lessons are learned in unusual circumstances. His bus ride after school was the "second load" which meant that he had to wait at school an additional forty minutes or so until the bus returned from the first load. Sometimes, he walked home if he had to stop to pick up little things like bread and milk for his mother. Other times, he waited so he could hang around with one or more of his buddies. One Friday afternoon, Pierre and his buddy Joe were walking near the football field to see if anything interesting might be happening there. "Friday is my favorite day," he told Joe, "because it is the first day of the weekend." Little did Pierre know that he would remember this particular Friday as long as he lived.

One of their classmates, a large boy, was walking towards the back of the schoolyard on his way home. Joe said, "Look, there's Wayne, let's beat him up." Pierre was not normally a bully or a fighter although he had had several fights in the lower grades, most of which were prompted by his older cousins to provide them with entertainment. Nevertheless, he said, "OK." He must have been auditioning for fool of the year. Wayne was the class crybaby, and boys picked on him. He would do nothing to defend himself and often cried. Pierre and Joe caught up with him and pushed him a few times until he cried and ran home. Satisfied with their less than noble actions, they turned around to walk back to the front of the school.

They had walked about fifty yards when they heard a woman calling them. It was Wayne's mother, and Wayne was next to her.

Y'all wait right there," she shouted to them, "I want to talk to y'all!"

They walked toward the pair and met on a gravel street that ran parallel to the school fence. Wayne was still bleary-eyed and red faced.

His mother said, "You boys still want to fight?"

"Yeah!" they answered.

"Okay, Wayne will fight you one at a time. Who wants to be first?"

Pierre said, "I'll fight him first." He thought this would be a piece of cake. He would give him a few licks, and Wayne would run crying to his mother.

"Ok, you two will fight until one of you quits. Son, you are going to fight!"

Pierre, one of the lightest boys in his class, was faced by an opponent who outweighed him by at least twenty pounds. That didn't bother him, but the stance Wayne took surprised him. He held up his fists like a boxer and moved like one, too. Still, he thought one good punch would take care of him and send him and his mother back home.

They squared off in the middle of the road and began trading punches. Wayne was no longer the gawky crybaby. He was fighting like a pro and not anywhere near crying. They fought on the road and in the ditch, they punched, wrestled, and did anything to hurt each other. They each had a bloody nose and scratches, but Pierre was well beaten and finally called it quits. Wayne's mother made them shake hands and told Joe his turn would be on Monday. As they walked back to the school building, Joe proclaimed with bravado, "Don't worry, I'll take care of him Monday. I'll beat the crap out of him!"

Worse than getting beaten up was going to school Monday morning and facing his classmates. Everyone would have heard that he had been in a fight and the class crybaby had beaten him. To exacerbate matters, he had a black eye—visible proof of his loss, and it would remain there for a week or more. But the damage he had inflicted on Wayne was no longer visible as bloody noses could easily be cleaned up. The final insult was that Wayne sat across from him on the next row, and Pierre just knew that each time Wayne looked at him he was relishing the memory of his victory on Friday. And of course, Pierre was teased all day by what he felt was the whole school. He did get some consolation from Joe, who assured him that he would finish Wayne off after school. He repeatedly said, "I can't wait to beat his ass. I'll show him."

After the longest school day in his entire life, the 3:30 bell finally and mercifully rang. He and Joe started walking to the back of the school yard as Pierre was assured once more that revenge was about to arrive. He had never seen Joe fight, but he was a little bigger and a year older than Pierre. Perhaps he could get it done. One thing he knew for sure, Joe would have to do more than he had done last Friday.

They got to the site of last Friday's slugfest, and Wayne and his mother were already there waiting. They walked up to them and crossed the fence to get on the road. The mother gave the rules again—they would fight until one would call it quits. Each got into his fighting stance. Once more, Wayne held up his fists like a trained boxer. Joe had a weird stance—left hand held at chest level and the right hand at his side below waist level. Pierre remembered enough from the *Friday Night Fights* to know that this was not a preferred stance. They circled a little, and Joe rushed in flailing the air with both hands, and unfortunately, hitting nothing but air. Wayne delivered a solid punch that landed with a resonating "whack" on Joe's left cheek. He winced in pain as he held his hand to his face and shouted, "I quit for right now, but I'll be back tomorrow!"

Francis's mother said calmly, "Ok, we will be here tomorrow."

As they walked away, Joe told Pierre, "I'll get him tomorrow, you'll see."

Walking back in silence to the front of the school, Pierre said to himself, "What a disappointment. I fought my ass off for such a long time, got some good licks in and took a beating. Then he comes here, never lands a punch, and quits after getting hit only one time. What makes him think he can do better tomorrow?"

There was no fight the next day—Joe didn't show up.

After further review much later, Pierre realized he got what was coming to him. There had been absolutely no reason to bully Wayne even though it seemed the thing to do at the time. Perhaps it was another manifestation of the adolescent pox. This fight was the last one Pierre would ever have. He learned it was better to sharpen his tongue rather than to sharpen his sword. Wayne profited immensely from that fight. No one picked on him again. He became a changed person with his newly found self-esteem. With good parenting and winning the fights with Pierre and Joe, Wayne was healed.

Like many schools of that era, his school had a store across the street which catered to the students. Students were allowed to cross the road at certain times of the day to purchase refreshments. Pierre was especially fond of the lady who, along with her husband, owned and ran the store. She was cordial and always ready to give advice to the students. She probably did as much counseling as the school counselor. Despite seldom having any money to spend on non-essentials such as refreshments, he did get money to buy school supplies like paper or pencils. Often, he went there with his friends just to hang out a bit.

On some of the rare occasions when he had a spare nickel, he would buy a Popsicle, the kind that had two wooden sticks and could be broken in half to share with a friend. On one of these occasions, he had a friend with him and shared half his Popsicle with him. Several days later, he saw that friend coming back from the store with a grape Popsicle, which looked almost freshly bought—it had been licked only about four times. Since he had shared with him a few days before, he assumed his friend would reciprocate. He went over and asked for his share. His friend replied with a curt "no," and walked away licking his sweet treat in complete satisfaction while Pierre walked away in disappointment. He couldn't understand why he didn't want to share. He had not yet learned that financial poverty was not the only type of poverty with which one could be afflicted. Despite his own relative poverty, Pierre had always been taught to share. His friend, though from a large family, did not, for some reason, have that opportunity.

In late spring, Pierre was lucky again; he was promoted to ninth grade. This time, at the end of the school year, he would graduate from eighth grade. To his delight, this meant that they got out of school earlier than all the other grades. They used this time to organize and practice for the graduation ceremony. The class was paired off boy/girl to march into and out of the ceremony. He would later remember nothing of the commencement speeches (who ever does?), but he would remember looking up at the girder that he had crossed earlier in the school year with amazement at his feat. He would also remember that his parents had come to the graduation, the first time they visited the school campus. To no one's surprise, including himself, he received no achievement awards. He didn't expect anything. To pass and graduate was good enough.

Pierre, eighth grade

CHAPTER 7
GRADES 9 – 12,
A MODICUM OF MATURITY

"The future influences the present just as much as the past."

Friedrich Nietzsche

THE summer after eighth grade was one of cutting grass, fishing, swimming, and reading, and it ended once again with the ritual of getting new clothing and shoes for the new school year. There was a trip to the next town to buy things like shirts, underwear, and socks, and a trip to the general merchandise store to get two pairs of jeans. The sharp scent of new denim was reinforced in Pierre's mind, and so was its stiffness that practically caused students to walk around like the Tin Man.

This school year they would have a different teacher for every subject. He did not see an advantage or disadvantage in this; it was just the way it was. Another difference was that the adolescent pox seemed to have loosened its grip somewhat on the class. They were a little more mature and a little less obnoxious to each other and the teachers. It was remarkable what a difference three months had made. Finally, some of the subjects were different, as in addition to math, English, and social studies, there were organized physical education classes and typing classes and a choice of agriculture or industrial arts. Farm boys usually took agriculture, and other boys took industrial arts. Girls took home economics.

Not being a farm boy, Pierre was placed in industrial arts. He liked these classes and enjoyed mechanical drawing and the projects they got to make. It was wonderful working with good tools for a change, especially the power tools which made work much easier. The teacher was a kindly, little-past-middle-aged man of whom many of the boys took advantage. When one misbehaved, he took him into the little tool room in the shop to give him a "talk." Unfortunately, the behavior modification from this little talk was short-lived. Most of the boys felt that they had done wrong and promised to do better, but once they got back with their peers, they continued to do and say stupid things. Nevertheless, the skills Pierre learned from these classes would serve him well into later life.

The typing course was a total self-inflicted wipeout. He did learn the keyboard and acquired decent typing speed, but he did not like the class and saw no purpose in it. He just didn't know enough to envision typing as a useful skill. Just getting to graduation was a stretch. No one in his family had ever graduated from high school. Additionally, he could never see himself typing at a desk for a living —that was for women. Predictably, as the typing lessons got more complicated, Pierre fell farther and farther behind. Then he got an eye injury that necessitated a bandage over one eye. He told his teacher he couldn't type that day because of his injury. She yelled,

"Well, get out!" He then went to the library and read books for several days before the teacher finally called him back to class. Could he have typed with his eye injury? Perhaps not well, but he probably just wanted to miss typing that day. He does not remember passing the class.

The English class was a combination of grammar and literature. The teacher was young, cute, and diminutive at around five feet and could control her classes like a puppeteer controlling puppets. Even the wisest mouths were frozen shut by her mere gaze of disapproval. It was interesting to see and hear big boys, who could not be controlled by their male teachers, become docile in her classroom. Pierre had liked English well enough, mostly because they sometimes read interesting stories, but this class presented some challenges for him, especially when they got to Shakespeare's *Julius Caesar*. It had been hard enough for him to learn English and even now French words would still pop up unexpectedly among his English words from time to time, but Shakespeare's English was vastly different from the English he had been struggling to learn. The words were not the same—some were weird, and the syntax was different. If he had known about genetics at that time, he would have concluded that he had a genetic deficiency for Shakespeare. Surprisingly, through the efforts of his teacher and his decent reading ability, he managed to learn and enjoy *Julius Caesar*. Some teachers were just plain miracle workers.

The P.E. class was very different from P.E. as he had known it. Up to now, the classes were more like playtime. Now, it was more organized; regimented would be a better adjective. The coaches taught the physical education classes, and his teacher was a young former football player with an imposing voice, temper, and strength. The boys were required to wear shorts, tee shirts, and tennis shoes. Pierre forgot his uniform once, and the consequences were dire. The coach brought him to the dressing room to give him some whacks on the butt with a broom. Then he gave him a tongue lashing that would have made a WWII Army drill instructor sound like a social worker. Finally, the coach said, "Stand up on this bench!" Apprehensively, Pierre did so. The coach continued on as he shouted inches from Pierre's face, "Now you are as big and tall as I am. What do you have to say for yourself?" Pierre said nothing, but he did not believe he was as big and tall as the coach. He did not forget his uniform again.

The P.E. class was more about physical fitness rather than sports. After getting dressed out in their uniforms, the students were given about 20 minutes of calisthenics for exercising all parts of the body. Then the class was sent for a mile run off campus without supervision. Needless to say, some boys did things in addition to running—like having cow and horse dung fights (they didn't know the word "dung"). After coming in from the run, some in a less than fragrant condition, it was time to play the coach's favorite game—"knockout," or dodge ball. In this game, the class was placed in the middle of the gym floor as targets for the coach and several older students who threw balls at them to knock them out of the game. Once a student was hit, he could throw balls at those left on the floor. Then, it was off to the showers where the students compared the red spots on their bodies obtained by being struck by the ball.

More "stuff" happens in a locker room than in a regular classroom. Pierre was walking into the dressing room where he saw a clump of boys surrounding another boy. Naturally, he walked up to see what was going on. In the middle of the group was a taller, older boy who had something in his hand that he was showing to the rest. Whatever it was, it attracted the rapt attention of all the boys. Pierre moved in a little closer for a better view of the show and tell session. The center of attention was what the tall boy held in his hand—it was a condom. One of the boys exclaimed, "Wow, he has his own rubber!" The demonstrator's face had a self-satisfied, gloating, expression that seemed to say, "Look what I've got, bet you don't have one, and if you did, you wouldn't know what to do with it." The coach came in, and everyone quickly dispersed.

During the morning run, the boys talked about what they had seen. One of the boys said, "That's no big deal, anyone with a quarter can get one of those at the Billups Service Station." No one knew if the boy would use his condom, but the consensus was that it would probably dry rot in his wallet.

Pierre enjoyed his science class in which he could have had a better than average grade. Unfortunately, he talked too much in class, and his teacher took points off his grade as a punishment that knocked him back into the realm of mediocrity. He thought it was crappy and unfair to reduce his grade as a punishment. No other teacher did that. Of course, he could have stopped talking. Well, at least his grades were uniform—except for typing and math.

Math was a disaster because they now were into algebra. The teacher was a very bright man with a mustache who often spoke and taught above the average ninth grader's ability to understand. One of his expressions was, "If you guys paid more attention culti-vating what is between your ears rather than what grows wildly on the tops of your heads, you would be much better off." The expression went well-above most of the carefully-coiffed heads. Pierre started off OK, but then it quickly got more difficult. When they proceeded into equations, the problems were easy as he could see the answer without working the problem using the rules and steps. He couldn't understand why he should learn all those rules and steps when he could see the answers. Unfortunately, he could no longer see the answers as the problems got more complex. He also didn't realize that a student needed what he learned today to learn to do tomorrow's problems. Not doing homework didn't help a bit either. As a result, he struggled through every math course for the rest of his academic career. He convinced himself that he was not smart enough to do well in math.

One class he enjoyed was the driver's education class. Like most adolescents of that era, he was looking very much forward to learning how to drive and eventually having a car of his own. His father, on several occasions, had allowed him to steer the pickup truck, but he knew he would not own a car for a long time as very few students from his school were given cars by their parents. No more than a handful would own a car before graduation. Most parents did, however, allow their children to drive the family car for outings.

Nevertheless, the prospect of actually driving from behind the steering wheel instead of holding on to it next to his father was exhilarating. Additionally, this was not like a real class, but more like an activity divorced from school, and that was good. There was some class work required, but it was more interesting and more relevant to an adolescent boy's frame of reference. It was no wonder most made an "A" in the class no matter what their ability level was.

The classroom instruction started; their amiable teacher helped them to quickly master traffic laws, safety, and defensive driving. The real fun came with the actual driving instruction. Three students and the teacher got into a five-year-old Chevrolet with a manual shift to begin the day's driving lessons. Once in the car, most vestiges of normal classroom behavior were happily abandoned. Most of the students had driven before, and those who hadn't, learned very quickly. They drove around the countryside at first and later into town to learn to drive in traffic and to parallel park. It was fun for the students, especially when they stopped to pick pecans and oranges from the nearby groves. They often drove faster than they should have. All of this was going on while listening to very adult stories from the teacher. They knew he was at odds with the administration and liked him all the more for it.

The class and the school year ended, and they would never see the driver's education teacher again. The school system released him. Pierre was not surprised because he had sensed a rift between the teacher and the principal. Even as a student, he realized that some of the activities in the class were not kosher, but he made a good grade to pair up with his good grade in P.E. Now he was good at driving and P.E. Not exactly college bound.

Outside of school, he and his brother-in-law Charles, Bertha's husband, were becoming very close. In the way that his second sister was like another mother to him, Charles became his second father. He was Cajun, eleven years older, and had a very difficult childhood. His father was even more out of step with the present than Pierre's father was, and as a result, Charles had a very difficult time at school. He was primarily a French speaker when he started school, and at that time, French was strictly forbidden in public schools. Because of these differences, he was often humiliated by his teachers and peers. Like many boys from similar backgrounds, he dropped out of school as soon as he could. He never recovered from his negative school experiences, but he was a smart, sympathetic, and talented man. He could play the violin and accordion and artfully carve figures from wood with his pocket knife. With proper encouragement, he could have had a much easier life. Pierre could talk to him about any of his adolescent problems and receive a sympathetic response. His life would have been very different without his remarkable second set of parents.

In addition to discovering Shakespeare, another reading form of "literature" came to his attention. Somehow, probably from one of his friends, he came upon a copy of a male adventure magazine, and he was instantly infatuated with this genre of writing. Soon after, similar magazines were passed on to him by friends, and he passed them along as well when he finished reading them. He found these magazines far more interesting than comic books and even better than *Peyton Place.*

The adventure magazine stories often seemed to be rousing tales of soldiers of fortune, explorers, or a group of men lost on a trek in an unexplored part of Africa, South America, or an isolated Pacific Island. It seemed they often found themselves in these exotic places, lost and captured by beautiful, blonde, amply-bosomed Amazon warriors festooned with machine guns and with bandoleers of ammo strapped across their bounteous chests. The women led the adventurers to their camp where they were forced to make incessant love to them. Pierre found this very interesting and, stimulating. How lucky these guys were! Perhaps he could join the French Foreign Legion when he got older. Then he read some *National Geographic Magazines* whose photos of women from these countries were nothing like those described in the adventure magazines—especially the bosomed part. Well, the illusions were fun while they lasted. It did serve some purpose—his reading continued to improve. But now it was time to create some new illusions.

Though he was a little taller than average for his age, he remained rather thin and wiry. He was not happy with this circumstance, especially since most of the men and boys in his family were strong and muscular. The vast majority of his classmates were larger and even heavier than he. From his copious reading of magazines and comic books, he had seen ads promising rapid muscle growth if one subscribed to a certain training program. The most popular ads were those of Charles Atlas, which presented a sketch of a skinny man with his girlfriend at the beach getting sand kicked in his face by a more muscular man, after which his girlfriend left with Mr. Muscles. Angry and indignant, the man with the skinny arms subscribed to the training program and in a short time gained a new powerful physique. He returned to the beach, found his tormentor sunbathing with his former girlfriend, punched him in the face and walked off with his girlfriend as she cooed, "What a man!"

He was very intrigued with the idea of being muscular like the hero in the ad. Of course, he did not have the money to subscribe to the training programs, but one program offered free trial exercises. He sent off for these and waited impatiently to receive the magical exercises that would make him look like the men in the magazines. To him, and to most of small town America, weight training and bodybuilding were practically unknown. Even coaches frowned upon their athletes doing any weight training out of fear that they would get muscle-bound and therefore too slow for sports.

He checked the mailbox every day for two weeks before he finally found the large envelope addressed to him. He recognized the address immediately and anxiously ripped open the envelope. It contained several exercises for each body part and encouraged him to buy the full course for even faster results. He knew he could never enroll, but at least he had some exercises to do which he just knew would transform him into a new muscular self—but there was one immediate obstacle. He had no barbell or dumbbells. He had never even seen any except in the magazine pictures. He came up with an idea. There were leftover bricks from their new house built a year ago. These bricks had holes in them through which he could slip a broomstick to make an approximation of a barbell.

In the privacy of the garage, he began to do the demonstrated exercises as he imagined his new body being formed. After a few days, he carefully examined himself in the old armoire mirror on the wall of his bedroom. He was very disillusioned. The image looking back at him was the very same scrawny kid with the pipe-stem arms. He just couldn't understand; they promised quick results. Perhaps bricks were not as effective as iron in building muscles—after all, who had ever heard of pumping bricks? Discouraged, he gave up the idea of being like those "magazine guys," but a seed was planted.

After a summer of his usual activities of fishing, swimming, grass cutting, spending time with his friends, and brooding about his perceived problems, he and his family were preparing for a new school year. It was time once again for new jeans, shirts and shoes. As usual, he was ready to go back to school. Now that he was older, Pierre had less anxiety about the first day of school. For the most part, he would be reuniting with the same students he had been with since first grade. That was the good thing about a small town; everyone knew each other and even knew each other's parents, grandparents, and relatives.

He began his sophomore year, and his classes were English II, Civics, Industrial Arts II, P.E., Math, and Biology. He liked most of his teachers, but he still was not inspired enough to spend more time studying. He didn't know how to study. So far he had gotten by, even if just barely, by his reading ability and whatever he absorbed in class when he was not daydreaming.

It was a new school year and a fresh start, but unfortunately, he did the same as he had always done—the bare minimum. The problem this time was that he misjudged his efforts, and the bare minimum was not enough to pass. By midterm, he was in the worst academic predicament of his life. He was failing half his subjects, barely passing two, and only P.E. saved him from a complete wipeout. And he had not seen it coming. His teachers had tried to warn him, but they had always done that, and he had always managed to pass to the next grade. Then he was called into the principal's office. That was a first for Pierre; he didn't know what he had done to deserve this.

With butterflies in his stomach and scared as a rabbit on the first day of hunting season, he walked into the office. The principal was rather young, wore glasses and had a crew cut. The community and the students had great respect for him, but a visit to his office was not on most students' wish lists.

The principal said, "Sit down, Pierre."

He sat down in a chair in front of his desk. He could see the principal's magnified eyes behind his glasses which sat on a face with a most serious demeanor. Pierre's heartbeat felt like multiple explosions going off in his chest.

The principal continued, "I guess you know why you're in here."

Shakily, he said, "No Sir." He truly didn't know why he was called in.

"Pierre, I'm looking your midterm report card, and at this rate, you will not graduate from high school."

He was stunned. He had always managed to pass each year and he took it for granted this would continue on until graduation.

"Your grades are some of the worst I have ever seen. You failed three subjects, and the two Ds you made, if examined more closely, should probably have been Fs." Those two classes were taught by teachers who seldom gave Fs. "Your only good grade is in P.E., but everyone makes a good grade in P.E. What do you have to say for yourself?"

"I don't know." He didn't know enough to explain what was happening to him. How could he explain something he would not understand until much later in his life?

"Well Pierre, you will need to study more if you expect to graduate. It will not be easy to bring up failing midterm grades."

"Yes, sir, I will do my best."

He was excused and left the office with a sense of abject hopelessness. He wanted to graduate. It would have been helpful if someone could have shown him how to study. His sister was in seventh grade and had always done well in school. She was always sitting at the kitchen table doing homework—which he thought was a girl thing. It did not occur to him that homework was a part of studying and was the reason why she was doing well. And anyway, the thought of doing school work at home did not appeal to him.

Miraculously, his grades began to improve slowly after his talk with the principal. He began to pay more attention in class and give a little more attention to homework, but he still had a problem with bringing work home. When a test came up, he reviewed materials while walking from one class to another. He thought he was studying. Whatever he was doing, it worked, if just barely.

Probably the most metamorphic class of his sophomore year was P.E. While P.E. is not normally known as a "metamorphic" class, what made the difference was the teacher. Last year's coach and P.E. teacher had resigned to go to law school, and a new coach was hired to replace him. Coach K was young, about twenty-six years old, and instantly became popular with the students. He was stronger, faster, and more athletic than any of his students. He had also been a pilot in the military. Pierre admired him immensely and wanted to be like him. He would never get to be as athletically talented as the coach, but due in part to his inspiration, he eventually, at least, improved considerably.

The physical education classes had been barely adequate at his high school. There was practically no equipment—no bats, balls, gloves weights, or anything necessary for a good program. Of course, a lack of funding was the primary reason for this, so one of the first things the coach did was to organize a P.E. club to address the issue, and about fifty boys joined right away. Each student paid a nominal fee of one dollar to join the club. Then he initiated several other fund-raising activities to raise more money. Pierre did not know for sure, but the coach probably found donors to contribute funds. With the money he raised, he then bought an astonishing variety and amount of equipment to meet the needs of every student. When baseball was the sport, each student had a proper glove—and many, like Pierre, put on a glove for the first time. Weights and weight benches were bought. Very few small high schools had weights at that time. The most spectacular purchase was a Nissen full-size trampoline that cost three hundred dollars (about $3,000.00 today). Most of the students didn't know what a trampoline was, let alone had ever jumped on one. Only a few of the more affluent, large city high schools had trampolines. Most remarkable was the purchasing of equipment necessary to learn lifelong sports such as bowling, badminton, and archery.

The coach immediately incorporated the equipment into all P.E. classes. This remarkable man coached every kid as if he were one of his varsity athletes, even the clumsiest, most awkward students, and he formed intramural teams which then competed for medals.

But perhaps the most enjoyable event he initiated for the students was the end of the year campout. These overnight campouts took place at Evangeline State Park in St. Martinville, and activities included lively sporting activities, a barbeque, and, of course, a requisite amount of carefree horsing around. Most students would never forget the fun they had at these campouts, and even more would never forget Coach K. Certainly, Pierre never would.

Throughout his school career thus far, Pierre had always had a few close friends. These changed from year to year, but beginning in ninth grade, he formed friendships with fewer boys but ones that were longer lasting. Two friends, in particular, were very close to him and would remain so for many years after high school. The first of these was Donald, the son of a Cajun family who lived three miles up the bayou from his house. His father was a successful farmer of soybeans, which had become the main cash crop of the area. Farming had changed since his father's sharecropping days. The explosive new demand for soybeans required the clearing of vast forest acreages and the buyout of small farms. In contrast to the sharecroppers who depended on mules and horses for power, modern-day farming was heavily mechanized and required huge capital outlays for the purchase of equipment such as gargantuan tractors, combines, and cultivators. As a farmer's son, Donald had begun driving heavy equipment at a very young age. They had much in common aside from their Cajun heritage. Pierre and Donald were both daredevils and influenced each other to do unusual things. They spent a lot of time swimming in the bayou, fishing, and climbing anything with elevation. They became close and sometimes spent nights at each other's house. They often walked the three miles to visit each other. If they were lucky, a passerby would give them a ride, but the traffic was so sparse they usually walked the distance without seeing a single vehicle. The influence of this friend would be pivotal in Pierre's life.

The other friend, John, was totally different. He was a non-Cajun from a well-educated family who lived about three miles down the bayou from his house. They had known each other casually from school, and he often saw him coming and going on the road in front of his house. He was considered to be one of the smartest kids in the class but was not very interested in getting the best grades. Pierre saw John as fortunate—his family was relatively affluent, and he got to drive the family car. John was like a race car driver, going into controlled slides around the curves on the bayou road, but fortunately, he never went off the graveled roadway. He also had a fetish for "burning rubber" that he achieved by revving the engine and popping the clutch to lay down a perfect pair of rubber streaks on the highway which he admired in his rear view mirror as he sped away. On one occasion, he burned the clutch, and the car became immobile, necessitating a tow to the repair shop.

Pierre often visited John at his home which was the first non-Cajun home he had ever visited. It was a large two-story house and sat on a large tract of land with cattle and a few horses. His parents were well-educated and spoke perfect English with no local accent. When he had lunch or dinner with them, his friend's father always read something at the table. He ate as if the food was secondary to the reading, and with complete dispassion, like a praying mantis chewing on a bug. The whole family ate like it was not particularly pleasurable, but rather a necessity used to sustain life, so dissimilar to the Cajun homes he had eaten in before. There, they generally ate with gusto, like this meal might be their last, and they commented on the taste of each dish. Even the mood was different; the former, one of quiet reserve and the latter, one of celebrating the main event of the day. In retrospect, the table manners were also quite different—for obvious reasons.

John had 'chores' to do each day. Pierre soon found out that this meant little jobs, and John was given an allowance for doing these little jobs, which to Pierre seemed like easy work. He would have loved to have had a situation where he would get an allowance for the work he did at home and then also get to drive the family car. Pierre still had a lot to learn.

Thanks to the jolt received from his principal, he passed his sophomore year. Certainly, many students' lives were redirected by his principal. Pierre was acutely ready for summer vacation after that close call. The summer after his sophomore year differed from that of his contemporaries in large towns and cities, as well as unlike the summer of any sophomore from more recent times. He and his friends built tree houses, which only pre-adolescents would do today. Their tree houses were not truly tree houses, but platforms built high up in suitable trees. Over the years, they had built several tree houses in different locations. They had used them in the past for their 'wars' which they fought with slingshots. There would be a team on the ground and the one in the tree, and he remembered the sting of being struck by rocks from the opposing faction. Parents, of course, knew nothing of these wars.

The tree house for this summer was the best yet. It was in a huge willow tree on the edge of the bayou about one hundred and fifty yards from his house. He had three buddies that summer. One, like Pierre, would be a junior when school started, and the other two were going to be seniors. They would spend hours on the large platform in the tree, looking at the bayou and watching for splashes made by the brawny garfish that lived in it. Mostly, though, they spent a lot of time playing bourré for money. The problem was that they seldom had any money to play for, so they came up with a plan where each player received the same number of pebbles which were valued at a nickel each. When the game was over, each player's pebbles were counted, and the losers would owe the winners five cents for every pebble lost, whenever, or should they ever, have any money. In one particular instance, they had a very exciting game going on, and there were some heavy winners and some heavy losers. It began to drizzle lightly, but they kept on playing. The rain increased, and they held a large piece of cardboard over their heads to keep the game going. After a few minutes, it began to pour, and they were getting wet. No one wanted to quit, since the winners wanted to keep on winning, and the losers wanted to get their money back. They agreed to make a run for Pierre's garage where they could continue the game. They climbed down from the tree and began to sprint to the garage. About halfway there, Pierre looked around for one of the players and didn't see him. He looked back and saw the missing player several yards behind kneeling in the gravel picking up small pebbles and stuffing them as fast as he could into his pockets. He was not surprised, as this friend was known to cheat, and they often practiced cheating each other. He claimed he was tying his shoelaces—yeah, right! Needless to say, there was no game in the garage that day. Winners, losers, and cheaters all went home unhappy.

That summer, he watched TV more than ever before. It seemed like everyone in the world had a TV except his parents. He spent a lot of time with one of his card playing friends watching *American Bandstand*. He enjoyed watching the dancing and listening to the music. It also put a face on the many singers he knew from the radio. He was up to date on the music, but he could not identify with his contemporaries on the show. They were just so cool. It was something happening far away and would certainly not ever happen in his own hometown. These kids were not building tree houses and swimming in muddy bayous, but he just couldn't see himself dancing on TV even if he could dance. Nevertheless, it was fun to watch the singers sing the songs he knew so well.

He began his junior year, and virtually all of his classmates from last year returned. This was great because previously, many students would drop out of school over the summer, but not this year. There would be one new student that school year, a young man who owned the coolest car. It was a fifty-five Chevy with special paint and "Wild One" inscribed on it. It was like some of the California cars he had seen in magazines. Everyone was intrigued with this new student. He had lived in several other states, and his level of sophistication was beyond the vast majority of his classmates. Every word he uttered became known to the whole class. He did not get to be close friends with many of his classmates.

Pierre did not have many new teachers since most of his teachers taught several grade levels in their subjects. He did get a new English teacher who would be very important to him. He still had the industrial arts class that he enjoyed. At this time, industrial arts classes were taken by all the students who did not take agriculture. It was not a place to dump non-achieving students. Some of the class's best students took industrial arts. Unfortunately, in later years, shop and industrial arts classes were indeed used as a dumping ground for the weaker students and stigmatized them. It was like a red-lettered sign saying, "I'm stupid."

Pierre did make more of an effort to make better grades, and there were some improvements. He was passing everything even if there was not much room to spare in some subjects. He still did not know how to study, and his goal was to get by and graduate on time. To him, studying meant looking at his notes a little more and trying to get his homework in.

He had a vivid memory of a test he took in his English class. His teacher was a very demanding, older teacher, and the only teacher in high school who wore her hair in a bun. The test papers were being handed out after grading, and that was not one of Pierre's favorite activities. At that time, teachers often called out the students' grades as the papers were handed out, but Pierre, for obvious reasons, preferred to keep his grades private. The teacher came to his desk with his test in her hand. His heartbeat quickened. She threw the paper on his desk, and he saw he had made a B-, a rare grade for him. He felt relieved because he thought she would be pleased with his improvement. But as she walked away, she sternly said, "You can do better than that!" His first thoughts were those of disappointment. He thought, "Damn it, I finally get a good grade and she is not happy with that. What else can I do?" Later, another thought came to his mind, "Well maybe she thinks I'm smart and can do much better." Certainly, he didn't think he was smart, but his self-esteem did take a baby step forward. No, it was not like a fairy doused him with magic dust changing him into an academic whiz kid, but he did take the first step to a very long journey. He regrets not having told her "thank you" for this rather unorthodox encouragement.

Coach K was again his P.E. teacher, and he continued to expand the program as he purchased more equipment for his classes to enjoy. They even had a session of square dancing. Pierre and most of his buddies were not exactly wild about that activity—they thought it was, well, square, but the trampoline was very popular. The coach was amazing on the trampoline. He could do all sorts of backward and forward flips that they had never seen before, except perhaps on television. Every student, no matter how clumsy or non-athletic, had an opportunity to try it out. They started with simple moves like knee and seat drops and moved on to more complex ones. A few students got to be pretty good.

Then there were sessions of organized weight training. As noted before, Pierre was super keen on that activity. He remembered his unsuccessful efforts in weight training two years ago, and he was hopeful that these "real" barbells would do the trick. Each P.E. class had training sessions consisting of stations where they performed certain exercises and then moved on to the next station to different exercises. The exercises were basics for the major muscle groups. Pierre was excited about the prospect of improving his still-thin body, but unfortunately, after a few weeks of training, his mirror did not reflect any progress. He still looked like the guy who got sand kicked in his face. He didn't understand that it would take years of consistent hard and progressive training to realize his dream. They had weight training for a few weeks and went on to another sport. He and some friends would go to the weight room in the mornings to lift, but, unsupervised, all they did was compete to see who could lift the heaviest weight overhead. Not a sound training technique.

Pierre and his best friend Don continued to spend a lot of time together. They swam a lot when the weather allowed, which was most of the year, and even when the water was icy cold in early spring, they took brief plunges. Though he was a good swimmer, he was not as good as Don, who had better technique. They still seemed to push each other in doing exciting and dangerous things. Near Don's house, the bayou bank at a certain spot soared high above the water. On that bank was a huge white oak tree with a large limb stretching perhaps twenty-five feet out over the water. They climbed the tree and went to the end of the limb and attached a steel cable to it. To the other end of the cable, they attached a large stick to it as a seat. The distance from the water to the tree limb was over fifty feet. The seat end of the cable was pulled up to the lower tree limbs of the oak where they straddled it to swing out over the bayou. It was the most exhilarating thing they had ever done! The cable swing made a long arch over the bayou and, like a giant pendulum, continued to swing until it slowed to a stop. Sometimes they would swing until the motion stopped and then drop down into the water. Other times they would wait until the swing reached its highest point over the water and then drop off for a twenty-foot plunge into the water. Many such swings were set up by boys up and down the bayou, but their own swing was the most awesome. Many boys came over to see it, and a few even dared to swing on it.

Perhaps because of thrill adaptation, the fun of the swing diminished, so Don decided he would climb the oak tree to the cable's origin on the limb and drop straightaway into the water—a more that 50-foot drop. He got there, thought about it for a little while, waffled a bit, but then dropped into the bayou. He emerged from the water with a scream of joy.

Of course, Pierre also had to do it. He climbed the oak and made his way to the end of the limb and looked down at the bayou below. He realized he was much higher than the girder he had walked across in the gym. His pulse rate quickened as he thought about the drop. He then took a deep breath and let go of the limb. He had never dropped this far before. He felt like it took a long time to reach the water, and he could hear the air whistling past his ears. He kept his body straight as he knew a belly bust could be fatal or at least very painful. He hit the water with an arm slightly extended sideways and felt a sharp sting as the arm slapped the water. He went down deep into the water and came up with the same exhilaration Don had felt.

Weeks later, Don suggested they dive from the limb. This idea was not attractive to Pierre. Don went up the tree to the end of the limb to make the dive. He hesitated a moment to visualize the dive and then dove into the bayou. It was a good dive as he hit the water with a small splash. Pierre did not make that dive—he had reached his limit in his quest for thrills. Perhaps he had his first intimation of the possibility of his mortality.

The rest of the school year went on, and he was doing okay in his classes. He was passing every subject, and for him, that was good.

He continued reading an assortment of magazines passed on to him by his friends. He still read male adventure magazines, and once in a while, he got a *Playboy Magazine*, usually with the centerfold ripped out. Beggars couldn't be choosers. He got an occasional *Mad Magazine* and enjoyed *Mad*'s type of humor. He would often check out the *Reader's Digest* magazines and condensed books from the school library, some of the few books he brought home.

His home life was about the same, and though he was not as deep into his adolescent angst, he was still moody at home. Many of his classmates were driving the family car, and a few had cars of their own, but his father would not even let him drive alone. He continued spending time alone along the bayou. This was his "safe place" for brooding about his lack of money, a car to drive, and not being able to do and have what his classmates did and had. Despite his thinking, he found no solutions. He would just have to wait, finish high school, and then get a job or perhaps join the military to achieve independence.

His father did allow him to get a driver's license, which turned out to be a rather memorable experience. He and his father got into the pickup and drove to the parish state trooper headquarters for a driver's license. His father and family knew the trooper in charge of testing and evaluating driving skills. Pierre passed his written test and then the trooper took him for a drive to evaluate his driving skills. The trooper was a redheaded, freckled, rather roundish man with a cigar that was almost a permanent extension of his mouth. For his driving test, they drove the truck to the next town and did a few blocks of town driving with some parallel parking. He did well even though he was quite nervous. His driver's license was almost in the bag.

About a mile away from headquarters, things went awry. He was distracted by something he saw in a field next to the road and didn't see a slow-moving vehicle in front of him. The trooper must have also been looking at the field because when he shouted, "Look out," their truck was only about twenty yards from the slow-moving car. He slammed on the brakes and came to a screeching stop a few feet short of plowing into the vehicle. The trooper turned even redder and almost swallowed his cigar, but he took a couple of deep breaths and didn't say anything. When they pulled up into the parking lot and got out of the truck, the trooper said, "Well, Pierre, I can't give you a license with you driving like that." Pierre was devastated. None of his friends had ever failed a driving test. He didn't dare tell anyone. The trooper told his father that Pierre would have to come back and take the driving test again.

Two weeks later, he retook his driving test and passed it. He now had a driver's license, but unfortunately, his joy was short-lived as he did not get to drive often, and those few times it was allowed were usually short trips to the store to pick up items for his mother. His father, still the eternal pessimist, was convinced that Pierre would almost certainly wreck his truck. Additionally, he did not want to pay the additional insurance cost to cover an adolescent driver. Fortunately for Pierre, both Don and John drove their parents' cars, and he spent a lot of time with them.

Midterm was an exciting time for him and his fellow juniors. They would soon receive their graduation rings. That meant two things to them. First, most of the boys and some of the girls had never had any form of jewelry, and that made the prospect of getting a gold ring with a red stone very exciting. And second, getting a graduation ring meant that they were actually going to graduate. But Pierre had never had any certainty of graduation; after all, no one in his family had ever done that. He remembered how difficult he thought it would be to ask his father for money to pay for his ring. He hated asking his father for money because this usually resulted in a "no" answer or a begging session to extract the money from him. Where were the "Jaws of Life" when he needed them? The cost of the ring was $35.00, a sizable amount of money in his family.

His father was sitting at the kitchen table counting his winnings from a card game the previous night. He loved playing cards, and having played since he was a young boy, he was very good at it. He won more than he lost by virtue of not drinking while playing, knowing the game very well, and quitting the game if the cards were not there. His family did not suffer financially from his little hobby. Pierre saw that he had around seventy dollars on the table. He screwed up his courage and blurted out, "Daddy, I-need-thirty-five-dollars-to-pay-for-my-graduation-ring." His father looked at him for a moment and then counted out the requested amount. He couldn't believe he got the money so easily. Perhaps his father thought it was easy come, easy go.

The rings came in, and without ceremony, the juniors received them. They showed off their rings to each other as they expressed their glee. Pierre was really happy with his ring, it was real gold, looked good on his finger, and perhaps he might graduate after all.

His delight with his ring was fleeting. About three months after receiving it, he and Don were crawfishing with drop nets near the Atchafalaya River. He took precautions against losing his ring by removing it and placing it under the car seat. They set the baited drop nets and picked them up after ten minutes or so and emptied the crawfish into a small tub. When the crawfish stopped biting, they moved to another location and reset the nets. They continued this process perhaps eight to ten times. After doing this for several hours, they decided to pick up the nets and go home. They hadn't made a huge catch, but it was enough for each family to have a boil or an étouffée. As they were leaving the area, Pierre reached under the seat for his ring. He couldn't find it. They stopped the car, and both searched diligently for it, but it wasn't there. They knew it must have rolled out of the car on one of the stops while fishing. They went back and searched each area they had fished but found nothing. Pierre was crushed.

He got home very disappointed at the price he had paid for his crawfish, but there was nothing he could do. There was no way he would ask his father for money to replace it. He would be ringless on the bayou for a long time.

In a flash, it seemed, the junior year was near its end and the time for the junior/senior prom had arrived. Pierre was not excited about attending the prom. One had to wear a coat and tie to attend, and of course, he had no coat and tie. Even more uncomfortable was the fact that he was not prepared to ask a girl for a date. There was some comfort in the fact that he was not alone in this situation as many boys in that little town on the bayou had not yet started dating. He resolved his fears by renting a white sports coat and getting a ride with three other boys to attend the prom dinner and ceremony. This tradition at the school consisted of a meal and a ceremony in the school cafeteria and a drive to a popular night club for dancing.

About two weeks before the prom, he bought a half pint of Seagram's VO whiskey for about $2.50. Though there was no alcohol in his house and his father rarely drank, Pierre had a little experience with alcohol. He had tasted a mixed drink or two and had had a few beers. He was well aware of the effects of alcohol; several of his relatives were heavy drinkers. Nevertheless, he looked forward to drinking his little bottle of VO. A few times before the prom, he took down the bottle he had hidden in the closet and fondled it as he carefully read the label over and over again.

The anticipated event finally arrived, and the juniors and seniors of the little town were busy getting ready for the occasion. It was lucky that he had been able to rent a white sports coat, as it was doubtful his father would have given him money to buy a coat for only one occasion. Pierre looked and felt awkward and gawky in his white coat and tie, something like a fish in the desert. His friends picked him up, and they drove to the school cafeteria. The cafeteria was nicely-decorated, and the cafeteria cooks had prepared a "fancy" meal for the participants. He did not remember the menu, but he remembered it contained asparagus. This vegetable was not part of Cajun cuisine in this area, and he was not particularly fond of its taste. He would taste it again soon. The ceremony was nice and included the usual prom activities such as reading the class will, announcing the class favorites, and a guest speaker. Most of the students were waiting for this to end so they could get to the night club to start the "real" celebration.

At last, he and his buddies got into the car and took off for the club, about eight miles away. Within minutes of their departure, Pierre reached under the seat and pulled out his whiskey. He cracked the seal and sniffed the strong alcohol scent emanating from the bottle. He took a sip, and the undiluted whiskey burned his mouth and tongue. He passed the bottle to his friends, and they took light sips. By the time they got to the club, the bottle was empty; he had consumed most of it. He did not yet feel the effects of the alcohol.

The club had a bar in the front with a huge dance hall and band-stand in the rear. Tables and chairs were on each side of the dance floor. Any teenager who put money on the bar could buy a drink. Most boys bought a beer—usually, a small bottle of Schlitz called a "Little Joe." There was no parental supervision at these prom dances; none, at least, that Pierre was aware of. The liquor flowed freely to anyone who wanted it. The rhythm and blues band struck up the music and it filled the building. The noise was loud, the smoke was thick, and prom students from several schools filled the building. Waiters delivered set-ups (liquor, ice, Cokes and Seven-Ups). Anyone who wanted to drink did. The dancing started, and the liquor flowed. Pierre, who already had a head start, was given an assortment of mixed drinks that began taking effect on him.

As in most of these "clubs," the restroom was the most popular place—largely due to the drinking. These restrooms were usually less than clean, had walls covered with vulgarities, and made one want to stop breathing upon entry. He remembered reading a mes-sage on the wall, "Don't throw toothpicks in the urinal, crabs use them for pole vaulting." As large as the urinals were, they were often missed by the less than steady men and boys.

The beat of the music went on, and the jollity and dancing increased. By this time, Pierre was doing weird things like jumping on the tables and dancing with the chairs. Later, his buddies took him to the car to sleep it off before he got in trouble. He was placed in the back seat and dozed or passed out for some time. He could hear the crunching of feet on the graveled parking lot—a replay of the sounds he had heard when he slept in the car at the dance as a child. In what seemed like a short time, his friends returned to go back home. It was in the morning hours, and after a few miles, Pierre felt like he needed to throw up. They stopped the car, and he stuck his head out the door to heave and vomit. He tasted everything he had eaten and drank that evening all over again—especially the asparagus. They then drove him home where he barely managed to get into the house and find his bed.

Early in the morning, his mother came in with a cup of coffee as she normally did. She looked at him and asked, "Did you get drunk last night?"

Pierre, in the steadiest voice he could muster, said, "No, why?"

Through gritted teeth, she said, "Because you went to bed with your sports coat on."

He looked down and saw a white, wrinkled sports coat with a smashed carnation. For some reason, she didn't push him for additional information. He drank the coffee she left thinking it would help his head and stomach, but his condition worsened as his nausea catapulted into the stratosphere. He knew he would be sick again, and he did not want his mother to see him in that condition. He got dressed and walked to the bayou where he heaved and got another awful taste of coffee—and asparagus.

He had to pull it together to go to school (the prom was not on a Friday). To ask to stay home would have meant he was sick, and that, he did want his mother to know (as if she didn't!). He got ready and made it to school on time. Of course, everyone in school knew of his condition. He spent the morning in the sick room. When he drank water, he vomited all over again. He could not eat lunch. That afternoon, he felt he could not miss his P.E. class. He went to P.E. and Coach K, knowing many of the boys were hungover, had the class do more calisthenics than usual to make them hurt and hopefully teach them a lesson. When the exercises were over, he said, "I want all of you to run to the goal post, and the last one back will have to run it again." Pierre, being the sickest, felt the coach wanted him to be last so he could have him run again, but he was thin and normally a pretty fast runner. He resolved to put everything in it not to come in last. The class took off and stayed fairly close together out to the goal post, but on the way back there was some separation among the boys. He did not finish last. His pain and nausea did not allow him to enjoy his victory, however, but he at least felt good in knowing he would not have to run again.

It would be several days before he would feel normal again. It's possible he had a mild case of alcohol poisoning—a term not known at that time. His classmates would remind him forever of that episode. The good thing that came out of this was that he had learned a lesson. For years, the taste of whiskey was abhorrent to him. He became very wary and careful when he had liquor. He did not ever want to get that sick again.

His school junior year came to an end, and he passed all his subjects. Though not impressive, his grades got a little better which considerably improved his odds for graduation. He spent the summer doing the usual things, such as fishing, cutting grass at home, and swimming, but not as much. He spent more time reading, hanging out with Don and John, and watching TV with his neighborhood friends. Somehow, the summer was not the same as all the others when he relished not being in school. He was bored and in a holding pattern, not knowing what he would or should do next.

He did some work in the soybean fields at Don's father's farm. The job consisted of walking up and down the rows and chopping down coffee weeds that flourished among the soybeans. Despite all the mechanization, the only way to destroy them was to cut them down manually with a cane knife. Don's father hired seven or eight workers to work for about three to four hours each morning. It was a hot job with a lot of walking, but he didn't mind the work. He was paid two dollars and fifty cents per morning, and for him, that was good money, since he had picked cotton all day for three dollars in seventh grade. This gave him a few dollars to keep in his pocket.

One of the things he spent his money on was bowling, and he and John did it fairly often. Bowling was not cheap, but the bowling alley in the next town had specials where one could bowl tons of games very early in the morning for a greatly reduced rate. He enjoyed it and became a fair bowler despite his lack of good form and proper training.

The most unforgettable event of the summer was, unfortunately, a tragic one. In one automobile accident, five students from his high school lost their lives. As everyone in the little town had known each other forever, the sadness and grief were overwhelming. Pierre would always remember the shock and sadness he felt when he saw the mournful row of five caskets. To exacerbate this sadness, another student lost her life in a car/train accident later in the school year. All of this in one very small school.

Finally, the summer ended, and his senior year lay before him. In the past, he had been interested in getting back to school to be with his friends, but this time, it was less that than wanting to finish high school and go on to something else. He had no idea yet what that something would be. He had never given serious thought to what he wanted to do after high school. At his school, most graduates went to work in the oil fields, moved to a large city to work in the chemical plants and refineries, or stayed local and farmed. Only ten percent or less went to college. A few went to trade school or joined the military. Some of his older cousins had gone to Baton Rouge and had done well; he gave some thought to that. He was certain he didn't want to do the work his dad did. He never even dreamed college was a possibility as this was so far beyond his aspirations. This just didn't happen in his family. One thing was certain, he couldn't just stay home.

The school year started, and he found out he was not the only one who was concerned about his future. As seniors, they knew they would soon become independent of their parents and that major decisions would have to be made, but they were nowhere close to making them. The top handful of students and their parents, however, had already made their plans.

Classes started and the forty-one seniors were ready to start up. They had no idea how quickly the year would go by compared to previous years. The teachers were the same as last year's; only the subjects were different. Pierre had English IV, P.E, Industrial Arts, Chorus, and French I. He didn't have to take another math course, and that was a good thing. His chances for graduation were greatly improved.

The band director taught the chorus class, and like many band directors, he was very much a drill sergeant or a little Napoleon. Pierre enjoyed the songs they sang even though singing was not one of his yet-to-be discovered talents. On one occasion, the director told him just to move his mouth and not sing. Pierre was not offended.

The French class turned out to be greatly consequential in his life. He knew there were some differences between Cajun and standard French. He was told several times in a demeaning manner that what he spoke was not real French but some trash language. The French teacher was also his English teacher and probably spoke Cajun French first herself before learning standard French in college. Pierre was hoping that because of his Cajun French fluency, he could coast in that class and get by with very little work. Wrong! He was actually expected to read and write the language. There were some differences in vocabulary and, of course, grammar, and when he translated an English word into an incorrect Cajun word, she would say, "No, that's colloquial." Nevertheless, most of his translations were correct because Cajun and standard French have very much in common. He did learn some new vocabulary, grammar, and some spelling, but regrettably, he did not apply himself as he should have. He knew he could pass the class with minimal effort, and that was good enough. It never did occur to him that he should make a good grade to boost his anemic GPA. It was, however, his initiation into the gradual transition his life would take in the future.

There was another new student in school this year, an unusual one. He was a Hispanic sophomore student. There had never been a Hispanic student in any of Pierre's classes, and few Hispanics made their way at that time to the little town on the bayou. He spoke English well but had a different accent and darker skin. It was amazing how many male students, including Pierre, were suspicious of him. Perhaps it was because he was cute and the girls liked him a lot. Pierre should have known better, after all, he knew he was different from half of his class, and while he was accepted, he had been made fun of for these disparities. The difference was that he and his classmates had known each other ever since first grade. It took Don to explain to him that the Latino student was really like everyone else and meant no harm to anyone. In maturity, his friend was light-years ahead of him.

During the school year, Pierre sometimes got to go to a popular nightclub with four or five classmates for a night of dancing and meeting the girls. As always, alcohol was available to anyone who walked in, but he had learned his lesson, and he confined his consumption to three or four small beers for the night. He was not a fan of dancing, and that was unusual since most Cajuns were fond of it. His older sisters had danced at home when he was a small boy, and his father still enjoyed dancing. Even his mother would sometimes dance at a wedding. Pierre realized that if he wanted to hold a girl, he would have to dance. Certainly, if he walked up and grabbed a girl without dancing, he would get slapped.

For obvious reasons, he preferred slow dances. Fast dancing was usually the jitterbug, which was a confounded mystery to him. It was evident he had not inherited the dancing genes of his family. So, under the cover of the heavy crowd on the floor, the dim lights, and the inebriation of others, he developed a rather unusual dance. If cell phones would have been in vogue, undoubtedly there would have been dozens of videos going viral of a skinny kid following the beat of the music with strange contortions, jumps, convulsions, with perhaps a bit of St. Vitus dance thrown in—he seldom did the same thing twice. He would never "dance with the stars."

In late spring of that year, he had what would be his final major crawfishing excursion. Pierre, Don, and Don's father and younger brother would experience a phenomenon they would never see again. They left early in the morning because they were going farther than usual to fish. Up to this time, they had always fished the Atchafalaya Basin area. This time, they would drive to another parish northwest of their little town.

The truck, loaded down with three boys, an adult, two dozen drop nets, lunch, a twenty-two rifle, a twenty-two revolver, a pile of burlap sacks, some galvanized tubs, a boat and motor, and their bait arrived at the fishing site in Avoyelles Parish. In the cool morning air, they parked on the bank of a small bayou and proceeded to unload the boat, motor, and the rest of the equipment. They all got into the boat and traveled a couple of miles down the bayou to where it spilled out into a swamp. They tied the boat and started to unload the equipment. In a few minutes, they saw an enormous number of crawfish crawling on land, out of the water. They caught a lot of the huge, red 'mudbugs' even before putting a net into the water. They put them in the tubs, then baited their drop nets and began to drop them into the water leaving only the top of the wire pyramid above the water.

They ate a little snack while waiting to run the nets then went out and saw that some were so full of crawfish that they protruded above the water. They had never seen so many crawfish! This was going to be a good day! They pulled the nets out of the water by hooking a stick through the top of the wire pyramid and emptied the crawfish into the tubs, which were quickly filled up. Exotica abounded, and every so often a huge snake slithered out of a net when pulled out of the water. Needless to say, these snakes rapidly accelerated their pulse rates! Snakes in crawfish nets were not all that unusual, but the size of these snakes was. They were sometimes well over three feet long with a body diameter of over three inches, far larger than normal. As the day warmed up, these huge snakes began to appear everywhere—in the water, on the banks, and on tree limbs hanging over the water. It was almost like magic as there were snakes where there had been none just a few moments before. Rod Serling, had he been there, could have written an excellent episode of "Twilight Zone." Empty limbs that were bare one moment were swarming with huge snakes the next. The boys began shooting the huge reptiles with revolver and rifle. When the bullets struck the snakes, raw flesh exploded outward. The crawfish surely must have exacted their revenge and eaten very well for the next several days.

Shortly after noon, they had all the crawfish they could carry home. They loaded the boat with the fat sacks of crawfish and all the gear they had brought. On the way back to the truck in the boat, a large mullet jumped into the air startling them as it landed with a thud and flopped among them in the boat—an appropriate ending punctuation for this most unusual day.

For many years after, they discussed that day and tried to figure out what had happened on that trip. Although all of them had lived around snakes all their lives, they knew what they experienced was not normal. Don's father was a very rational man not given to exaggerations, but the most logical explanation he could come up with was that the superabundance of crawfish that spring allowed the snakes to gorge themselves and grow larger than normal. The snakes were mostly non-venomous water snakes like those they had at home, only a lot larger. The only sure conclusion that they could arrive at was that they would never forget that day.

Sooner than anyone in the senior class had expected, graduation day was only two weeks away. They would take final exams one week and then go to school for a couple of days the next for graduation practice. It felt so good to be out of school while the rest of the student body was still in class. When practice was over, they went to a bayou where they could swim and ski board, since one of Pierre's friends had made a ski board in industrial arts class. It was not a safe contraption as it was attached to a rope and pulled by a boat. It was important not to fall forward because the boat could pull the ski board and rider under water.

Graduation day came in late May, and students and families filled the gym. As there was no air-conditioning, it was very warm, especially for the seniors in their heavy caps and gowns. Pierre's parents were there for his graduation which was the first high school graduation they had ever attended. There were the usual quickly-forgotten speeches, the obligatory handing out of the diplomas, and the march from the stage across the gym floor among the parents and relatives. It was difficult to believe that high school was over, and Pierre felt happy but also a little bereft. He knew he was the first from his father's family to graduate from high school, but he did not know enough to fully understand its significance.

The best part of graduation was the money he had received from family and friends as graduation presents. He received a surprising total of about one hundred dollars, and that was equivalent to about one thousand dollars today. He had never before had this much money at his disposal. He would make that money last until September.

Pierre, high school senior

Part II

Becoming an Educator and Assimilating into French Culture

CHAPTER 8
DECISIONS, CHALLENGES, AND GETTING BY WITH A LITTLE HELP FROM HIS FRIENDS

"Life is the sum of all your choices."

Albert Camus

PIERRE was now a high school graduate. He finally managed to leave the little school that he'd attended with little enthusiasm for most of his life. What next? He didn't know. During the last month of school he had told his teachers and friends that he was going to enroll in college to become a teacher. No one believed that, including himself. He knew they thought that he would end up in the oil fields or perhaps register for college and flunk out after one semester and then go to the oilfields. His counselor had told him he lacked preparation for college. He found out later she was right—he wasn't prepared. He didn't blame them for thinking the way they did because he knew logic was on their side. If a sixth grader told his parents that he was going to be president of the United States one day, they would at least humor him by saying,

"That's great. You can be whatever you want to be if you work hard enough." Of course, they didn't think the kid had a shot at becoming President of the United States.

He had begun thinking about college because Don was going to start school that fall. In their senior year, they had talked about going to college together. They had been such close friends, more like brothers really, and they had talked about joining ROTC while in school, getting a degree, and then starting a career in the Air Force. They even had dreams of going to flight school. The most immediate obstacle was that except for his graduation money, he was penniless. His father had never indicated he would help him pay for college, which was not unusual because no one in his family ever had reason to fathom that possibility. In his father's mind, Pierre getting a high school diploma was the ultimate achievement and now it was time to go to work.

But right now, Pierre could not even go to work because he was underage. He was still seventeen years old and would not be eighteen, the minimal legal age for employment, until the last day of September. His father told him he could go to work with him when he turned eighteen. So he thought about it, and after, he and Don worked up a plan. He would work until the end of the university's fall semester, save his money, and then register at USL in the spring.

He spent the next four months doing the same things he had always done in the summer such as cutting grass, spending time with friends who were not working yet and playing cards with his aunt and cousins. He enjoyed the card games because they played bourré for money. They would play for hours, but no one ever won or lost much money as everyone had a turn at winning or losing. It was a good pastime.

He never gave up the idea of weight training to gain some weight and muscle. When he finished high school he weighed one hundred thirty pounds despite eating gigantic amounts of food. So now, he and Don got together to make a set of barbells. First, they mixed pieces of cast iron with concrete and poured the mixture into cut cans to make plates of five, ten and 20 pounds. Then, when the concrete hardened, they cut the tin cans just above the cement line and crimped the edges over. Lastly, they painted them black, and they had a very functional set of weights—much better than his first attempt with bricks and a broom handle. They made a weight bench and placed it under a cedar tree at the end of his house. They worked out in the summer heat and sweated profusely. But again, he made little progress due to lack of proper training techniques.

When the fall semester started, Don left for college, and Pierre had only a month or so before he would start working with his dad in the oilfields. On weekends, he and Don got together, and he learned a little something of going to college. He realized that the news was not good when he learned about all the work and studying the courses required. It put doubts into his mind about his ability to succeed. If he barely got out of high school, how in the hell would he fare any better in college? Maybe they were right about him flunking out the first semester.

His eighteenth birthday finally arrived, and it was time to go to work. The pay would be minimum wage, one dollar per hour, and he had doubts here, too, about being able to do the work. All of his life, he had heard his father talk about how hard the work was. His father woke him up around five in the morning to get ready to drive to the contractor's headquarters to prepare for the first day's work. Men were milling around chatting and waiting to be assigned to a foreman and a job for the day. Some of the men grumbled when assigned to work for his father. They complained that he worked them too hard. His father replied, "I'm not hard, the work is hard." The reality was that the work his father supervised was the hardest and dirtiest work in the oil field. Pierre had no choice; he had to go with his father. Once the crews were assigned, large cans of ice water were prepared to take to the job sites and tools needed for the job were then stored in the "doghouses"—steel cabins with benches on each side for the men to sit on in transport. The doghouses were then winched up onto a gin pole truck and secured. His dad, the driver, and a senior worker rode in the truck cab while Pierre and the others rode in the doghouse.

The ride to work was not a comfortable one. It was a rough ride in cramped quarters, and of course, all the men were much older than he. Most were French-speaking Cajuns, and all had no more than a few years of primary school education. A few of the workers had mental challenges. They were rough-looking men, and practically everyone smoked strong self-rolled cigarettes. One smoked a pipe, and one or two would chew tobacco and spit on the doghouse floor. The main topics of conversation were sex, food, and various gripes. They looked at Pierre with an air of suspicion, probably because they thought his father would give him the easiest jobs. They were not bad people, just disadvantaged ones condemned to the hardest, lowest paying, and least desirable jobs. Pierre did not feel the least bit out of place among these men—they were the kind of men with which he was most familiar.

Before they got to the job site, the driver stopped to give the men an opportunity to buy lunch and perhaps a cold drink or coffee. Most men's lunches consisted of sardines, Vienna sausages, beanie weenies, pork and beans, cookies, and other cheap, convenience foods. A few men brought their lunches of sandwiches or prepared foods. His father always brought his lunch.

They got to the job site in about forty minutes and all the men disembarked, lowered the water coolers and the tools—the axes, shovels, picks, pry bars, and sometimes a crosscut saw. The truck driver unloaded the doghouse and set up his gin poles which would be used to lift heavy stacks of lumber or pipes. The men who had gloves put them on and either hauled heavy boards from the stack and placed them on the ground to make the board road or nailed the boards together. The purpose of these board roads was to allow trucks to access the drilling site with heavy equipment. The road could be fifty feet long or as much as half mile or more. At the end of the road was a platform where the actual drilling site was. Depending on the firmness of the ground, the board road could be made of two to four layers of wood.

His father took his job seriously and expected his men to work steadily. Workers could take water as needed, but he frowned if the breaks were longer than necessary. If too many men went to the water cooler at one time, his father would shout, "If lightning strikes that water can, I'll lose half my crew!" As locations were often in wooded areas, bathroom breaks were taken in the woods

—there were no porta-potties. If a worker spent too much time in the woods, his father would ask, "What happened to you, got bit on the butt by a rattlesnake?" The work was hard and boring. The oak boards were two and one-half inches thick and 12 to 16 feet long, and as they were often coated with drilling mud, or fresh-cut and loaded with sap, they were always heavy.

There were no breaks during the day except for lunch break, and those lasted for only thirty minutes. The men sat under the trees or in the shade of a truck to have lunch. They ate their lunches rapidly so they could lie on the ground for a few minutes, the fastest few minutes the men would ever experience. Pierre compared the speed of time at school to the speed of time at lunch—a metaphorical light year of difference. At precisely 12:30, his father made the most unwelcome announcement of the day, "Ok men, it's time to get back to work."

Sometimes, one of the men would ask, "Can't you give us another ten minutes?"

His father did not even respond to that. In slow motion, everyone got back to work.

As the son of the foreman, Pierre got no special treatment; he did the same work as everyone else. On the contrary, he worked harder because his father often gave him extra chores to do. At times when the men were waiting for a stack of boards to arrive, his father would tell him, "While you're resting, go back and pick up the scraps." Perhaps he did not want him to fall in love with the job, but the odds of that were not great.

Despite his meager one hundred and thirty pounds, he was a good worker. He had strength and endurance, plus, he was making money for the first time. Many of the men did not want to partner with him in hauling boards because he worked too fast. Time went by slowly, and the men joked a lot to help kill time. If the weather was hot, they shouted, "Come on clouds, come on rain." Around three in the afternoon, fatigue would set in, and the men would get irritable. Arguments would break out between friends who had worked together for a long time. When the last hour before knock-off time arrived, moods got better as they could now say that they were only minutes from quitting time.

The days and the weeks wore on as Pierre began to get accustomed to the work and learned the little nuances that would make the days go by a bit faster. Payday was every two weeks, and his check was around eighty dollars after overtime, social security, and taxes were factored in. He had never made that much money before. He realized grown men with families were living on this same amount of money. While they could subsist, there were few luxuries for these families. Pierre, living at home, felt fortunate to be able to save virtually every penny he made to start school.

Not every job was building board roads; some were tearing them down after they had served their purpose. After the teardown, the boards were recycled to build another board road. The teardown was even more difficult that the building. Often, the boards had been pounded into the soil by heavy trucks and equipment, and the heavy drilling mud used to resist well pressure often covered the boards. The mud was slimy, heavy, and loaded with a long list of chemicals unknown to them. It made getting a grip on the heavy boards difficult, plus, it created a suction effect on the submerged boards. It was tedious, back-breaking work that consisted of tearing up, walking with, and stacking the lumber.

The workers' clothing was coated with the slimy mud as they groped into it for the end of the boards. They would have been suitable characters for a recasting of *Les Miserables*. Pierre remembers looking up at the two truck drivers who wore clean, pressed, khaki pants and clean boots looking down at them as they groveled in the mud. At that moment, he wanted to be a truck driver, and he would later remember this moment when he read the poem, "Richard Cory." One redeeming factor in this situation was that one of the drivers had a tremendous sense of humor. He lacked education, but was very intelligent and had the ability to make the most mundane situation hilariously funny. During the brief time he was there, he told jokes and stories that kept the men laughing and relieved them of their fatigue and boredom. It quickly returned after he left.

Winter came and presented a different set of challenges—the cold and the rain. The cold was bearable due to the heat generated by the laborious work, but the rain was a different issue. Some men had slicker suits that kept them dry, but a few men had no rain gear and got soaked. His father had mercy on one man who had no suit and was shivering from the cold by telling him to go to the dog house for shelter. The man never did buy a slicker suit. He was one of the too many men who, after pay day, returned to work only when he ran out of money after paying for his alcoholic binge.

Among the many things he learned on this job were the different nuances of hunger. He was never hungry for lack of food as it was always available to him in copious amounts. He knew about the hunger pangs one experienced sometimes between meals. For one to say he or she was hungry simply meant that it was time to eat something. He also knew about the adolescent appetite that required constant nutritional appeasement. The new kind of hunger he learned about was the hunger produced by many hours of hard physical labor and insufficient caloric intake. The light lunches the men consumed ran out quickly, and snacking on the job was not done. By the end of the day, they had a consuming appetite that Pierre called "a peasant appetite." It was a sharp pain in the stomach which felt like the stomach and intestines were trying to digest each other.

When he and his dad pulled up to the house around six o'clock, they could smell and identify what had been cooking. As they walked into the house, they went to the stove for verification. There was always rice with chicken, beef, or pork gravy, fresh beans or corn, or perhaps rice and gumbo. On Friday nights, it might be catfish stew or crawfish *étouffée*. Reacting like Pavlov's dogs, they had to keep their mouths closed so as not to drool into the pots. They could not eat until they had washed up, and with only one bathroom, one of them had to wait his turn, and usually that was Pierre.

In a short time, they were at the table seated in their usual places—father at the head of the table, Pierre on the side, mother opposite him, and his sister at the other end of the table. With appetites whetted to the sharpest edge, they could taste every ingredient in the food. His mother was not a great cook by modern standards, but everything she cooked was consistent, well-seasoned, plentiful and most importantly, it was his mom's cooking. The meal was passed in almost complete silence except for exclamations on how good each dish was. The focus was on appeasing the stomach, not on conversation. Each plate was piled high, and he and his father ate two or three servings of everything. It was an absolute pleasure to calm their ravenous appetites, a pleasure known only to those who labor all day or athletes who compete in events like triathlons, marathons, and long-distance cycling.

They left the table with distended stomachs, like lions of the Serengeti after they consumed a zebra. There was no TV to relax before going to bed, so they sat on the glass porch to talk some as his mother and sister cleared the table, washed and dried the dishes, and put away any leftovers in the fridge. They would not stay up late. By nine o'clock, or sometimes earlier, they were already in bed. Wake-up time at 5:00AM would arrive in the blink of an eye. For Pierre, wake-up time would instantly arrive because he was asleep as soon as he hit the pillow. His wake-up alarm, his father tapping his forehead, seemed to come seconds after he had fallen asleep.

By early January, his first work experience came to an end, and it was time to register at the university in Lafayette for the spring semester. Though he had been uncertain about going to college, he was now ready to give it a go. He chose to major in history with the idea of becoming a teacher, an odd choice for one who had never been particularly enamored with school. His major made sense though, because history was his favorite subject. His choice of a teaching career, though unknown to him at the time, was also logical, as often the first educated of under-educated families goes into education. Certainly, teachers were the educated people Pierre knew best, because there were no college graduates in his family. Pierre knew about doctors and lawyers and engineers, but it was just too much of a leap for him to go in that direction. He could not dream that large.

CHAPTER 9
THE UNIVERSITY EXPERIENCE

"Education is learning what you didn't know you didn't know."

George Boas

D ON came to pick him up to go to Lafayette for spring registra-tion. After loading his meager belongings in a small suitcase, they were on their way. Record cold temperatures had invaded the South, and ice covered many roads. Don's car constantly lost traction and swerved from side to side. Once safely in Lafayette, they went to the home of Don's aunt where they would be lodging for the semester. She also had several other rooms which she also rented out to other college students. Don paid no rent as he was family, while Pierre would pay twenty dollars a month.

They unloaded the car and walked into the big two-story house which was about three blocks from the university. His aunt Wilma was a large Cajun woman who also had a small daycare business in addition to the room rentals. Pierre's room was not a bad room, but he wasn't comfortable there yet. He went downstairs and chatted with his new landlady, a warm, welcoming person, and he felt comfortable with her because they spoke both English and French as they conversed.

Then, the horrors of registration reared its ugly head. Before computers, college registration was a nightmare and often took a full day to complete. One had to stand in a long line to register for each course desired, and after waiting in line an hour or more, the desired course was often filled. Then one had to stand in the same line again to change to another course. Next, there was the wait to secure the required signatures. Finally, there were long lines to pay tuition fees. Pierre was fortunate to have received a tuition exemption scholarship from his state representative—obviously, there were no academic requirements for this small scholarship. Finally, late in the day, the process was completed, and, bewildered and exhausted, Pierre stumbled back to his room. In the registration process, his plans to take ROTC were dashed because, as an education major, he could not substitute the ROTC classes for PE classes. He would have to do both ROTC and PE, which meant more time in school, and with his limited finances, he felt he could not do both. Nevertheless, he was now a college student.

He was fortunate that when he finished high school in 1961, the qualifications for college entry at this small university were few. A pulse rate, a warm body, and any high school diploma were all that was required—no ACT or SAT, no GPA requirements, nothing. Not surprisingly, the dropout rate, as he would find out later, was huge. Pierre didn't know much about his new university. To him, college meant going to school, doing a lot of studying to get a degree, and then going to work. He did know about his university's athletic program but nothing about its fraternities and sororities or any other campus activities, and when he found out about them, he realized that there was no way he could afford to join them. He could just imagine asking his father for money to join a fraternity. If he had, the conversation probably would have gone something like this:

"Hey Dad, could you give me money to join a fraternity?"

"A what?"

"A fraternity."

"What does that word mean?"

"Well, it's like a club where you go to parties and meet girls."

"You mean you want me to give you my money, which I busted my butt to earn, for you to go to parties and meet girls? When I was your age, I met all the girls I wanted by going to the dance, and it just cost me fifteen cents." Pierre would have had a better chance getting money by panning for gold in his bayou.

The next morning after registration, he woke up in his new bed, which was more comfortable than his moss bed at home, but he felt depressed. There was no cup of coffee waiting for him, and he felt lonely, discouraged, and anxious. "What am I doing here?" he thought. "How am I going to pass all these courses I registered for?" He could not see any path to graduation. He missed the familiarity of home and his family. But after a talk with Don, he felt a little better.

Classes started, and he walked the three blocks to the University. Most of his classes were close together, which was convenient. He took the same generic classes most freshmen take—math, English, history, science, and P.E. Most of the teachers handed out a class syllabus (a new word for Pierre). The syllabus alone raised his anxiety when he saw everything he would be required to do, like reading tons of books, writing papers, and taking tests. For someone who had done so little in high school, it was overwhelming. Despite this, he had no thoughts of quitting, and he hoped he never would.

He got his first glimmer of hope in his first English class of the semester. The professor had all the students write an essay to determine if they would take English 101 for credit or go to a no-credit remedial course. Feeling less than secure, he automatically assumed he would be put in a remedial course for no credit and still have to pay for it. Everyone wrote the essay, and at the next class, they would be informed who would stay and who would go. The next day, he nervously walked into English class feeling he would certainly be in remedial English. To his surprise, he heard his name mentioned among those taking the for-credit class. The non-credit students went to another classroom.

He got accustomed to attending classes on Monday, Wednesday, and Friday, or Tuesday, Thursday, and Saturday. Obviously, no one wanted Saturday classes, but sometimes they were unavoidable. He seldom missed a class and was attentive during class, but he felt like he didn't really belong there—like the dog whose fake horns were torn off at the horned animals' party and was chased away.

He was impressed with his professors—they were so damned smart, but they seemed disinterested in the students. Additionally, most of the professors came from outside South Louisiana. They were probably flummoxed when they first faced a class composed mostly of Cajun students with strange-sounding accents and names who often were unprepared for college. Certainly, Pierre was one of those. To him, the work was overwhelming. He had to make up for twelve years of less than stellar academic effort. The college textbooks were written on a much higher level than his high school books had been. Fortunately, his decent reading skills allowed him to keep his head above water.

He went home most weekends. If Don was also going home, he rode with him. If not, he hitch-hiked the thirty miles back home with his suitcase filled with dirty clothes for his mother to wash. It was common to see college students hitchhiking, and they were usually quickly picked up, often by a man and his family. Once home, it was so good to be in his lumpy moss-mattress bed and eat his mother's cooking again. It was good to see his bayou; after all, he had never been away from it before. For many years after college, the last thing he would do before leaving home was to take a last look at the bayou.

He got into the routine of college life. He lived off-campus and was on campus only for classes or going to the library. He loved the library and often got absorbed in reading non-cogent books and magazines before he got to his assignments. His circle of friends was small and consisted, besides his hometown friend, of other students who roomed in houses next to his. He never ate breakfast, lunch, or dinner in the college cafeteria a single time during his college career. He sometimes had lunch at a nearby mom-and-pop restaurant a block away which catered to college students. The food was good and relatively inexpensive. Often, he ate with Don and his landlady which saved him a little money. There were no fraternity parties, which was not particularly his choice, but it was just as well because he could not afford these activities, and he needed all his time to keep up with his school work. The only break he enjoyed was playing gin rummy with Don and his landlady's adolescent son, and having an occasional quart of chilled Jax beer in a frozen mug. Compared to his life at home, he didn't perceive himself as particularly unfortunate. He ate much better at home, but at school, he was independent and had money, at least for the time being. He also had solace in knowing several other students who were in the same boat as he. He had spent his life having less than most of his classmates, so it seemed to him that this was the natural order of things.

His first semester of college ended, and he passed his courses with average grades. He was not displeased with his grades—to approach mediocrity in college courses was a great achievement for Pierre. Don encouraged him by telling him that he could indeed succeed at the university level. To finish college as soon as possible, he decided to go to summer school with the little money he had left. Also, he planned to take eighteen to twenty-one hours per semester in the future to expedite the process. That is, if he could continue going to school.

He passed his courses in the summer session and went home for summer break. The problem was that he had very little money left and thought that this could well be the end of his college career.

The last thing he wanted was to ask his father for money. There had been no precedent in his family where parents helped pay for college expenses because, in his family, young men were expected to work. He and Don had tried hard to find any job available. They had applied at several supermarkets and other types of businesses for part-time and weekend jobs during his first semester, but they never got a response from any of these applications.

Fall registration came, and Pierre's prospects looked bleak. Don was a little better off financially; he had support from his family and aunt to continue. On the day before registration, Don stopped by to pick him up to go to Lafayette. Don, of course, knew about his predicament but stopped regardless just in case things had changed.

He asked Pierre, "Are you coming with me to Lafayette?"

"No" Pierre responded dejectedly, "I don't have enough money to pay for the semester."

"You can't just give it up like that," Don said forcefully, "go ask your father to help you this semester."

"I've always hated asking my father for money," he replied

"Look, goddamn it, you have to try!"

"OK, I'll try," he agreed unenthusiastically.

His father was sitting in his rocker on the glass porch. Pierre was leaning on the counter that separated the kitchen from the glass porch. His mouth was dry, and he had butterflies in his stomach. He could not envision a positive outcome. His father was always frugal with his money and had worked very hard for it.

He took a deep breath to calm his nerves and asked, "Daddy, could you lend me some money to go back to school this fall?" As his father always did in the past, he did not reply right away, took a couple of deep breaths and made that familiar facial expression which projected his internal conflict over possibly parting with his money. He and his sisters knew that expression well, and as a result, they would ask for money only when absolutely necessary. His father still had not responded. As usual, he would have to ask again.

"Well, can you help me with a loan for this semester?" Pierre thought if he could limit his request to a loan for one semester, his chances of getting money would be a little better.

His father took another couple of deep breaths, reinforced his negative facial expressions and then said, "OK, I can let you have fifty dollars a month."

Pierre felt like a ton of bricks was lifted from his shoulders. He would get to go to school another semester. Fifty dollars at that time was equal to five hundred dollars today, but it was still not enough money because after he paid his twenty dollars monthly rent, he would have thirty dollars, or one dollar per day, for the rest of the month. But he did not complain and would never ask for more; he was just happy to be still in school.

They got through the registration process. It had not changed or improved much from the spring semester—there was still a lot of waiting in line. They would have a new address this semester because Don's aunt had bought a house only one block from the university campus. The house was a two-story one, and they shared a room upstairs. There was no air-conditioning, but that did not matter since they had never had it at home. There were several other rooming houses surrounding them. Overall, it was a pleasant area.

Classes started, and Pierre immediately noticed the absence of several friends he had during the spring semester. He asked about them and was told that they had flunked out. It was like a war with many lost in action. He knew it would be a hard semester because of the twenty hours he was taking, but he did feel a little more confident than he had before the spring semester. It was challenging, keeping up with all the reading, studying, paper-writing, and test-taking, and he still had not learned to study efficiently. He was still paying, and would continue to pay for his lack of effort in high school. His goal was to get it done, graduate, and get a job. College would not be fun for him. He would be in academic purgatory until graduation redeemed him.

He and Don brought the weights they had made back home earlier and placed them in an empty room across the hall from them. He was still enthused about weight training since he continued to weigh only 130 pounds, and he still believed if he worked hard and long enough, he would see some improvement. Don trained with him, but he was not as enthusiastic as Pierre was. They didn't have the same needs, or they used different avenues to meet those needs. Sometimes other boys would train with them, and he tried to help them with what he had learned. At the university, many boys were into weight training, and it was obvious by the number of muscular young men on campus.

He did okay in most of his classes, except for math that he would end up dropping because he had no chance of passing it. Of course, he enjoyed his history classes the most, which was great since history was his major.

He was usually reticent about taking part in class discussions. He felt he could not express himself well or at the level of his classmates. There was a girl in particular in his psychology class who tended to dominate discussions. He thought she was a genius. She would unleash a volley of polysyllabic words and complex concepts which stymied students, especially Pierre, from taking part in the discussions. From his reading experiences, he thought he had a fair vocabulary, but now it was just not enough.

After class, he went to the bookstore and bought some large sheets of white poster paper. When he got to his room, he made lines with a pen and ruler across the poster sheets and divided those into two columns—one for "word" and the other for "definition." Then, he attached the poster sheets to the wall. The plan was that, while reading, he would look up each word that he came across that he did not know and write the word and definition on his poster sheet. Soon, he had a multitude of words listed there. He would look at these words each time he walked near them. His vocabulary increased rapidly, and he continued this process until he graduated. He learned that some of the words could not be used in everyday conversation. His friends would tell him to please speak English.

He got settled in his new home, and his landlady continued to be very helpful. On one occasion, she invited him to a crawfish boil in her little back yard. Her son-in-law was a fisherman and had brought her twenty-five pounds of select, fat crawfish. The crawfish were boiled and placed in the center of a table around which were about eight eager Cajuns ready to commence eating. Everyone reached to the center of the table to grab the well-seasoned crustaceans. After about twenty minutes, Pierre looked up and saw that there were no crawfish left on the table, and everyone was staring at him. He looked around the table and saw small, neat piles of crawfish hulls in front of the other participants. He then looked down at his untidy mass, and it was huge. He didn't mean to eat more than everyone else. He thought everyone would be able to get his or her share—that's how it worked at home. Perhaps while peeling hundreds of pounds of crawfish for the freezer at home, he had developed uncommon speed. He was never invited for crawfish again.

Besides the academic challenge, there was the constant financial challenge. The biggest issue with the thirty dollars he had left after paying his rent was not having enough money left to eat well. Fortunately, his landlady often invited him to eat with her and Don. Unfortunately, though, she was a horrible cook—rare for a Cajun woman of her generation. She could take the most wonderful fresh meat, fish, or crawfish, and render them practically inedible. She would put something on the stove and only come back to it when she smelled it burning. Despite that, he was grateful for the food and her generosity. Bad food certainly trumps no food.

On weekends, he continued to hitchhike home with his dirty clothes in a suitcase. For two days he would try to make up his food deficit by eating at Bertha's house in addition to his regular meals at home. His mother made sure to prepare all his favorite dishes while he was there.

While home, he and his father often went fishing for *sack-a-lait* (crappie) and usually caught a long stringer of them. As was the family tradition, these fish were cooked in light tomato gravy with onions, garlic, and lots of red pepper. They seldom fried fish, unless they were very small. With a large fish and tomato gravy over rice, a whole family could be fed. The same was true for chicken, as they seldom fried it. Undoubtedly, this was a custom carried over from the lean years of sharecropping, the Great Depression, and large families.

His second semester ended, and he passed everything except math. He would have to repeat the math course, but the good news was that he was now a sophomore. Perhaps he belonged here after all. The other good news was that his father continued to give him fifty dollars a month to continue going to school. Perhaps he now believed that Pierre could eventually graduate. His father also continued paying for his clothes, shoes, and books, which was very helpful. His father had never told him he was proud of him, but Pierre knew he was.

Spring semester brought another heavy course load of sophomore classes in English, history, science, speech, PE, and education. The workload and study time increased, and it seemed each course required reading five to seven books. They truly wanted him to learn something.

He was in absolute dread of his speech class. He had anxieties speaking to a group of people he didn't know, but the course was required, and he could not dodge it. The class started off okay since they didn't have to give a speech right away. Then, the horrifying moment arrived when the professor assigned students their first speech—a mere ten-minute affair, but the idea of preparing and giving that speech dominated his psyche for several days before the event. He wrote a talk according to the professor's criteria and began to practice in front of a mirror as recommended. He timed himself, and after several attempts, he got it up to ten minutes.

After dreadful anticipation, his turn came up. He had the worst case of anxiety ever. Most of the other students had given really good speeches. He just knew he would look like a bumbling fool in front of the class. Butterflies that had knots in their stomachs filled his stomach, and his mouth was as dry as a just-opened bag of flour. With weak knees, he shakily walked up to the front of the classroom and faced his classmates which to him were an assortment of blurry faces. As he began his anxiety-driven speech, a torrent of words erupted from his mouth like a burst of machine gun fire. Unfortunately, it was a burst of about four minutes—six minutes short of the suggested time. Nevertheless, greatly relieved that it was over, he quickly walked back to the security of his desk. The next student up was a friend of his. He was much older, perhaps in his late twenties and he wore loose-fitting, brown, dress pants and a white shirt. He was also a Cajun and spoke English with a very heavy accent. And like Pierre, he was extremely nervous, perhaps even more so. As he began his speech, his voice was afflicted with stress, and he began to shake and stutter. He was shaking so vigorously that his car keys and coins began to jingle in his loose pants. Pierre could truly feel his pain, but he still thought it was funny and had to suppress his laughter. Mercifully, the speech ended, and he nervously walked back to his desk. His speech did last longer than Pierre's.

He got his speech evaluation from the professor the following week. Pierre read, "Too staccato, slow down!" The professor was from outside Louisiana and was probably new to Cajun speech patterns. French-speaking Cajuns often speak English very rapidly due to Cajun French being a rather rapid language, and this tends to make their English rapid, too. Additionally, the last letter of most French words is not pronounced causing them not to pronounce the last letter of English words either. Finally, French is spoken with evenly spaced rather than sliding syllables. Of course, Pierre did not know this at the time of his less than spectacular performance. He did know that he would probably not make an "A" in the course.

A short time after the speech debacle, he got a notice to report to the speech therapy department. He was puzzled and wondered why he got this notice. He knew speech therapy as something handicapped children or adults needed to correct speech impairments. He didn't see himself in that category as he had been talking since he was two, and no one ever had a problem understanding him. There must be some mistake.

He made his way to the Speech Department and showed the notice to the receptionist. She looked at it and said, "Oh, you need to see the speech therapist. Go to room 114."

He walked to the room and knocked on the door. A young man, a graduate student, greeted him and told him to come in and sit down.

"Pierre, you have been recommended for speech therapy."

Taken aback, Pierre exclaimed, "What? Do I have to do this?" He felt he had enough to do and didn't want to spend his limited spare time doing whatever would be required of him here.

"Yes, you have to do it. You have a serious speech problem, and you will never be certified as a teacher unless you have it corrected."

Incredulously, Pierre said, "Well, what's the problem?"

"You are not pronouncing the 'th' words correctly."

"What do you mean?" He thought he had been pronouncing these words correctly; no one had ever mentioned it was a problem.

"To pronounce the 'th' words properly, you have to place your tongue between your teeth." He then demonstrated the "th" sound.

Pierre thought it was weird. There were no sounds like that in French and he never really noticed them in English. Perhaps the first French speakers didn't invent this sound because they didn't want to endanger their tongues.

The therapist then gave him a schedule and said, "You will need to see me one hour per week on Wednesdays at 2:00 PM."

Irritated, he took the schedule and walked out of the office. He thought, "Just what I needed, another (expletive) class, and a non-credit one at that."

The next week, he met the therapist at the appointed time. He handed Pierre a list of words with "th" sounds in them.

"Pronounce these words for me." The list included them, those, there, they, that, mother, another, month, strength, and theater.

Pierre looked at the list and thought this was going to be easy as he knew most of these words since second grade. He said, "Dem, dose, dare, dey, dat, mudder, anudder, munt, strent, and teeater."

"You see, you didn't pronounce the 'th' sound in any of these words. That's what we need to work on."

The therapy began. First, he had to learn how to place his tongue between his teeth to make the proper sound. This process was very alien to him. Next, he had to pronounce long lists of "th" words with "th" in the beginning, middle and end of words. He sputtered, spat, stumbled, and got tongue-tied in his initial attempts. He felt like he was trying to learn German. Each week, he got better, and within a few weeks, he was pronounced "cured."

During one of his workout sessions, a group of three students from across the street came in to visit. One of the boys had obviously been bodybuilding for a long time. He was like the men he admired in the magazines—suntanned and muscular, with a well-proportioned physique. His name was Glen Viltz, and Pierre and Don would later call him "The Little Greek God." They talked about working out, and Glen ended up inviting them to train with him in his room. They agreed to meet with him for the next workout.

A couple of days later, they worked out with their new friend. Glen had real weights and a lot more equipment, such as dumbbells and an adjustable bench. Pierre learned for the first time what real training was. They did multiple sets of exercises for each body part until they felt a burning pain. He learned what it was to get "pumped up." They trained on a regular basis for about a year, and for the first time, Pierre could see that he was making progress and getting stronger. He even gained a few pounds. It was not spectacular or as fast as the guys in the magazine ads had promised, but it was encouraging. He credited Glen, who went on to win many titles in bodybuilding, for giving him the first push toward his physical fitness goal.

The spring semester came to a close, and his grades were getting better. He managed to pass the math class that he had had to repeat. The good news was that this was his last required math course and also that he was in good academic standing. He was also able to include the "th" sound in his speech, but he would never lose his Cajun accent, though, over time, other experiences and environments would modify his speech. He and just about everyone who knew him couldn't believe he was still in college.

The rest of his college career would remain similar to his past semesters until his senior year, except that his classes varied. One course that had a great impact on his life was sociology. Learning and understanding human interaction was transformative. Some of the concepts the professor taught were completely contrary to what he had believed all his life. Probably more prejudices were exposed and broken down in that course than any other class in the university.

As for his college existence, it remained a very Spartan one. It was not a joyful experience, but instead one of obligation. Money was a constant issue. It was impossible for thirty dollars a month to pay for food and incidentals. At times, he was just about out of money by the third week of the month. With the little money he had left, he would buy a large loaf of Evangeline Maid bread and a three-pound package of the cheapest bologna he could find. It tasted like soap, but it got better as he got hungrier. Sometimes he ate with his landlady, which was a great big help and was greatly appreciated. Sometimes, his sister and brother-in-law would give him a few extra dollars to help out, also greatly appreciated. On one occasion, he met a young man who worked at a barbecue stand a block away from his lodging. The young man had an interest in weight training, and Pierre invited him to join him for a workout. They worked out a few times together, and he coached him on proper techniques, and in return, the young man gave him free barbecued chicken, baked beans and potato salad on several occasions. Nirvana. On some occasions when studying late at night, he and Don got hunger pangs so bad that made it difficult to concentrate. They went downstairs and got a thick piece of government commodity butter or cheese from their landlady which they ate with a slice of the Evangeline Maid bread. The fat was effective in assuaging the hunger pangs.

While he was determined to get a degree, and worked hard toward that goal, he still did not have the right attitude about education. He still felt the professors were lining up hoops that students had to jump through. He wanted to get it done and get a job. A friend of his, a distant relative who was also financially limited expressed it properly.

He said, "I want to hurry up and graduate so I can jump into this thing called 'life.'"

He and Don made a poster for their bedroom wall. It read, "School is Hell."

His junior year brought more new friends into his life. His landlady had built a little apartment in the backyard that she now rented to students. The first renters were boys from towns not far from Pierre's. Their hometowns had a much heavier Cajun population than his. They spoke French unabashedly which was normal in these towns with Cajun majorities. They would get together and talk up a storm. It was interesting how different Cajun French could be among people who lived only 10 to 15 miles apart.

He also met two Italian brothers, Mike, and Joe from the New Orleans area, who had classes with him. Joe was a varsity weightlifter, and his younger brother was an advanced bodybuilder. In a conversation, Joe told Pierre that they had to move from where they were because the landlady no longer wanted the barbells on her property. He asked Pierre if he could bring his weights to his room where they could train together. Pierre thought it was a great idea as his former workout partner, the "Little Greek God," had graduated. A few days later the boys showed up at his room with an adjustable bench and a ton of weights. The weights were not what Pierre had envisioned. The plates were much larger, and the bar was much longer. These were Olympic weights. The room was not large, but they managed by taking the weights apart after the workout. The boys were stronger and larger than he was, but he was eager to train with them. They worked the hell out of him, and he slowly made a little more progress.

Finally, he was a senior and the end was in sight. He felt like he had been in school forever. He was so ready to finish and hopefully get a job somewhere near the university. His situation had improved dramatically after applying and receiving a student loan. The loan was a good deal; he would only have to pay half the loan back after he started teaching. He didn't borrow a large amount, but it made all the difference in the world. For the first time in his college career, he had enough money to buy something besides a little food. No way could he afford to live high on the hog, but he could now afford to eat at the little restaurant nearby and even get a cold drink with his meal. He had always been embarrassed when the waiter asked him what he wanted to drink. He had not been able to afford a quarter for a drink with his meal.

He did his student teaching that year and enjoyed the experience. His supervising teacher was thin and meek, but very helpful and easy to work with. The school was, at the time, one of the best high schools in the university area and populated mostly with the children of professional families. He made an "A" in that course.

He also tutored a freshman high school student in English grammar that year. He thought it was ironic for a person who was once challenged by English grammar to end up teaching it. The extra money along with his loan put him in a relatively good position. The extra grammar practice didn't hurt him either.

Pierre got his first car this year—not just any car, but a brand new 1965 Ford Mustang. No, he did not win a lottery or get lucky in a big stakes *bourée* game. He did not need a down payment or have to pay notes, and no one bought it for him. One of his good friends, Phil, who graduated a year ahead of him and had been his mentor, had bought a new 1964 Mustang at the end of his senior year, and Pierre thought it was so cool. He knew Phil was just as financially strapped as he was and wondered how he could buy such a car. Phil told him he had a guaranteed job for the next school year, and the local Ford dealership would sell him a car, no down payment, and no monthly payments until after he started working. Of course, Pierre would remember this when the proper time came.

During the second semester of Pierre's senior year, the superintendent from the St. Bernard Parish Schools, located near New Orleans, visited the university to recruit teachers. After the interview, the superintendent gave him a contract, told him to sign and mail it to him, and he would have a job. Pierre shouted to himself, "I have a job! I can get a car!"

He had just agreed to work in a place he had never seen before and hadn't known existed. He did know, however, it was one of the best-paying parishes in Louisiana at the time. His mother was not pleased with his job location.

"Why did you get a job so far away," she asked. "We will never see you again."

"Mom, it's only about three hours away," he responded, "and I will visit you often."

In Cajun culture, children were expected to stay close to home. His three sisters were no more than fifteen miles away. Often, children built their homes next door or a few blocks from their parents' home.

When he got a copy of his signed contract, he and Don went to the Ford dealership. A salesman quickly swooped down upon them as soon as they stepped out of the car.

Pierre asked, "Can a graduating senior with a guaranteed job buy a car with no down payment."

"Yes, indeed!" the salesman replied.

"Well, then, I want to look at a Mustang."

"I have a yellow one right over there—take it out for a test drive."

The salesman knew he was about to make a sale. They got into the car and headed out of town to test drive it. Pierre was ecstatic as he looked at the black bucket seats, black carpets, and smelled the wonderful new car aroma. He couldn't believe he was about to own a car, and not just any car, but the hottest and most desired car in America. He floored the accelerator to test its power, and the V8 engine quickly obliged. He stomped on the brakes to test its stopping power. He and Don took turns giving the car a thorough workout. Pierre made up his mind that he had to have this particular car. They drove back to the dealership where the salesman was waiting for them.

"Well, what do you think?"

"I'll take this one," Pierre said.

They entered his office where they signed the necessary papers before driving off to their room. It was still early, so Pierre and Don decided to drive home to show the car to his family. The first stop was at his parents' house. They were happy for him, but his father was not in agreement with the concept of financing the car. Pierre knew it was not the ideal way to buy a car, but he had waited long enough. He hoped he would never have any regrets, because this was one of the most cherished moments of his life. Next, they went to Bertha and Charles's house to show them the car. And last, they went to show the car to Linda and her husband of eight months,

Nicky. Pierre took them for a short spin in town to impress his little sister.

Before leaving town, they stopped at the town saloon to get a celebratory beer. It was a real old West-type saloon complete with a false front, bullet holes in the walls, long bar with brass spittoons on the floor and a set of regulars, who, like props, could be found there at almost any time. One of the props was sleeping with his head on a table next to an empty T&T wine bottle. Clint Eastwood could have easily filmed one of his spaghetti westerns here. Pierre and Don each ordered a Jax Beer, which, like always, was ice-cold. Because each was wearing a sports coat, they were incongruous in this setting, but they were known, and there were no problems.

Before they left the saloon, they went to the restroom, and it was the same as it had always been—primitive. The whole room was a urinal, nothing but a sloped concrete floor with a drain. One did not linger here and tried to complete the operation without breathing. Pierre imagined that perhaps once a year, someone held his nose, opened the door, and threw in a large bottle of Pine Sol which shattered on the concrete like a grenade to discharge its deodorizing content. He then ran away with the satisfaction of knowing that he would not have to do this again until the same time next year.

They got back to Lafayette in time to get ready for classes the next morning, but he had a hard time sleeping that night. The next day he got up and looked out the window to see if his car was still parked under the oak tree. It was still there! What a relief. He was afraid he had been dreaming and there would be no Mustang there. Why, just last week, he was still a penniless college student hitchhiking back home with his dirty clothes in a suitcase. Sometimes students he knew and who knew him would see him by the side of the road and not pick him up. These were very demeaning experiences for him. Once again, sand was being kicked in his face! But now, those days were over. Yes, it was worth it getting a car when and how he did.

He finished his last spring semester and needed six hours of electives to graduate. He lived at home for that summer session and drove to Lafayette every day for his classes, but driving was a pleasure. With the completion of summer school, he was finally finished. He had been in college three years and three months. As he was a summer graduate, he would not receive his diploma until next year's graduation ceremony. He was OK with that. It was a wonderful feeling to escape from purgatory at last.

Pierre, university senior

CHAPTER 10
THE WORLD OF WORK

"Work spares us from three evils: boredom, vices, and need."

Voltaire

OVER the summer, Pierre and Don visited the school system in St. Bernard Parish where he would start working in the fall. He had been to New Orleans once before to see his aunt who was in Charity Hospital, but he hadn't been the driver. This was the farthest he had ever driven since he'd gotten his driver's license. All went well until they got into the city. He was very nervous and had heard that all the drivers were crazy there. He felt like a conspiracy of maniacs were all colluding to plow into his new car. They would pull out in front of him without warning, and others would hug his bumper to within inches. A few gave him the middle finger salute. He had no idea why. He would have liked to return the salute, but he was too afraid to release one of his white-knuckled, sweaty hands from its death grip on the steering wheel. Then things got worse when he somehow took a wrong turn and ended up in the French Quarter. He was completely overwhelmed by the warren of narrow, one-way streets. It was intense stop-and-go driving with a lot more stopping than going. He expected someone to run into him at each intersection.

Somehow, they found their way out of the French Quarter with his car still intact and got back on track. They finally found the school board office in Chalmette, parked, and went inside. Pierre found the superintendent's office and just walked in. The superintendent forgave his lack of protocol and greeted him warmly. He told him he would be teaching English until there was an opening in his major. Pierre asked if he could see his school, and the superintendent gave him directions.

They left in search of the school which they understood was not far down the road. They drove for what seemed to them a considerable distance but didn't see a school. They stopped for directions and were once again told, "Oh, it's a short distance down the road." They drove farther and finally saw it. They had not gone that far, but it seemed to them they had because it was unfamiliar territory. It was a dismal, gray, and rather forlorn-looking three-story building that looked more like a prison than a school. There were some menacing looking boys hanging around and he wondered if they would be in any of his classes. After looking at the school for a few minutes, they turned around to go back home. Pierre said, "I'll fulfill my contract and get the hell out of here after a year." He would end up staying thirty-three years.

His first school year began around mid-August, earlier than the school he had attended in his hometown. On the first day of school, all students and faculty assembled in the gym where the principal gave his welcome back talk and introduced the faculty. Then, each teacher went to the middle of the gym floor to call out the names of his or her homeroom students. When Pierre's turn came to call out the names of his ninth grade students, he had a problem right away. Many of the students were of Spanish Canary Island descent. The "Isleños" had settled in the area here around the same time that his ancestors had come to Louisiana. Like the Cajuns, many of their descendants had kept the language and customs of their ancestors. Additionally, other students had Italian names that were also alien to him. These were descendants of the great Italian migrations of the early twentieth century. He commenced his roll call and heard giggles from the student body and saw no one coming down to the gym floor. He could pronounce anything in English or French, but not these names. The more he tried, the worse his pronunciation got. Thankfully, a veteran teacher came over to him and finished his roll call. It was not a particularly auspicious beginning for Pierre.

One advantage of being an English teacher was that he had only four classes to teach to give him the time to grade themes and essays. He had two ninth grade classes and two eighth grade classes. As were the eighth graders of his day, these students were a challenge due to their hormonal changes. The ninth graders, on the other hand, were a dream to work with. What a difference a year made! For the most part, the students were well-mannered. Even the threatening-looking upperclassmen he had seen on his initial visit were respectful. It was helpful that he was only twenty-one years old; the students could relate to him more easily.

He was just getting into the teaching groove when on September 9, one of the deadliest hurricanes ever to make land-fall on the Gulf Coast, Hurricane Betsy, struck Southeast Louisiana. Pierre had never experienced the pandemonium of a hurricane, as such storms did not often occur in his hometown area. Everyone was looking for a place to flee. Since he shared a small mobile home with a fellow teacher, they knew they had to pack up and run. This was a small job for Pierre. He could put everything he owned in the small trunk of his car within a couple of minutes. His roommate had a cousin in Covington, Louisiana where they went to weather the storm. Though they experienced strong winds, heard trees snap, and lost electricity, they were unharmed. In the morning, they went to Lake Pontchartrain to see huge waves of the still-angry lake crash relentlessly onto the shore.

The next day, he left to stay with his parents until he could get back to his job. They were well and had had no damage. He later learned about the damage in New Orleans Metro—it was horrific. Many lost their lives. Not far from where he lived, numerous homes had taken on ten to twelve feet of water. He had no idea how his trailer had fared. He had heard news that some homes disappeared or were torn apart and dispersed into the marshes. There would be no school for him for three weeks.

His father suggested that he go to work with him while he was "unemployed." He liked the idea because he could use the extra money. He had worked in the oil fields the fall and winter before college, but he had never experienced the full Louisiana heat. He was soon to find out what it was like. The job was building a drilling location down the Atchafalaya River. They got into the doghouse for a short drive to the river where they boarded a crew boat to reach the downriver location. On arrival at the location, they saw it was along the river in a patch of small willow trees which would stymie any breeze trying to reach them. The white sand would reflect the heat and sun into their faces. The early morning hours were tolerable. Then the sun came. Many of the men who were blond or freckled had sores on their faces and around their mouths caused by the sun. As the sun rose in the sky, the heat factor multiplied as it beamed down on the struggling, toiling figures on the tiny island circled with the breeze-stifling willow trees. The sweat-soaked men proffered silent prayers for clouds to move in to shield them from the jealous, fiery devil in the sky who intercepted their prayers and annihilated the last wisp of a cloud. They toiled on in silence.

Fortunately, Pierre was in good physical condition and was able to do the work. One had to drink gallons of water each day to remain hydrated. The men could not eat a regular lunch because to do so would initiate a session of retching and vomiting later in the afternoon. Their lunch consisted of a can of tomato juice, a small bag of Fritos and a Coke which was not nearly enough calories to perform the heavy labor. When they got home, they were in "peasant appetite" mode again. Even in college, he had never felt this hungry. When he started eating, he could almost feel a primordial instinct urging him to growl at anyone who approached his plate. They didn't talk very much at the table. Once again, his father said after eating, "You know, rich people don't eat like us. All they eat is soup." Pierre had no idea where his father had seen "rich people" eat.

After about three weeks, he was notified by his school system to come back to work. He packed his car and set out for St. Bernard Parish. He didn't know what he would find or not find there. He was almost certain his small trailer would be only a memory. After all, if the hurricane had destroyed large homes and buildings, what chance did his little trailer have? But lo and behold, his trailer was still there, unmoved, not flooded, and undamaged. That was the irony of a hurricane—the most unexpected outcome can occur. He unloaded his car and moved back in. The trailer had no air-conditioning, but the heat was nothing like what he had experienced over the last three weeks while he was working in the oil field. There was a fan to pull and exhaust air through the trailer. He was home again.

His school, which had served as a shelter during the hurricane, was cleaned up, and he resumed his job. Academically, everything got back on track rather quickly, but there were many residual emotional scars—reminders of Hurricane Betsy's savage visit. To these victims, Betsy was analogous to his parents' Flood of 1927. It would never be forgotten.

He got his first paycheck, $430.00. Due to the disruption caused by the hurricane, the retirement, state, and Federal taxes were not deducted and would be prorated over the next nine paychecks. His succeeding checks would be around $300.00 per month. After paying his rent and car note there was not much money left, but he could still eat well, have a little money for occasional amusements and save a little each month. He was happy with his situation. Most importantly, he had a job and independence.

In addition to teaching his classes, he sponsored many extracurricular activities. As a novice, he didn't know that new teachers were often dumped on by older teachers who wanted to unload their extracurricular duties. He participated in all school activities, and he and a group of friends followed the football and basketball teams all over the state. These were very happy times for Pierre.

He got in touch with his two college workout partners, Mike and Joe, who happened to live not far from him and they invited him to resume his workouts with them along with their brother, Dennis. When he got to their house, he was treated like family and felt very welcome there. He recognized the familiar Olympic weights that had been in his room in Lafayette. They also had a squat rack and a pull-up bar. It was a nice setup, but they did have to wash the weights before each workout because the family poodles peed on them. Perhaps the resemblance to a car tire was too much to resist. He immediately resumed his workouts and found out what real workouts were. They trained over two hours per day, six days a week. They pushed him beyond his limits, and his strength and size increased at a steady rate. On several occasions, he was treated to wonderful Italian meals after workouts.

Not all of his improvement was due to the increased workouts; having adequate food played an important role. While he did not have the Cajun food he had grown up with, he quickly adapted to the local fare. At school, the cafeteria ladies adopted him and loaded his plate with all he could eat. For dinner, he often ate out at various little restaurants in the area. His favorite was an Italian restaurant that served a huge amount of food for a very low price. At first, he was not very fond of the thick, omnipresent sweet tomato sauce and parmesan cheese, but he soon learned to love it. He especially enjoyed the veal cutlets, macaroni and cheese, and wop salad. The interesting thing was that the Italian owner, a native of Sicily, never charged the same price for the same food, but whatever the price, it was always a good deal.

His environment changed drastically. Living in his little town on the bayou of perhaps two thousand people was so different from living in New Orleans Metro, where the population was over a million. He came in contact with so many more people than he would have in his little corner of Louisiana. They all influenced him in different ways, most of them positive.

He met very few French-speaking Cajuns. Certainly, there were many Cajuns dispersed among the New Orleans area's million plus population but he seldom ran into them, and the majority of these had lost their language many years ago. At his school, he met an older Cajun-speaking lady, Mrs. Robin, with whom he could converse, and they formed a friendship that lasted for many years. Her husband was a commercial fisherman, and she often brought him wonderful fresh seafood. He had a few students over the years who spoke a little French, and the mother of one of the students brought him some seafood gumbo as she knew the Cajun propensity for it. She was from the Southeast Louisiana group of Cajuns, and her gumbo was thinner than that of Southwest Louisiana cooks. Her gumbo was chock-full of fresh seafood and was much appreciated.

Unfortunately, not all of his acquaintances were as pleasant. Many denizens of large cities felt superior to those from the smaller cities and towns. Pierre often met someone and after a few words of conversation, the dialogue would be something like this:

"Oh, you're from the country aren't you?"

"Well, not exactly, but I am from a small town."

"You have an accent; you must be a boogerlee."

Pierre never found out exactly what a "boogerlee" was or its correct spelling, but it was certainly less than an endearing term. He could understand why many city dwellers considered themselves as being superior—large cities provide more opportunities for education and sophistication compared to rural areas and small towns, but that is not a universality. It was certain that those who branded others with terms like "boogerlee" and "coonass" were not sophisticated themselves.

Near the end of the school year, he officially became a college graduate. It was rather anti-climactic for him as he had completed his graduation requirements almost a year before. Since he had finished school after the summer session, he could not officially graduate until the end of the following spring semester. He and his college roommate, Don, attended the ceremony in a hot, stuffy coliseum. The graduating class was huge, and graduates and their families, including Pierre's, filled the coliseum. With the heavy graduation gown on, Pierre nearly fainted for the first and last time in his life. He couldn't believe that despite his conditioning and the hard physical work he had done in the full summer heat, that he was about to pass out. But he survived, and he and Don congratulated each other outside the Coliseum in the fresh air.

The year went by quickly and the end of the school term was hectic with final tests, grading papers and turning in grades. He had enjoyed his first year and found it very satisfying. Due to hard, assiduous training, he had put on twenty-five pounds of muscle. Of course getting enough to eat helped his progress. He was not like the guys he remembered from the magazine pictures, but he was in much better shape than he had been before.

Now, with the summer off, he started looking for a part-time job that would last until the next school year started. He read an ad in the paper from a Ford dealership in New Orleans wanting to hire and train salespeople. He had no clue about selling cars, but he decided to give it a try. He applied and was accepted. The manager gave him and several other applicants some lessons in salesmanship and a schedule giving them time on the floor and time to make contacts by phone and mail. He quickly learned that this was not what he had trained for at the University. It was a very cut-throat job as commissions determined the amount earned. Some of the sales personnel were "characters" and sometimes fights occurred when a salesman perceived that a customer had been "stolen" from him. It was a learning experience for him, and he did manage to sell a few cars, but he was not going to change careers. A few made a lot of money, but most made very little.

It was obvious to him that the ploy of the dealership was to bring in a large number of new salespersons who would go out and make a few sales to family and friends. Once that played out, most found other occupations. He also learned that the pay was very irregular, and as a result, some salespeople lived at the level of their best sales months and had to borrow money during the slow months to continue their accustomed lifestyle.

The second school year started, and his school system went from co-educational to separate boys' and girls' schools. He would have preferred teaching at the boys' school because most of his friends were going there, and he liked the principal; however, he chose the girls' school because he would get to teach in his major, social studies—and this turned out to be a good decision for him.

He also changed his living quarters. A friend's brother had moved a new, wide trailer only three trailers away from his. The man was single, was away most of the time and wanted someone to stay in his trailer. The price was right, and the trailer was so much better and nicer than the one he had. It was even air-conditioned. He moved in, and despite having nothing in common with the owner, it was a good arrangement.

He enjoyed teaching civics, world history, and geography to girls. He found girls easier to teach than boys and much easier to manage. He became department chairperson, which meant a lot more work and responsibility but with no extra pay. One of his responsibilities was to sponsor and organize the annual social studies fair. Every student in the school was required to do a project. Since the janitor had a bad back, and there were no boys in school to do the heavy lifting, Pierre did it all himself. He moved thirty-five sheets of three-quarter-inch plywood and all the saw horses from the storeroom to the gym floor, removing the junk atop the pile of plywood first. Then there were judges to recruit to judge the projects, donations for trophies to solicit, and a million other details to attend to that fairs like this required. It was hard work, but not near as hard as the oilfield work he had done. He didn't mind it, and he still found the energy to do his usual weight training.

During the school year, he spent some of the money he had saved to buy his mother a new bedroom set. At their local furniture store, she picked out a walnut, three-piece set. The store delivered the furniture the same day, removed the old bedroom set, and replaced her moss mattress with a nice, new one. He was not sad to see it go. She was happy with her gift, and he was even happier to give it to her.

Outside work, his life was busy. After Joe, Mike and Dennis had gone on to their careers, he needed a new place to train. He had made good progress, and he wanted to maintain it. A health studio opened up close to his house, and he drove over to check out the facility. The owner, Vic, showed him around, and was one of the most considerate men he had ever met. Pierre would learn a great deal from him. His wife Wanda, who he met later, was equally genial. After he toured the gym, which was complete with the latest equipment, plus sauna, whirlpool, and of course, the obligatory mirrored walls, Vic asked him if he would like to work part-time for him as an instructor. He was happy to accept the offer because he did not want to pay monthly dues. His job was to set up training routines for members and teach training techniques. He got a small commission on members he signed up. He met a lot of people there and enjoyed the experience.

At about the same time as he was working at the health club, he made a visit back home to see his parents. As he often did when he visited, he would go to a local lounge to have a beer with some of the home boys. One of his former classmates, Danny, the big boy who had pinched him in first grade, walked in. He had not seen him in years as he had been away serving a hitch in the US Navy. They had a couple of beers and caught up on what had been going on in each other's lives. Pierre told him about the big house with three bedrooms he had recently moved into just outside the New Orleans city limits and offered Danny one of the bedrooms if he wanted to move to New Orleans Metro.

Pierre didn't expect him to show up; after all, most things said by guys drinking beer at a bar didn't or won't happen. Additionally, not many young men from his hometown wanted to move to New Orleans Metro. At home a few nights later, he heard a knock on the door. He opened the door, and there was Danny standing with a huge duffel bag in his hand.

"Hey Pierre, can I move in with you?"

"Sure."

Plasticity is one of the best attributes of youth.

They would spend two years together before Danny got married. They bought a boat and motor together and did a lot of very successful fishing in the marshes. He and Danny competed to see who could catch the most fish—Danny usually won. The fish in the marshes were so much more abundant than in the freshwater lakes and bayous back home. One measured his catch not in numbers caught, but in the number of ice chests filled.

The abundance of fish led Pierre to develop an entirely new skill —cooking. To this point, he had never cooked anything except for fried fish, and with all the fish they were catching, they finally got tired of fried fish. He heard a friend describe how he baked fish in the oven. It was simple. He put a mixture of olive oil and lemon juice in a shallow pan, seasoned the fish with salt, pepper, and cayenne. The fish was then put on a baking pan in the oven and basted on a regular basis. With fresh bread added to dunk in the juices, it was a wonderful meal. Danny was not interested in cooking, so he washed the dishes and cleaned up. For Pierre, that was a heck of a deal.

Even with the wonderful fish they had access to, one could not live on fish alone. He had to expand his culinary repertoire. He got some Spam, sliced it, placed a slice of canned pineapple on it and baked it in the oven. Along with the instant mashed potatoes and heated up green peas he prepared, they felt like they were in the realm of haute cuisine. With his discovery of "Shake and Bake," they got relief from fish and Spam. He shook and baked chicken, pork, or fish to go with the instant mashed potatoes and canned corn or peas. Now, they were really living! He then started trying to duplicate some of the dishes his mother cooked at home. He often called his mother or sisters for instruction. As he soon mastered the finer points of gumbos, étouffées, stews, smothered potatoes, and fish stews, he realized he had a knack for cooking. All of his uncles and male cousins cooked, so perhaps it was genetic.

Despite his heavy work schedule, he started working on a master's degree during his third year of teaching. Several of his friends were going to Nichols State University in Thibodaux to work on their master's degree. They asked him to join them, and he did. A master's degree was important to teachers because it brought more pay and qualified them to become administrators. They took turns driving once a week on Monday nights to attend classes for three hours. The round trip was a hundred miles. They would then attend two summer sessions at the university to complete the requirements.

For the first time in his life, he developed a good attitude about education. He no longer felt that he was being made to jump hoops. Now he was interested and applied himself more fully. He saw his professors as fellow educators. He completed his master's in about two years and made all A's, and B's in his graduate courses. Perhaps being a teacher himself helped to improve his attitude.

For the fourth time, he graduated, and for the fourth time, his parents attended his graduation. The drive from the little town on the bayou to the university in Thibodaux was not one his parents would normally make. His mother had never been there before, and his father had only been there on a job some time before. Pierre was moved by their presence as he realized that they were proud of him and that they had done everything they knew how to support his education. He felt very grateful.

In 1971, after having worked six years, his superintendent, Mr. Davies, asked him if he wanted to go to Ecuador as part of an exchange program they had with that country. He was so surprised that he didn't know what to say. He replied by saying that he didn't know. He was too insecure just to say "yes." The superintendent told him to think about it. A little later, a senior supervisor came to him and told him he should not turn down the superintendent's offer—a very good opportunity and at no expense to him. He agreed to go with the selected group that summer.

He and seven other teachers chosen by the superintendent were set to go to Ecuador as consultants. It did, indeed, turn out to be a wonderful opportunity. It was the first time he would fly internationally and visit a foreign country. They flew first class, and that was the last time he would fly first class despite the numerous times he was to fly subsequently. They spent one week in a huge coastal city and one week in the Andes Mountains. In the coastal city of Guayaquil, they visited a school and did some activities with the students and teachers. He was able to connect with the students by telling them he liked the popular Spanish rock group, "Santana." He wished he could have been fluent in Spanish.

It was in the large coastal city of Guayaquil that Pierre got his fifteen minutes of fame. While touring the city with his group, he wore his sleeveless workout shirt. As they were walking down the street sightseeing, a crowd of boys and young men began to follow them. Some in the crowd, talking excitedly, were pointing at Pierre. The crowd got larger as they walked. He asked the guide what was going on. She told him that they were impressed with his physique. Due to the small stature of the inhabitants, and knowing nothing about weight training, they probably had never seen anyone like Pierre.

The second week in the Andes was as spectacular as the drive there was frightful. Two drivers in old, beat-up cars were assigned to take them to Quito. Pierre knew what could happen to old, nonmaintained cars. He remembered how the tie rod end would disconnect on his father's old pickup causing the two front wheels to turn in opposite directions, making it impossible to steer the vehicle—very frightening. The roads were often more like gravel trails that snaked high up in the high Andes and the drivers seemed to drive as if they were preparing for the Pikes Peak Race. There were crosses all along the road where hapless drivers (and worse still, passengers, he thought) had met their doom. If a carload of five passengers went off, he wondered, would there be five crosses or only one cross for the car and driver? He kept waiting for the tie rod end to drop. Perhaps because wire instead of string was used to hold the car together, they reached their destination. The Andes were amazing! They were the first mountains he had ever seen. Where he was from, the highest point always had been a bridge or an overpass. Their week in the mountains was eventful as they visited some of the native Indians and the beautiful colonial city of Quito. They also learned the high altitude was very taxing on physical activity.

Pierre was indeed fortunate to participate in that teacher exchange. To him, at that time, this was a once-in-a-lifetime stroke of good fortune. He certainly could not afford to travel on his own in the foreseeable future. He had no clue that in nine years, lightning would strike again, and this time the consequences would render him changed forever.

To supplement his salary, he got a part-time job teaching adults the skills necessary to take and pass the GED test for a high school diploma. He worked three hours twice a week from 6:00 to 9:00 PM. He enjoyed the work, teaching every student on a one-on-one basis. He had some remarkable students who came to him on a fifth to seventh grade level and earned a high school diploma within a school year. Many of them would go out and get jobs for the first time or improve their position in existing jobs. His satisfaction was great as he was their only teacher for all subjects as opposed to being one of the six teachers his students had in high school.

In June of 1973, at 29 years old, Pierre and Anita, the mother of two children, Lisa and Rudy, married. Most of his cousins and hometown friends had married just out of high school or by their early 20's. His cousins thought he would be a lifetime bachelor. He had no regrets waiting. Don was his best man; his parents, sisters, and one niece came to the wedding along with many of his school friends and Anita's family. They went to Toledo Bend for their honeymoon, and he was back to work on Monday.

Two years after the marriage, his supervisor, Mr. Fernandez, appointed him to initiate a full-time adult learning center. This concept would allow more students, especially women, to attend classes, and the program reached many more students. Pierre taught full-time in the learning center as well as administrating the whole adult education program. He had some very good help from his secretary, Kay, who could also teach, and an aide who was a superb teacher as well. For several consecutive years, they graduated over 100 students, mostly women, from the adult learning center alone. Pierre would often see his graduates getting jobs for the first time—very rewarding experiences.

One of his colleagues, Mr. Helsher, from the central office told him, "I hear that you're a home wrecker."

Taken aback, Pierre replied, "What do you mean?"

"Well, you're graduating all these women, and now many of them are getting a job and leaving their husbands."

His colleague, a consummate jokester, chuckled at Pierre's reaction.

Pierre worked closely with his supervisor, Mr. Fernandez, a descendant of the Canary Island migration of Spanish origin, and they became good friends. While visiting him in his office, he noticed he was writing something in Spanish at his desk. He knew he was a fluent Spanish speaker, but had no idea he could also write in the language as well. He asked how he had learned to write in Spanish. He replied that he had spoken Spanish as a child, had taken it in high school and college, and had even taught it in high school at one time. Pierre was impressed because even though he spoke French and took courses in high school and college, he could not write it very well. He thought to himself that he, too, would like to be able to write well in his first language.

Pierre's adult learning center was first located in Chalmette High School which had an excellent French teacher. Pierre envied her because she often had French nationals with her and he was fascinated listening to them speak. Pierre knew she had also visited France on several occasions for training and visiting friends. He thought that he would really like a lifestyle like that, but could not foresee when he could ever do such a thing.

Pierre's career had taken a shift from a high school teacher to a full-time adult education teacher and administrator. While he still enjoyed teaching high school students, the move turned out to be a life-changing one for him. His supervisor was a board member of the Louisiana Association for Public Community and Adult Education and took him to some of the board meetings. He met fellow adult educators from throughout the state of Louisiana and some of the leaders at the state department of education. He became a board member of the adult education association when his supervisor retired a few years later. As a board member, Pierre would come in contact with many people who would facilitate his professional growth.

Each year, as part of the annual state adult education convention, the board members would "roast" the incoming president. Hundreds of adult educators from every parish in Louisiana attended this event. Pierre had become proficient at speaking to his classes and at other school activities, but speaking to his peers from throughout the state was another matter. His turn came up, and he felt a little like he had for his "memorable" speech at the university. His fellow board members had done roasts several times and were good at it. His latent insecurity popped up at an inopportune time, but he delivered his part of the roast, not eloquently, but passably.

A year or so later, a state supervisor, Bobby Boyet, asked Pierre to help him put on a teacher training workshop in north Louisiana. He was honored to be asked by the person many considered to be the "guru" of adult teacher training in Louisiana. Previously, Pierre had written an article on student recruitment, and Bobby wanted Pierre to present it at the training session. He was apprehensive because he felt incapable of matching the skills, poise, and speaking ability of the presenters he had in the past. He felt a little like he did in high school when he felt certain things were for others to do, not him. However, he was able to get comfortable and deliver a good presentation. He felt so good being one of the presenters because to him it was a step up in his profession and confidence. He would do many other in-service activities throughout his career.

While Pierre was busy with his work, hobbies, part-time jobs, and life in general, his mother, now in her 60's, learned how to read.

He couldn't understand how this could have happened. She had only gone up to fourth grade while going to school very irregularly over fifty years ago, still spoke very little English, did not drive, and certainly hadn't taken adult literacy classes. He had worked with students his mother's age in his adult classes who had made good progress, but they were English speakers and still needed a lot of one-on-one instruction to progress. He knew his mother was considered by both sides of his family to be the family encyclopedia since she could remember practically everything she ever knew or heard—such as the birthdays of every child born on both sides of his huge family. He knew she remembered the cost of every item purchased for the house and also its date of purchase, no matter how long ago it had been bought, and often, even the weather on that day. But to Pierre and his sisters, she had always been "just Mom" and they hadn't seen any particular significance in her rare memory. It was just something she had always had.

What he did know, after talking with his sisters, was that she would pick up magazines they had left in the house and was later seen looking at them on several occasions. They had thought she was only looking at the pictures. They had also seen her looking at newspapers they had left at home every so often. A few times, she would ask to have a word pronounced. Then, she just read —and she read well. She remembered everything she read and what section and page it had been on. She subsequently even got a subscription to the newspaper and read it completely every day. She didn't know what subjects, verbs, vowels, and consonants were, nor could she write anything but her name. But obviously, she understood English well. How mysterious!

As a son and educator, he was overjoyed with his mother's achievement. She would continue being a reader for the remainder of her life. But chained to that joy was a profound sense of sadness and regret. He was sad because it happened so late in her life. Regret, because she never had the opportunity to develop those remarkable abilities, and that he, as a literacy teacher, was not the one to help her with her reading. Her fourth-grade teacher was correct when she told his mother that she would do very well in school if she attended regularly. Who knows how many individuals from throughout the world with unusual abilities and talents did not and will not get the opportunity to develop them? His mother's sharecropper parents believed the labor of a nine-year-old girl was more important to them at home than sending her to school. Her parents were not bad people; they were merely victims of the sharecropper lifestyle which required the labor of the children to help eke out an existence for the family. Survival trumped education. Such was the insidiousness of sharecropping.

CHAPTER 11
FRANCE AT LAST

"To travel is to discover that everyone is wrong about other countries."

Aldous Huxley

PIERRE was in the 15th year of his education career in 1980, and he had still not visited France. Most Cajuns aspire at one time or another to visit France, but most don't. From childhood to present, Pierre had dreamed about going there, but it always seemed to be something out of his reach. He certainly wanted to, but there were complications. With the responsibility of the wife and kids, it was not that simple to just pick up and go to France. Additionally, the cost of such a trip was not inexpensive.

He had been very involved with his job as a teacher and administrator representing the New Orleans metropolitan area on the Louisiana Association for Public Community and Adult Education (LAPCAE). Each year the Louisiana State Department of Education conducted two conferences with the parish directors of adult education programs, usually in Baton Rouge. At one of these meetings, the state department staff and parish directors had breakfast at the hotel restaurant. Pierre had finished his breakfast and had just begun walking to his room before the meeting began. After a dozen or so steps, he reached the table where the state director was finishing his breakfast. He motioned to Pierre to come over. After a few words of small talk, the director inquired, "Pierre, would you like to go to France this summer?" Pierre didn't think he had heard right. Like, is this for real?

"Well, I would love to, but I really can't afford it at this time."

"Oh, this won't cost you very much," he explained, "All you have to do is pay your plane fare."

Pierre was getting excited. He could manage the plane fare.

"OK, I will talk to my wife about it," he uttered, trying to seem casual.

"Give me a call Monday."

Pierre was floating on a cloud all weekend. His wife, Anita, was also excited at the prospect of visiting France. They couldn't believe this was happening. The opportunity to visit France—incredible! He called his family back home about their good fortune, and they were happy for them but hesitant because they didn't like the idea of them going on a trip so far away from home. Except for their short excursions to East Texas, no one in his family had ever even gone out of state. His father was especially anxious as he was convinced most planes crashed soon after takeoff. He saw it on television.

On Monday, he called the director to get more information about the trip. He learned that the France visit was a cooperative venture of the state department, the Council for the Development of French in Louisiana, and France. The venture provided exchanges between French and Louisiana educators. Approximately thirty Louisianans would visit France that summer. A similar number of French educators would visit Louisiana next summer. The trip consisted of a one-week tour of western France with several stops in host communities. The second week would be spent in Paris studying French language and culture. He got more and more excited as he absorbed the itinerary. He still could not believe this was happening.

He was not sure why the director selected him for this exchange. He was not a person of great influence or connections with the powers that be. Certainly, many others would have loved being selected for such an experience. He knew the state director on a professional basis, but they were not exactly bosom buddies. It was possible, he thought, that since not all participants were French speakers, he might have been selected to help with interpreting.

The school year ended, and shortly after, the group of educators met at the New Orleans airport to depart for Paris. Pierre had to pinch himself to make sure he was not dreaming. His first trans-Atlantic flight took forever, and the food was very bland. Little did he know that airline food would later plummet from bland to awful and then to nearly disappear. He slept very little during the flight.

They finally landed at Orly around 8:00 AM where a large tour bus awaited them. They boarded, and as tired as they were, began the one-week excursion to destinations from Tours to the Atlantic Coast. Pierre was way too curious, however to rest or sleep on the bus. Unlike his father's visit to Texas, he was not disappointed —he was astonished by what he saw! He was constantly looking out the window to see the countryside and towns. He was already amazed by the blend of antiquity with modernity in towns, cities, and countryside. It was so different, even for a person who lived near New Orleans, one of America's oldest cities. The charm of the ubiquitous, narrow, cobblestone streets never ceased to amaze him.

Their first stop was in Tours, a large city where they would visit and spend the night. They visited what he thought was a large cathedral. The stained glass windows left them in awe. They walked the streets, and to Pierre, everything was of interest. Thanks to the French courses he had taken in high school and college, he could read most of the signs on the buildings. There were certain scents that he would find in common in all French towns and cities he would ever visit. These were the scents of freshly baked bread, the pastry shops, restaurants, and perfume shops, and the diesel fumes of trucks and buses in the usually heavy traffic.

He had his first French cuisine in Tours. He had been eager to taste French food which he expected to be similar to what he had at home. He was somewhat disappointed to discover it was rather bland and unlike the "in your face" seasonings of Cajun cooking. Of course, he would manage to eat it without a problem. He quickly learned to *vivre la différence!*

By now, he had met the rest of the people on the tour. Most of them were educators from Orleans and Jefferson Parish. Several were French teachers, and two were from the state department. Traveling together most of the day brought a quick cohesiveness.

The next stop was Orléans, where Joan of Arc had rallied the French forces to defeat the English near the end of the Hundred Years' War. Pierre was destined to cross paths with Joan of Arc many more times in the future. Orléans was an attractive city along the Loire River, and the beautiful cathedral with its twin spires, was most, well, inspiring.

Another visit was a stop at the largest chateau in the Loire Valley, Chambord, built by Francis I. The Renaissance chateau, which had four hundred and fifty rooms, was meant to be a hunting castle. During his visits to the chateau, a staff of 2,000 accompanied the king. As there was no furniture in the castle, everything had to be transported for each hunt. Francis spent only about seven weeks during his life there for his hunting events.

They visited several other chateaux in the Loire Valley before leaving for western France. Here they would stop in several towns for receptions with officials and locals. Since this was the Charente region that specializes in the production of Pineau (a liqueur of cognac and grape juice), they were greeted at every stop with Pineau. Then the officials, proudly wearing their sashes, gave welcoming speeches to the group. In Jonzac, they were welcomed with a ceremony, folk dancers, and a wonderful and copious meal.

They had a wonderful visit on the island of Oléron just south of La Rochelle. This large island was very diverse, having the usual beaches in addition to fishing villages, oyster cultivation farms, woods, marshes, villages, a lighthouse, and vineyards. The French

Kiwanis Club received them for a soirée. After the usual speeches by the sash-wearing officials, they were treated to a most unusual appetizer. The natives placed mussels in single layers on a concrete park table and covered them with dried pine straw. They ignited the straw which quickly burned down to ashes and perfectly cooked the mussels. They were wonderful. He would never see this again.

After the mussels, they joined some inhabitants of the fishing village for a sit-down meal of a variety of seafood. Pierre and Anita sat with a fisherman, his wife, and son. They had a wonderful time and a lot of conversation. Pierre was pleasantly surprised at how well he was able to communicate with the family as they ate. The fresh seafood was wonderfully prepared and delicious, especially the baked fish with white cream sauce. He would keep in contact with the couple for several years.

They then began their journey back to Paris stopping in other places of interest. One was a country restaurant for lunch. Their visit there was pre-arranged, and the meal and location were excellent, but the lunch lasted three hours. Pierre, of course, loved to eat, but he found three hours a bit much for lunch. He still had a lot to learn.

For Pierre, the arrival in Paris was mind boggling. He had never seen such a magnificent city. He was not totally naïve. He had read a lot about Paris and had seen movies set in that city, but still, to be there in person was such a moving experience. The tour bus drove by many monuments that he recognized. The Place de La Concorde, the heart of Paris, was different from the many pictures he had seen of it; it was so much larger and busier. The architecture surrounding the site was a precious horde of neo-classical art treasures. The fountains in the center were stunning with their massive bronze sculptures jetting out continuous streams of water. He wondered if this water was symbolically washing away the blood of those beheaded during the French Revolution.

They got to their accommodations in Sevres, a community about six miles from central Paris where they would spend the remainder of their trip. Their accommodations were in a huge four-story building that was originally the famous Sevres Porcelain Factory and which now housed the Center for International Pedagogical Studies. The factory had provided fine porcelain for the royalty and the wealthy classes of Europe. The concierge showed Pierre and Anita to their room on the fourth floor. There were no elevators.

The week would be spent attending classes on French language and culture and visiting the most important sites in Paris. There would also be some dinner functions. The classes were interesting and fun. He was supremely motivated and learned a great deal to improve his French. Unfortunately, Anita was not able to profit from the French classes, but she did enjoy the French history lessons.

The visits in Paris were unforgettable and emotionally moving for Pierre. He felt a connection with the wonderful culture of this country of his ancestors, which is the envy of the whole world. Pierre had been well aware intellectually of the wonders of Paris since high school. But emotionally, it was utterly vindicating, for after having been demeaned for most of his formative years for being a Cajun, he could, in some strange way, feel proud to claim a connection to this wonderful culture and people.

Advanced French speakers led the excursions into Paris. That was a good thing as Pierre had no idea how to navigate the city. While he spoke standard French fairly well, there were certain situations he had never encountered in the language. He was impressed by a couple in the tour group who could handle everything in French. Pierre thought they were cool, and he made it his goal to become as proficient as they were.

They got around by bus and subway. The subway, which seemed so complicated at first, was extremely efficient and economical. The logic of the subway system made it easy to learn. Of course, one was always capable of going in the wrong direction or missing a train, but that was not fatal. On excursions, Pierre was a bundle of almost inexhaustible and curious energy. Everything was interesting to him. He would climb steps and towers to get the best photographs possible. He wanted to take a picture of everything he saw, but the expense of having the photographs developed back home would be exorbitant for him and his wife. He was in constant motion, like a bee gathering nectar for honey. He sought to maximize his experiences since he thought this would be his last visit to France. After all, how often could one be the recipient of such good fortune?

Sometimes, they were out until 10:30 PM, and he was amazed that there was still enough daylight to take pictures. They would get back to their building in Sevres around 11:00 PM, and Pierre, finally exhausted, had to pull on the mahogany handrail to help him climb the four flights of stairs. When Pierre and Anita entered the door, their butts entered the room three steps behind them. Sleep came with the first grain of sand from the sandman.

The evening dinners were a great source of learning for him. Their group and the French nationals sat six or seven to a table, and each table had someone fluent in both languages to interpret conversations. Pierre was the interpreter at his table, and he found out that it was hard work to be an interpreter as he had to speak whenever anyone spoke. He felt exhausted after those long dinners. He quickly learned to respond with the least amount of words possible.

Of course, there was always the appropriate wine for each dinner. To Pierre, the white wines tasted very acidic, and the reds like a bad tasting medicine his mother had given him as a child. He had tried wine before in the states, but it was usually sweet or semi-sweet. At one time, Strawberry Hill, which tasted like a soft drink, was popular with his group. But wine with meals was a practice practically unknown to him. Americans, except for the elite, had not discovered wine yet. But he was in France now, so he would do like the French and learn to appreciate it a little more.

The cheeses served at the end of the meal impressed him. His knowledge of cheese was limited to cheddar, Velveeta, and for those special occasions requiring sophistication—Swiss cheese! When the waiter came out with the cheese tray, it was populated with cheeses unlike any he had ever seen before. Some were the normal color of pale orange and white, but some were gray, some were green, some the color of ashes, and some were brown and crinkled. When the waiter placed a cheese plate on the table, it smelled like no cheese he had ever tasted. He expected all the street cats of Paris, domesticated and feral, to show up at the same time to commandeer the table. A few of the cheeses were mild and quickly favored by the non-French. But some of them had a green or gray mold on them and had a very strong taste. Pierre tried all of them. He didn't like every one at the first bite, but a bit of bread with a bit of the cheese, and a sip of wine, worked wonders. The fats in the cheese mellowed the wines and the wines cleansed the palate in preparation for the next bite. This was the first of many lessons he would receive on cheese, and by American standards, he would be considered an expert.

They visited several schools in Paris and learned about the differences and similarities between French and American schools. It seemed odd to them that French high schools and universities did not have organized sports teams, and that Catholic schools were state-supported. Each school placed its students on tracks according to students' ability and interest. Good students had the opportunity to get state support through their university degree. The French teaching process was much more formal than that of the United States. Students were well-behaved and the teacher was in complete control.

Sadly, the time was soon up for this dream—it was time to wake up. A bus took the group to the airport for the flight home. On the plane, the group was excited and anxious to reunite with family, friends, and home. There was a lot of celebratory drinking of wine on the plane. They landed in New Orleans and the group departed and went their separate ways. Pierre would maintain contact with a few of his fellow travelers.

When they got home that night, he felt like he would go to bed and sleep for days as he had gotten no sleep on the flight. However, that was not to happen. He did not sleep at all, yet he was not completely awake. He felt like a zombie suspended between life and death. In the morning, he got up and was scheduled to go to a church function. He managed to get there, but he felt like he was not present. He got back home and immediately jumped in bed feeling he would sleep at last. He didn't sleep, nor would he that night. He had a classic case of jetlag. It took days to get back to a modicum of normalcy, but this was the last time he would suffer from severe jetlag.

Chapter 12
New Directions

"Don't be pushed by your problems, be led by your dreams."

Ralph Waldo Emerson

PIERRE spent the remainder of his summer doing the usual summer projects around his house and yard. He and Anita visited his family and shared their experiences with color slides from their vacation. His family knew no one who had ever gone to France, except his uncle Isaac during World War II, so their vacation turned out to be a family learning experience for everyone. Then it was time to begin another school year, to resume his teaching and directing of the Adult Education Program. On the outside, he seemed to have returned to normal. But mentally and emotionally, changes were welling up within him. He constantly relived his trip to France. He wanted to do it again as soon as possible. He wanted to go full speed ahead to perfect his standard French, and he wanted to learn more about France and its people.

On the trip, he had met and befriended a man who was an assistant superintendent of the state department. They had talked about going on a similar trip next year, and he decided to follow up on that possibility. After talking to his friend, he learned that one of the criteria for participation was enrollment in a university-level French class. Since this was something he wanted to do anyway, he made plans to register for the spring semester. He also found out the trip would not be to France but to Brussels, Belgium. He was a little disappointed, but he knew that Brussels was a beautiful French-speaking city with many attributes.

Meanwhile, he got cable TV in order to access French television on TeleFrance. He could listen to the language and get all the latest French news as well as watch French movies. He also subscribed to a French newsletter to keep him up to date on the Francophone world. Additionally, he went to university bookstores and purchased grammar workbooks and books on French literature. He began the process of reading the great writers such as Moliere, Voltaire, Jean-Jacques Rousseau, Victor Hugo, Chateaubriand, Albert Camus, and many others in French. Initially, the reading was tedious, but he got faster as he got more practice.

During the second semester of the school year, Pierre learned to his great delight that he had been selected to participate in the Belgian exchange program. The program would consist of two weeks in Brussels where they would study the Belgian culture and French language. In addition, they would be taking excursions throughout the diminutive, but attraction-dense country. Pierre was taking the next step in his journey to French literacy.

Belgium shares a border with northeast France. There was no way he could resist the idea of spending an extra week in Europe to visit

France and Switzerland. Pierre planned a train trip that would take them to Paris for several days, a stop in Basel, and a visit of a few days in Lausanne, Switzerland. They would then take a train back to Brussels to board a plane for home.

After the school year had been wrapped up, the group of about 30 educators departed from New Orleans for Brussels. Besides Pierre and Anita, there were a few who had participated in last year's trip to France. The makeup of the group was different in that many of the participants were from areas outside of South Louisiana. They had an uneventful flight (the best kind) and landed in Brussels the following morning.

They were taken to a private boarding school which was now vacant due to the summer break. The accommodations were rather spartan but completely adequate. They were given a welcome and an orientation before they would go out to get a preview of Brussels.

They found Brussels to be an ancient, magnificent Francophone city. Belgium is a bilingual country of Flemish and French speakers. The French speakers are nearest the French border, and the Flemish speakers are mostly farther north. The ancient center of Brussels is called, "*La Grande Place*" (the big square), a large, cobblestone square surrounded by the most striking Flemish architecture. Unfortunately, the monumental buildings were covered with a layer of black soot caused by auto pollution, a problem found in most large European cities.

The Grande Place is the site of many activities throughout the year. One of the most beautiful is the display of multicolored flowers which cover the cobblestones. Nearby are some of the many chocolate shops to be found in the city. The chocolate was divine, especially with hazelnuts. Also nearby is the famous bronze statue of the Mannequin Pis, a small statue of a little boy urinating. The citizens consider him the first citizen of Brussels and have filled a nearby museum with hundreds of copies of him wearing different uniforms and costumes reflecting Belgian history.

They settled into a routine of classes on Belgium culture and French language in the mornings. Pierre enjoyed these classes and learned interesting information about this tiny country's culture and language. As he was still an avid fan of music, he especially appreciated the music of Jacques Brel, an internationally famous Belgian singer and songwriter of the 1950s and 60s. His songs and music transcended language as he had performed to sold out venues throughout the world, including the United States. Many of his songs were translated into English and became popular in the U. S. Rod McKuen translated Brel's song, "Ne Me Quitte Pas" into English for Neil Diamond, where it became, "If You Go Away."

Despite its diminutive footprint, Belgium had a plethora of interesting sites to visit. One of the most impressive was Bruges, a city often compared to Venice, Italy because of its many canals. A tour of this well-preserved medieval city in a small boat was one of Pierre's most remarkable experiences of all time. The medieval town with its Flemish architecture and birch trees hanging like weeping willows over the mirror-like surface of the canals was breathtaking.

After the canal tour, they ambled around and found a Belgian Fries stand. It felt strange saying "fries" without "French" as an adjective, but yes, the Belgians made wonderful fries—perhaps the best. The stands were small, about seven by seven feet. One of their secrets is that they fry the fries twice. The long white potato fries were sold in a paper cup holding a handful of fries. Most Americans are taken aback when they learn that mayonnaise is the default condiment for fries in Belgium. Pierre tried it and instantly preferred it to ketchup. It would become a lifelong preference.

One of the certainties in Belgium was the uncertainty of the weather. On the average, there is a 50 percent chance of rain each day. Often, while sightseeing, rain just popped up, and one either ran for cover or opened up an umbrella. When a bright, sunny day occurred, it was a topic of conversation among the natives. They appreciated good weather.

Pierre had some interesting conversations with one of the professors at the school. He was an older man and very interested in Pierre's Cajun language and culture. As they conversed, he would point out words Pierre used which were archaic words from the old French spoken in the 17th and 18th century. Pierre learned that these words were part of what made Cajun French different from standard French. Because his ancestors had been separated from France since the 18th century, their language had ceased to evolve in the path of the mother country's language. Pierre got the feeling the professor considered him a relic of the past and worthy of study.

Part of the exchange included a weekend stay with a pre-selected Belgian family. Their family was from a smaller town just outside Brussels called Jambs which was not far from the French border.

Pierre and Anita would receive the Belgian family at their home the following year. Their host, Monsieur Martin, picked them up for the trip to Jambs, while Madame Martin stayed home to prepare their dinner for the evening.

The ride to the Martin's home turned out to be quite an experience. The car was a blue Citroën 2 CV, which would later become a cult car in Europe. When they got to his hometown, they did not go straight home. He stopped at one of the local bars so they could have a beer and meet his friends. Like everywhere else in the western world, few have only one beer at a bar. They left and drove a few blocks when Mr. Martin announced he had some more friends he wanted them to meet. His buddies were sitting at an outdoor table enjoying small shots of pear liqueur. They insisted that Pierre and Anita have a drink with them. One of the buddies poured them drinks, and they learned that the liqueur had a definite fresh pear flavor and high alcohol content. After some conversation, they finally left to meet Monsieur Martin's family and have dinner.

His home was a neat two-story house in a residential area. Monsieur Martin introduced them to his wife and daughter. The daughter was about eighteen years old. They were very nice people—the Belgians have a reputation in Europe for being warm and friendly. Naturally, they had an aperitif before dinner and much conversation. Then dinner was served. Madame Martin had made beef stroganoff. Of course, wine was served with dinner. Then they had dessert and cheese followed by a digestive. Feeling sleepy and tired, for obvious reasons, Pierre and Anita excused themselves to go to bed.

The next morning, Pierre, Anita, and the Martins had breakfast before loading up in the Citroën for a tour of Namur. They visited the historical town center where there were considerable attractions, one of which was the Citadel high up on an elevated ridge. The architecture was very unique due to its Flemish influence, and there were period weapons and uniforms on exhibit. The view from the elevated ramparts provided great photo ops of the city.

They spent the rest of the day touring gardens, monuments, and churches. When they got back to Jambs, they visited Monsieur Martin's father who lived near their home. Pierre hit it off well with his father and shared many conversations with him. As they were preparing to leave, he gave Pierre a Nazi officer's dagger he had taken from a German officer in WWII. Pierre was deeply touched by this gesture as he could have given this valuable relic to any of his children or grandchildren. It was a memorable souvenir for him.

The two weeks in Belgium came to an end, and it was time to start part two of the trip, a week in Paris and Switzerland. They boarded a train for a quick trip to Paris. It was Pierre's first train ride, and he was amazed how smooth and quiet the ride was. He remembered the locomotives that ran near his grandfather's farm when he was a child, and how they made a loud click-clack noise. The modern welded rails eliminated the click-clack noise and produced a smooth ride.

From the train station in Paris, they took a taxi to their reserved hotel. Upon arriving at the hotel, he immediately noticed it was a seedy area populated by seedy characters. They felt less than secure. They checked in and went up to their room on the second floor.

They rested a little and then went back to the lobby to go for a walk in the neighborhood. He asked the receptionist if it was safe to walk around the area. The man said, "Oh sure, there are a few pickpockets out there, but no one's going to kill you." They felt much better.

After walking a short distance, he learned where they were—Pigalle, an area famous for every form of vice and perversion imaginable. Fortunately, most of its reputation had been earned in the past. American soldiers in WWII called it "Pig Alley." As Pierre and Anita walked, they saw many "working ladies" of every description plying their trade. The customer made the deal on the street, and the lady led the customer to a more private location to consummate the deal. Not far away, they saw the famous Moulin Rouge, which was another reason many came to Pigalle.

From the hotel, they visited many sites they had not seen before and some they enjoyed seeing again. Unlike last year, Pierre and Anita had to navigate the city on their own. The fastest, cheapest and most efficient method of navigation was the Metro. They bought a bunch of tickets and zipped around all over the city. Every day, they would return to the hotel exhausted from a full day of touring. The street noises penetrated into their room; nevertheless, they managed to get some sleep.

They left Paris by train to reach their next destination—Switzerland, which would be a much longer train ride. The scenery of the French countryside was fascinating to him. They got their first sight of the Alps—they were magnificent. While traveling, he had an extensive conversation with a Swiss national who discussed the wines and foods of Switzerland.

They arrived in Lausanne, a city located in the francophone area of Switzerland, and marveled at the view of this picturesque city hugging the coast of spectacular Lake Geneva (*Lac Leman* in French). The lake, fed by glacier melt from the Alps, had the clearest blue water he had ever seen. Their hotel was close to the lake, and they enjoyed the scenery and the activities associated with it.

Lausanne was a cornucopia of touristic treats. Neolithic man, Romans, and the Middle Ages have all left their footprints there as documented in the archeological museums. The cathedrals were impressive despite having lost their flamboyance after the Reformation. Lord Byron lived in Lausanne when he wrote "The Prisoner of Chillon." Pierre's thoughts were that Lord Byron, with his well-documented debaucheries, probably had even more fun in Lausanne than he did.

The cleanliness of the city was amazing—absolutely no litter on the sidewalks or streets. There were even signs that read, "No spitting on the sidewalks." Walking the streets was challenging due to their steepness. They learned to avoid some of these steep grades by going into a store, taking an elevator to the second or third floor and walking out of the building onto a higher street.

With sore legs, they took a train to return to Brussels. They stopped in Basel for a few hours and walked around the medieval section and along the Rhine River. The city was quite impressive with its quaint architecture and unique roofs crowned with multicolored tiles. They would have loved to spend more time there, but they had to get back on the train to complete their journey to Brussels. They had hotel reservations in Brussels for the night and would board a plane for home the next morning. It had been a great vacation, and they learned so much. He had had the opportunity to share extensive conversations with Belgian, French and Swiss nationals. He was making progress.

CHAPTER 13
TRANSITIONS

"All changes, even the most longed for, have their melancholy;
for what we leave behind us is a part of ourselves; we must
die to one life before we can enter another."

Anatole France

IN 1982, the year after their Belgian experience, Monsieur Martin and his family spent a few days with Pierre and his family in Louisiana which was another opportunity for Pierre to get extensive practice with his French as his guests spoke very little English. While Anita spoke Spanish, she had not learned French. Remembering how much Anita had loved the Belgian chocolates, Monsieur Martin brought her several chocolate bars of assorted flavors. She was delighted. They treated their guests to a tour of New Orleans to experience its diverse attractions. The Martins were awed by the Superdome, the French Quarter, the music, and the ambiance of the city. They also visited some of the fisherman's villages outside the city which they found very picturesque. At home, Pierre cooked some of the popular Louisiana Cajun dishes like gumbo, crawfish étouffée, and fried seafood which his guests very much appreciated. After their visit, they departed to spend a few days in Lafayette with another host family.

In the summer of that same year, an exchange student from France come to spend a month with them. Pierre's stepdaughter, Lisa, had taken a French course, and he thought a French exchange student would help her to progress. He also had an ulterior motive—he wanted to practice and improve his own French. Yvette, a sophomore in the French schools, arrived and quickly adapted to living in an American home. She was a good, bright student with a sunny disposition who wanted to improve her English. She could speak some English, but needed to improve her fluency.

They enjoyed her visit, and she enjoyed spending time with Lisa and her friends. She and Pierre spent time speaking in French and English. They visited Pierre's family and they took to her immediately. They had never spoken with a French national before. They had fun comparing the differences between Cajun and French words. They would never forget her and would always ask if he had seen her during his subsequent trips to France. He had to explain to them that when he did not see her, it was because she lived in an area he did not visit.

During her visit, a large package was delivered to their house. It was a case of Bordeaux wine from Yvette's father along with a letter of appreciation for welcoming his daughter. Pierre still did not know very much about wines but recognized that the consecutively numbered bottles in a wooden box indicated a very special wine. The wine was indeed superb and, thereafter, was brought out only on very special occasions.

When they took her to the airport for her trip home, there was not a dry eye in the group. Everyone, both Pierre's family and Yvette, felt like they would never see each other again. And they would not—not for a long time.

The year after Yvette's visit, Pierre's world was seriously shaken. He and Anita separated and divorced. His plans for Lisa visiting France and going to college went by the wayside. To her credit, Lisa would later go to work and climb the ladder to a very good position in banking. He was very proud of her determination and work ethic. As for Pierre, his work ethic carried him through this trauma as he buried himself in his work to keep moving forward.

He continued his study of the French language, history, and literature. He kept up to date on French culture through his French newsletter, and he read about French study programs that were relatively inexpensive. For some time he had wanted to do another study program, but now this would have to wait. With the divorce, he could not hope to visit France again soon. He already had gone to France twice through the exchange programs, but that was not going to happen again. Though he and Anita had been doing well financially before the divorce, the 1984 real estate market crashed and they were forced to sell their large, beautiful home for a little more than half its value.

In 1984, Pierre took Bertha and Charles to Gatlinburg, Tennessee for a vacation. He had been to the Smokies in 1975 with his own family and had enjoyed it, and he wanted his sister and her husband to have the same experience. Given the guidance and support they had shown him during the most challenging years of his life, he felt very good to be able to do something for them. They had never been on a vacation, and of course, never to Tennessee. They enjoyed being together and spoke only French to each other. Pierre taught them French words to replace the English words that had become part of the Cajun language. They had a lot of fun with that. They would visit Tennessee again several times over the next several years.

Once back home, Pierre decided to make some changes in his physical fitness routine. Despite always having been fit and healthy and with no weight problems, he changed his diet by decreasing the fat and eating less. He also incorporated cardiovascular training into his workout routine. He didn't like running, so he looked into the possibility of cycling. An acquaintance at his gym had a bike for sale. He didn't know much about bikes. The bike was an Italian one, a Bottecchia, and the owner sold him on the quality and reputation of Italian bikes. Pierre bought the bike for one hundred dollars. He took it home and began riding several times a week in his neighborhood. He had no knowledge of training techniques.

In 1985, he bought a house that had better access to open roads for cycling. He soon met fellow cyclists and began to ride with them on a regular basis. Most of them were young, in their 20's, while he was in his early 40's. He would have to become a better rider quickly. He loved the sport. He increased his bike mileage and speed. He read all the information he could to improve his cycling. He learned his bike was heavy, so he bought an aluminum Peugeot road bike. It weighed ten pounds less than the Bottecchia —a huge difference. He felt like he could fly.

Also, around 1985, he went back to college to earn thirty additional graduate hours for his Master's + 30 Degree. This would provide a raise in pay and additional qualifications for promotions. He enjoyed these classes and couldn't believe that he once was less enthusiastic about school, but better late than never.

With the addition of cycling to his routine, he was busier than ever. He still did weight training several times a week. He was teaching and administering the adult education program. He kept up his house and yard, fished on the weekends, and maintained his activities with the state adult education professional association. He also found time to read French literature and refine his French grammar.

In 1987, two important events came into Pierre's life. First, he was elected president of the state adult education association. It was not a position he sought because his first task was to organize and direct the annual state adult education convention, and that required a lot of work. Again, many of his friends came to his aid with assistance and advice, which he sorely needed because he had very little knowledge about the intricacies of convention planning. With the help and work of many, including his secretary, Kay, teacher's aide, Beryl, and one of his teachers, Dr. Jeandron PhD, they had a successful convention at the Intercontinental Hotel in New Orleans.

After the convention, he was preparing to go to France again. Finally, after six years, he would get to visit the country of his ancestors, this time for a study program in Angers, France. The study program was the type of program that college and high school students took to enhance their French language skills. He was forty-three and knew he would be one of the older students there—but he didn't care. While in the program, he would be staying with a French family to maximize his exposure to the language. The program would last four weeks with classes every weekday and excursions on weekends. Amazingly, the cost was very reasonable because the French government subsidized a portion of it. France had several such programs throughout the country where foreigners could go to learn French.

He departed alone from the New Orleans airport with two pieces of luggage. This would be the first and only time he would depart for France alone. His girlfriend, Carly, would meet him later in Paris after the study program. He felt ambivalent—he was happy to go, yet apprehensive about going alone. He had to be driven to do something like this. After all, he had a lot of things he could be doing at home, and there were a lot of other places he could have gone.

His flight landed at Charles de Gaulle International Airport, and he caught a taxi to the train station for the trip to Angers. He walked through a maze of stairs and tunnels to reach the Angers-bound train. He got on the train several cars away from his seat and had the hardest time manipulating his two pieces of luggage through the narrow aisles. They kept getting hung up on the seats. His suitcase had no wheels and this made things even more difficult. By the time he got to his seat, he was dripping with perspiration and exhausted.

The train came to a halt in Angers, and his hosts were waiting for him. The woman was perhaps in her 60's, and her son was in his 20's. They exchanged greetings before they got into his host's car to drive to their home. He was surprised how briskly she drove her little Renault. She did rapid-fire shifts to accelerate even though she had only a few hundred feet to go, and a rapid series of down-shifts before stopping. He thought about the song "The Little Old Lady from Pasadena." Upon arrival, Pierre observed a neat house surrounded with beautiful hydrangeas and other shrubs and flow-ers. There was a large cherry tree loaded with cherries behind the house. His host then showed him his room on the ground floor.

Later, they went upstairs and settled down in the living room to get to know each other. She was a widow who originally lived in Brittany, had worked for the university there, and had three sons. Pierre related his story to them and explained the Cajun culture in Louisiana.

"You speak French very well," she told Pierre, "but you have an accent different from any I've ever heard."

"That's because I spoke Cajun French first," Pierre responded, "and our 'r' is pronounced more like a Spanish 'r.' Additionally, we have a different rhythm, and some of our words are archaic French, or altered French in sound and meaning."

She thought it was very interesting and was happy that she had a boarder with whom she could converse since she spoke very little English.

The next day, at the campus of the Catholic University of the West, all of the international students—110 nationalities were represented —met in an auditorium for introductions of staff, administrators, teachers, and an explanation of the guidelines. Then the students took a test to determine their functionality in French. There were students at every level from French teachers to beginners. The evaluation staff assigned students to beginner, intermediate, or advanced classes. The staff assigned Pierre to the intermediate class. He agreed with that assessment as his grammar was far behind his fluency level.

The classes began, and he found out right away that these people were serious—they wanted people to learn. Imagine that! Students received instruction in grammar, reading, conversation, and French culture. There were heavy assignments every night.

As it turned out, he was not the oldest student in the class. There were several students older than he, and of course, many high school students from all over the world, including Louisiana. The Louisiana students he met were quite fluent, and Pierre was happy to see young Cajuns improving their French.

They also had a session on popular music, and the pop star of the moment was Jean-Jacques Goldman. He liked Goldman's music because his lyrics were so profound. Some of his songs were psychological studies. *"La Vie par Procuration,"* "Life by Proxy," was one such song and was Pierre's favorite.

They had their lunch in the school's cafeteria, and it was wonderful. One of his favorite dishes was rabbit with prunes. There were several courses at each meal, and this was the first time he had cafeteria food that rivaled that of a good restaurant. He had dinner with his host each evening. By her own admission, Madame was not a good cook. His first meal there gave Pierre pause when she brought out a dish and served each diner only one small serving. He thought he might starve to death with such tiny portions. At home, all the food was served at one time. He had not learned yet that the French serve their meals in courses even at home; this is not just done in restaurants. By the time she had served all the courses, he had had more than enough to eat. Despite her professed lack of culinary skills, he got to experience many different dishes and enjoyed the meals greatly.

The excursions with his group were enlightening; they visited some of the most interesting attractions in France. They left the school in several buses and visited Mont Saint-Michel on the edge of the English Channel, and it was stunning. The visit required climbing up a lot of steps, but the views of the channel, the marshes, the expanses of sand at low tide, and the base of Mont St. Michel were breathtaking. If one has the good fortune of visiting during the morning hours, Mont Saint-Michel may appear to rise out of a cloud initially pierced by the golden statue of St. Michael the Archangel. It was obvious why this site attracts over three million visitors annually. After the visit, they had a picnic lunch near the bus while they gazed back at the monument and the rising tides quickly reclaiming acres and acres of sand.

They visited St. Malo, a city on the coast which had been destroyed in World War II and completely rebuilt to look exactly as it did before the war. The panoramic views from the ramparts were exceptional. Pierre could see the blue English Channel, several small, rocky islands, the town of Dinard across the bay, the part of the city of St. Malo that lay outside its walls, and the restored city nestled inside the walls. Surrounded by so much history and beauty, he was ecstatic. He was just as excited during this visit as he was in his previous visits.

Coming down from his stroll on the wall, he and his friend from Ireland walked through St. Malo to meet their group for departure. They saw some of their fellow students sitting down at restaurants drinking coffee or cold drinks. Pierre could not understand how anyone in the midst of these historic and scenic treasures could sit down and have a cup of coffee. They had the rest of their lives to have cups of coffee, but only this moment to be enriched by the gifts that surrounded them—gifts that made memories which would last a lifetime.

Again, he was so disappointed when they were allowed so little time to see places of interest. It seemed like as soon as he got started, it was time to get back to the bus for the next destination. He felt like he was at the Rex Parade during Mardi Gras in New Orleans where the krewe members threw solid gold doubloons to him from the majestic floats, but there was only enough time to catch one before a hook yanked him out of range of the flying doubloons. He again promised himself that one day, he would visit France on his own schedule and spend as much time as he wanted in a destination of interest. Not that he was not appreciative; he certainly was, and he understood the situation fully. But, some day.

Perhaps the most memorable excursion was to the Puy du Fou, an evening sound and light show depicting seven hundred years of the Vendée's history through practically every medium possible. The thousands of period-costumed actors and performers were all volunteers from the region. The moving story narration, the light and sound effects, and the music completely riveted Pierre's attention. The castle ruins on a hill overlooking a lake provided a wonderful backdrop for the performance. Reservations had to be made well in advance to attend this spectacle.

He spent a lot of time exploring the city of Angers which had a population of about 150,000 and has been the site of human activity for forty thousand years. The medieval section had a renowned chateau, a cathedral, and other medieval structures. With its location on the Maine River, it was a scenic setting. The chateau was the home of the world famous Apocalyptic Tapestries. The city also had many green areas and parks for recreation as well as fishing, sailing, and other outdoor activities.

While walking around the city, he was often accompanied by a friend who was a French teacher from Texas. One day, he asked Pierre, "Why is it that when you speak French to the natives, they respond to you in French, but when I address them in French, they respond in English?"

Pierre didn't want to tell him the real reason. He did have perfect grammar, but he spoke with a J.R. Ewing Texas-like drawl that was an impediment to the natural flow of French. He diplomatically responded, "Well, they may think you are struggling, and they want to help you."

During his stay in Angers, he met and spoke with students from Sweden, the U.S., Spain, Poland, England, Mexico, Ireland, and several other countries. Everyone was encouraged to speak only French to facilitate learning. This was not difficult because French was the common language used among the diverse nationalities.

As a bonus, he got to watch the Tour de France on TV in real time. Heavy into cycling, he had become a fan of the tour. At home in the U.S., news of the tour was very spotty and limited to brief announcements. In France, it was as huge as the Super Bowl was in the U.S. He and many other students spent many hours watching the tour on television. The winner that year was Stephen Roche, an Irishman. His Irish friend was ecstatic.

He had brought his cycling shorts and helmet with him hoping to get a few kilometers in, but there was never enough time or roads suitable for cycling. He did get to do a lot of walking since his host lived about a mile and a half from campus. The walks were pleasant, especially when he went through parks and across a bridge which gave him panoramic views of the city. The Angers area is considered to have the best French spoken in all of France. On one occasion, due to a late function on campus, he hired a taxi to take him home. The taxi driver was a large man with a huge handlebar mustache. He might have been a barber in his other job, and perhaps he could sing as well. His diction was so perfect that Pierre felt that even a non-French speaker could have understood him. They talked all the way home. Pierre had a habit of talking to taxi drivers no matter where he was. He learned a lot that way—a talkative taxi driver is like a free tour guide.

He had some wonderful and enriching moments with his host. She was very knowledgeable and regarded him almost like a fourth son. She made a cherry *clafoutis* that was quite unique. It was very tasty pie-like dessert but one often made with non-pitted cherries. One had to be careful eating that pie, or spend thousands in dental repairs. On another occasion, she presented him with Antoine de

Saint Exupery's book, *The Little Prince*. Pierre knew about the book and always thought it was a children's book. When he saw the cover with a little boy wearing a nightgown, his thoughts seemed to be confirmed. But she said, "Read this book. It is much more than a children's book." He did, and what a flash of enlightenment he received. He had heard the expression, "Disneyland is not just for children." Well, *Le Petit Prince* is also not just for children. Unless extremely precocious, few children would fully understand the wisdom in this book.

On the last evening, before he was to leave Angers, he took his host to a restaurant for dinner. She had selected a quaint little restaurant outside the city which specialized in seafood. She decided to order boiled crabs and Pierre ordered a fillet of fish. Their orders arrived, and both commenced eating. Pierre was busy appreciating his excellent fish when he noticed she was not making any progress with her crabs. She was struggling. Being from an area blessed with abundant seafood, he assumed everyone could eat a crab, but she was picking at it and extracting only tiny morsels for her efforts. At that rate, they might never have left the restaurant. He asked her if she had a problem, and she replied that this was her first time to eat a boiled crab. He apologized and proceeded to show her how to break open the crab to extract the delicious, white flesh. When she got to the large claw, she vigorously cracked it open, held up a huge chunk of crab meat, and joyfully exclaimed, "Now that was worth the lick!"

Again, like all good things, his academic stay at the CIDEF in France came to an end, but the experience would influence Pierre for the rest of his life. He had grown and learned so much, and that was not only in the realm of language. He had gotten very close to his host and her son, and there were sad goodbyes at the train station. He had learned a lot from them during their countless hours of conversation. He promised to keep in touch, and he did for many years.

He boarded the train and waved a final goodbye from the window. The train would take him to Paris where he would spend a week with Carly who had never visited Paris or France. Pierre got to the train station and hired a taxi to take him to the hotel he had reserved while in Angers. He got to the hotel and saw that it was well-located and comfortable. It was about two blocks from Les Invalides, and there was a Metro station only two blocks away, however, Pierre could walk to most of the major attractions in Paris from the hotel.

After he had checked in, he went upstairs to his room with his luggage. The room was nice and had an unusually large bathroom. He unpacked the suitcases and put some clothes in the closet. Then he walked out to explore the neighborhood. Les Invalides, formerly a hospital for veterans built by Louis XIV and now a huge military museum and the burial place of Napoleon, was only a few minutes away. He walked in front of the huge structure and could see the Alexander III Bridge on the Seine. Beyond the bridge were the Petit and Grand Palais and not far beyond those was the Champs Elysées. He had been there before, but it was still one of his favorite vistas in Paris.

As it was getting late, he realized he was hungry. As he resumed his walk, he kept an eye out for a suitable restaurant. After looking at a promising menu, he walked into the restaurant. He ordered tripe. He had not had it in quite some time, and he wanted to see and taste how the French did it. He got his order and saw they did it quite differently from what he was used to in South Louisiana. It was very good, and he enjoyed his dinner. He got his check and was shocked at the cost of eating tripe in Paris.

Pierre went to the airport the next day to pick up Carly. The flight arrived and soon he saw her, looking visibly jetlagged, coming out of customs. They greeted each other warmly and took a shuttle to Montparnasse and then the Metro to the hotel. As there was a lot of time left, Pierre, not considering Carly's exhaustion, proposed they go out and see the nearby attractions. He was like a tour guide showing her the attractions aforementioned plus Les Tuileries, the Eifel Tower, and the Place de la Concorde as they ambled among world famous sites.

During their week in Paris, they would visit Montmartre, Versailles, Notre Dame, Napoleon's Arc de Triomphe, the Pompidou Center, the St. James Tower, the Luxemburg Gardens, the Pantheon, the Louvre with its pyramid entrance then under construction, and the Marais District. They also made visits outside Paris to Chartres and Amiens, sites of world famous-cathedrals.

They stored wonderful memories in their minds from this non-stop tour of Paris. They were both exhausted, but Carly, not being as fit as he, much more so. In his enthusiasm to maximize experiences, he did not realize until much later that he should have slowed the pace some.

When Pierre returned to his English-speaking world, he had to get accustomed to speaking English again. Of course, one does not lose his language in five weeks, but he was now thinking in French, and he had to pause a little to get back to the default mode. He made a quick recovery, as there was no French spoken in his world except for the brief times he visited his family.

The more he thought about these past five weeks, the more he realized how special and life-changing they were. Certainly not all of the many students who studied at the CIDEF that summer felt that way, but he felt like he had made giant steps in improving his standard French and his understanding of the French people. He knew this would not be his last visit to this wonderful country.

He got back into his usual routine of work, fitness activities, his professional association, and so on, but now he had a new interest —French movies. The Prytania Theater in uptown New Orleans specialized in screening French movies. He had been able to watch some French movies on television, but it was a lot more fun in the theater. The movies had English subtitles that gave him practice reading and listening to the language. If he didn't know a certain French word, the subtitles gave him the English meaning. An added bonus was that the subtitles helped whomever he brought with him to understand the movie. That was a good thing.

In 1989, another gift was bestowed upon Pierre. His longtime friend and cycling buddy, Salvatore, now a dean at a community college in New Orleans, called Pierre to tell him that they needed a French teacher and asked him if he wanted to teach the class. Pierre responded that he was not certified to teach French.

"You don't need to be certified," Salvatore told him, "this is a conversational course that is part of our Community Education Program."

Pierre thought he might be able to do that. "What are the hours?" he asked.

"You would meet for three hours, once a week for one semester," his friend explained.

"Yeah, Okay," Pierre said, "I'll give it a shot."

After he hung up, he thought, "What am I doing? How am I going to work this into my already overwhelming schedule?" He knew this would involve more than three hours per week. There was a two-hour round trip drive time through New Orleans for each class. Then there was the prep time and a syllabus to make. Student materials had to be made and duplicated. On and on.

He had the first meeting with the class and was amazed with the caliber of his students who were mostly professional people. He felt good about these people wanting to learn French, which in a way, validated his efforts to perfect his own French. Some were there to prepare for a French vacation; some had Cajun ancestry and remembered parents or grandparents speaking French. One lady taught Cajun dancing and wanted to learn the language. Some had already been to France and now wanted to learn its language as well.

Pierre got into the routine of teaching his class. He was enthused and put his energy into it. He taught standing up for the whole session except for a ten-minute break at the midpoint that he often spent with the students. He taught a lot more than the French language. He also taught French culture as well as coping skills for touristic situations in France. They learned the many details necessary to maximize enjoyment during a trip to France. He used many of the techniques he had learned at the CIDEF in teaching his students. Most importantly, he strived to erase the stereotypical images that many Americans had about France and its people.

There were many times when, tired from a long day's work and his daily activities, he felt like he could not possibly give the class and students justice. But, when he faced the class, it was like pushing a button which propelled him into his usual energetic self. He understood the expression, "the show must go on." But when he got home at 10:00 PM, he was totally drained.

Learning was not a one-way street. He learned a great deal from his students. One of his students who had just returned from France gave him a cassette of one of France's most popular singers, Francis Cabrel. The student had first heard Cabrel while riding in a taxi and just had to have his music. Pierre played the cassette at home and was immensely impressed. It was so much more than music. It was poetry with themes such as social justice, minorities, animal rights, environment, and of course, love. Francis's vocals were so clear and easy to understand that he began to use them as instructional materials for his classes. He anxiously awaited every new album he recorded. Unfortunately, he only recorded about every five years, but Pierre would eventually own everything Francis ever did. If he could have had dinner with any person in the world, it would have been Francis Cabrel.

Teaching the class helped Pierre to maintain and improve his own grammar. There are few methods of learning more effective than teaching what is desired to be learned. This was the most enjoyable job he had ever had, and he would do it for about ten more years until he moved away from New Orleans.

The new decade of the 90's brought Pierre new experiences and opportunities. In August of 1992, Pierre finally visited Nova Scotia. Like most Cajuns, he had long wanted to visit the source of his Acadian ancestors. From his genealogy hobby, he had learned several years ago that Nova Scotia was the link between France and Louisiana.

He and Carly flew to Bangor, Maine and rented a car to drive to Nova Scotia. It was a scenic drive through hilly forests, small towns, and finally Nova Scotia with its endless coastal vistas and forested interior. At first, Pierre was disappointed that they had not met Acadians or French speakers after several encounters with the natives. He thought that because his ancestors came from there, and the nearness of the francophone province of Quebec, there would be many French speakers. He should have known better, because after the Acadian's expulsion from Nova Scotia in the 18th century, their fertile lands almost immediately became populated with British subjects. The few French speakers still there were found mostly in Eastern Nova Scotia.

They had a nice experience at a lobster house on the Bay of Fundy. They chose a huge, live lobster which was expertly prepared along with the obligatory reduced butter and sides of potatoes and coleslaw. They enjoyed their feast on a picnic table as they watched the highest tide in the world almost race up the coast line with each lapping wave a little higher than the previous one.

For Pierre, the most moving moments came during their visit to the Grand-Pré National Park which commemorates the settlement and expulsion of the Acadians during the 18th century. In the museums nearby, he saw the many excavated artifacts of the exiled Acadians, such as pieces of broken plates and cups, clay pipe stems, tools, and other household items. He wondered if some of his mother's ancestors had owned some of these items before they became relics.

In front of the rebuilt church was the statue of Evangeline inspired by Longfellow and designed by a sculptor from Quebec in 1920. The statue depicts Evangeline crying for her lost land. Pierre walked slowly around the sculpture to observe the changes in her face. One side is the face of a young Evangeline full of hope while the other side is one of an older woman saddened by the tragic deportations. Tears came to his eyes. Carly did not notice his tears; his sunglasses kept his emotions private.

They walked around the park and could see the spot marked by an iron cross from which the actual deportations took place. He envisioned a large number of Acadian families with their few pitiful possessions being herded onto small boats to board ships for the journeys to the British colonies, England, and France. He could only imagine the hopelessness and fear they must have felt. Their homes would be burned and most would never see their beloved Acadie again.

Despite not having an opportunity to meet his distant cousins and speak French, Pierre was richly rewarded. Now, the deportation was not just a little piece of history or an abstraction, but an event which occurred 227 years before that would remain with him as long as he lived.

In 1993, a great opportunity came about, but with it, also tons of additional work. The state adult education association met and voted to sponsor an adult literacy national convention in New Orleans. The state association had sponsored a national convention about ten years previously with some success. The biggest obstacle was to have someone assume the responsibility of chairing the convention. No shoulders were disjointed from hands rocketing up into the air to volunteer for the job. Several were asked but each had a multitude of reasons not to do it. Then, Dr. Sam Dauzat, who had worked on a past national convention, asked Pierre if he would chair the convention.

Pierre didn't know what to say. He and Sam had been close friends and fellow board members for the past sixteen years. He was honored to be asked as it indicated Sam had confidence in his abilities. He thought about his already busy schedule. He remembered how much work the state convention he had chaired before his presidency required. No way could he chair a national convention with a staff of only two people.

"I don't know if I can," Pierre said. "I have a very heavy schedule already, plus, I don't know anything about national conventions."

"The board will be helping you," Dr. Dauzat responded.

He just didn't think he could juggle it all. "No, I'm sorry, it's just too much for me to handle."

"How about if you and I co-chair?"

He was done for. He just couldn't turn it down anymore. "Well, Okay, I'll do it," he responded less than enthusiastically.

Everyone else on the board released a sigh of relief—they were off the hook. Sam and Pierre were now on the hook. The work needed to bring this project to fruition was unimaginable, but they would get a lot of help from the board and adult education personnel from throughout the state.

The convention was held in June of 1993 at the Fairmont Hotel in New Orleans (now the Roosevelt). It was a huge success and was one of the best-attended adult basic education conventions ever held and the most fun, too. The entire convention boarded the steamboat *Natchez* for a tour of the Mississippi. There was gumbo, crawfish étouffée, red beans and rice, jazz and appropriate libations for all participants. During the convention, training sessions by the foremost authorities from across the United States were presented to the entire Louisiana adult education staff and other attendees from most states across the United States.

As a result of the convention's success, Pierre and Sam were asked to present training sessions on convention planning to other state adult education associations who were to host the future national conventions. They were well received, and their methods earned similar success in several states.

For Pierre, this was probably the crowning achievement of his professional career, feeling as he now did that he could do anything he set his mind to do. In addition to playing an important role in the convention's success, he later made several professional presentations at national conventions throughout the United States. He was very grateful to Dr. Sam for having conned him into this endeavor.

In 1994, Pierre's university, the University of Southwestern Louisiana, put together a group excursion for its alumni to go to the first *Congrès mondial acadien* (World Acadian Congress) in New Brunswick, Canada. New Brunswick hosted the reunion, and thousands of Acadian descendants from Maine, Canada, France, and Louisiana were expected to attend. There would be family reunions, dances, tours, seminars, and meetings with the locals. After not meeting any Acadians in Nova Scotia in 1992, Pierre looked forward to this excursion.

The reunion would be a double reunion for Pierre. First, he would get to meet and talk with his fellow Cajuns from Southwest Louisiana. Since he moved to the New Orleans Metro area, twenty-nine years ago, he had had very little contact with other Cajuns except for his family. During the many hours of conversation with his fellow travelers, he found it remarkable how similar their lives had been. Like Pierre, many spoke French as a first language and shared the same experiences and emotional consequences.

The second reunion was, of course, with the descendants of the Acadians who managed not to be expelled by the British in 1755 from maritime Canada, and also with those whose ancestors were dispersed throughout the world. It was amazing how many similarities there were between the New Brunswick Acadians and the Louisiana Cajuns, despite having been separated over two hundred years ago. Doppelgangers abounded—there was an uncanny resemblance between many of the two groups of long-separated relatives. Their French was remarkably similar, and they could easily converse. The New Brunswickers told Pierre how their ancestors had escaped the British by hiding in the woods with the help from the local Indians. A big difference between the two groups was that they had a choice of attending French or English language schools.

The Acadian cuisine, however, had few similarities with its Cajun counterpart, being rather bland for Cajun tastes. The differences were caused by the multicultural influences which altered the original cuisine that the Acadians brought with them to Louisiana. The Spanish, Africans, Germans, and Indians all had an influence on Cajun cuisine. But in spite of these differences, Pierre did not go hungry. The abundance of lobsters, scallops, mussels, and fish more than eased his hunger pangs.

During the Congrès, Pierre attended a family reunion of his mother's relatives, the Comeau family, where there was an abundance of genealogical information available. He discovered that his ancestor, Pierre Comeau, came to Nova Scotia from the Dijon area of France in 1632, and is the ancestor of all the Comeau's in North America. His relatives have been traced back to the 14th century. Pierre even got a photo of this first immigrant's home. Surprisingly, the home was substantial, like a small castle. He wondered why a man would leave such a home to come to the New World to live a hard, impoverished life. Perhaps the alternative was worse.

One of the activities Pierre attended was an outdoor concert of Acadian folk and rock music. The weather was perfect, and the attendance was high—in the thousands. While there, Pierre enjoyed speaking to many Acadians as well as some of his fellow Cajuns. It felt wonderful being there. All of a sudden, a thought occurred to him out of nowhere. He realized that this was his first time being in a large crowd where he was not in the minority. It gave him a certain warm feeling, perhaps because he did not have the feeling of being something "other" as he often did in other large crowds. The feeling of "otherness" was not a negative one—just a difference. He did not mind his differences, he embraced them. Could it have been the commonality of historical experiences they shared, such as their ancestors being uprooted and, like butterflies, cast to the mercy of the four winds? Or was it his subconscious mind resurrecting old feelings from the parallel world he lived in long ago where only French was spoken? Pierre was definitely not xenophobic as he was comfortable in any setting or among any people. But still, there were those feelings. He wondered if others experienced the same feeling. He regretted not asking.

While Pierre and the thousands of other Acadians from the world over were enjoying the many activities of reconnecting with their long-lost cousins and enjoying the Retrouvailles 1994, most were not aware that the British Crown was being petitioned by Cajun attorney Warren Perrin. Warren, the leader of Pierre's group, began the Petition in 1990 in order to to obtain an apology for the Acadian Deportation from the British Crown. If Las Vegas had given odds on this endeavor, it would have been a million to one against him. But the more he researched legal and historical records, the more he was convinced that the issue had to be addressed. Consequently, Perrin drafted a Petition requesting the following 1) restitution of the status of "French neutrals," 2) an inquiry into the Deportation, 3) an official end to the Acadian exile by annulling the Order of Deportation, 4) an acknowledgement that tragedies occurred that were contrary to existing law, and 5) a symbolic gesture to memorialize the end of the exile. He would persist in his efforts for 13 years, gaining support from many quarters, and ultimately, on December 9, 2003, Queen Elizabeth II's representative would sign the Royal Proclamation acknowledging the wrongs committed against the Acadian people in the name of the Crown, and would establish a "Day of Commemoration" to be observed on July 28th of each year.

The quest for the Petition added another dimension to the reunion for Pierre and the others aware of Warren's efforts. When they got together, they were apprised of the status of the Petition. These were exciting times! Certainly, every Cajun was hopeful, but cruel logic invaded their minds with reality—this was like David fighting Goliath without a sling shot. But sometimes, a miracle happens, and this time it would.

In the late summer of 1994, Pierre and Salvatore had just completed a fifty-mile bike ride in the hills of North St. Tammany. They were next to Sal's garage toweling off sweat and loading up Pierre's bike when the phone rang. Sal went into the garage to answer it, and Pierre continued tying down his bike. After his phone conversation, Sal came out and said, "That was one of my former classmates at USM. Do you want to go out with her?"

Pierre was taken aback by this out of the blue question as he was still recuperating from a mutual parting with Carly six weeks earlier. Additionally, Sal was three years older than he, and a female classmate of his could well look matronly. So, having over a half century of maturity, Pierre asked, "What does she look like?"

Sal said, "Well, I don't know, her name is Freddie, and I haven't seen her in several years, but she's coming to New Orleans in a couple of weeks for a football game."

"Could you meet with her then and give me more information?"

Sal had his meeting with Freddie and called Pierre to give his report. Pierre was anxious to get some information about this "mysterious" woman. Pierre asked, "What did you find out? What does she look like?"

In a nonchalant tone, he said, "She looks all right."

Two things Pierre really liked about Sal—his verbosity and copious use of adjectives.

Nevertheless, a date was set for Freddie and Pierre to meet at Sal and Rosalind's home in October.

Pierre joined Sal and Rosalind at the appointed time, and Freddie had not arrived yet. They chatted and had a drink and snacks while waiting. About thirty minutes later headlights lit up the long driveway. The driver rang the doorbell. Sal opened the door, and Freddie walked in, greeted Sal and Rosalind, and to Pierre, she said, "Hi, I'm Freddie and I'm pleased to meet you!" Pierre was also pleased to meet her—she was not matronly at all!

The foursome went on to dinner at an Italian restaurant where Pierre and Freddie would learn more about each other. He found out she was originally from Birmingham, Alabama and graduated from USM (University of Southern Mississippi). Uncharacteristically, for a woman, she was a rabid football fan, which was what brought her to New Orleans to watch her alma mater play. She was presently living and working in Nashville, and by coincidence, Pierre had a convention there in November. The odds of them meeting had to be at least a million to one.

They later met in Nashville where they had lunch and dinner, visited the touristic sites, including the Parthenon, and spent time with two of her closest friends. They later met for the Christmas holidays when Pierre was introduced to her parents and her two children, Scott and Lisa, both graduates of USM as well. As they say, the rest is history.

In the winter of 1995, Pierre met with a group of Cajuns who were laying the groundwork to host the World Acadian Reunion Congress in Lafayette scheduled for 1999. Many of those attending had been on last year's excursion to New Brunswick, and there were several others he met for the first time. Surprisingly, he also reunited with an old friend, Glen, (the "Little Greek God,") with whom he had worked out in college. It had been almost 30 years since they had seen each other, and they quickly caught up on what had transpired in their lives over the past 30 years. During the evening fish fry outdoors in very cold weather, several men and women had an informal discussion on what the effects of the expulsion from Nova Scotia by the English were on the Cajun culture. There were many theories and opinions expressed which were totally new to Pierre. He had not been aware of the cultural passion going on in his native region.

Several interesting questions were posed during the evening. What would the Acadian culture be like today if it had not been uprooted and dispersed throughout the world? Would the culture be better off today or less so? Did the Cajun culture in Louisiana continue, until modern times, to be adversely affected by the trauma of expulsion? There were many interesting opinions expressed in this lively exchange, but unfortunately, no definitive answers. One man opined that the Cajuns were a damaged people. Pierre had never heard of such a concept before, and it did not resonate with him at that time. He never considered himself to be "damaged," but he would never forget the concept. Much later he would begin to wonder if perhaps the slow assimilation of many Cajuns into mainstream American life was due, at least in part, to this damage. Was he damaged, he wondered? Interesting questions with no definitive answers, except, perhaps depending on whoever was asked about Pierre's damage.

It would be 1996 before Pierre would get back to France again, and the planning for that trip began in a most surprising manner and setting. He and Sam were at a convention in Kansas City, Missouri and visiting a nearby museum. Some of the exhibits reminded Pierre of the visits he had made in Paris. He mentioned to Sam that perhaps they should visit Paris together. Sam, not having been to Paris yet, liked the idea. They talked about it some more and made plans to make the trip the following summer. Pierre, Sam, Jo Ann and Freddie departed for Paris in August for their much-anticipated vacation. Pierre, not having been to France in over nine years, just couldn't wait to put into practice his improved language skills and relive his wonderful visits of years past. Sam, Jo Ann and Freddie were eager to get to France to see if it was indeed the cornucopia of wonders Pierre had been raving about. When they circled Paris to land, they got wonderful views of the city which heightened their anticipation to get there and start exploring. They landed, went through customs and hired a taxi to take them to the hotel. Pierre had made reservations in the same hotel he had used in 1987. They were pleased with their rooms, and he noticed there had been some remodeling done since he had been there.

Not wanting to waste time, they immediately put up the luggage and went out to tour the surrounding area. They would be in Paris for a week, and there was so much to see and do. Pierre led them to Les Invalides and all the nearby sites he had visited the last time he was there. For a partial first day, they had already seen a great deal.

They would be in constant motion for the rest of the vacation. Pierre knew how to get everywhere quickly with the metro. He felt like a professional tour guide. They had many memorable moments. One was getting sore leg muscles after climbing the tower to see the bells of Notre Dame and the spectacular views of Paris, in addition to getting up close and personal with the gargoyles. Their legs would remain sore for the remainder of the vacation—especially after they walked up the steps to see Sacré Coeur at Montmartre. Strange, Pierre didn't remember getting sore legs the last time he did these things nine years ago.

The visit to Versailles ended up being like a death march due to the amount of walking they did. They began by touring the Chateau of Versailles, which involved going up and down stairs in addition to a lot of standing up, to say nothing of walking. Pierre's tourists were impressed with the art and opulence of Louis XIV's whims. Then they were astonished by the formal gardens and fountains of the Chateau. They had all seen pictures of these iconic gardens, but to be there in person left them breathless. They walked to the rear of the Chateau and on to its forests and canals that stretched almost to the horizon. They visited the Petit and Grand Trianon. Louis XIV had built le Grand Trianon for himself and Madame de Montespan, his mistress. Le Petit Trianon, also built by Louis XIV, was where he and Madame de Pompadour and Madame du Barry had their liaisons. Le Petit Trianon is reputed to have a beautiful chapel—rather incongruous on the premises of their trysts, but perhaps convenient for prayers of contrition. While the Trianons were indeed impressive, Pierre's companions were most impressed with Marie Antoinette's whimsical little hamlet where she could pretend to live a simpler life. It was such a peaceful, humble setting in the midst of opulence and grandeur.

Reaching the most distant corner of Versailles, fatigue, like a thief in the night, snatched the spring from their legs. Even Pierre, who was in good physical condition from countless miles of cycling, was just concentrating on putting one foot in front of the other to simulate walking. When a jogger effortlessly ran past them, he remarked to himself, "How can he do that?"

As the death march continued back towards the chateau, they talked about how they should have rented bikes to get around. At that moment, riding a bike seemed like fun compared to walking. Several thousand slow steps later, they got to a bike rental stand where they each rented a bike. These bikes were not like Pierre's aluminum racing bike. They were old, heavy, and in disrepair. A Frenchman in front of them renting a bike called his rental a "P. O.S." Pierre agreed.

Despite the lack of quality transportation, they took off on their rusty, squeaky, warp-wheeled mounts. Freddie, Sam, and Jo Ann, not having cycled for years, did the obligatory weaving and wobbling for the first several yards before finally stabilizing. Pierre felt good being on a bike despite this one being a clunker. After activating his cycling muscles, he moved about down the path effortlessly. They giggled out of sheer joy like children as they rode around the grounds.

Every time they had dinner, it was an interesting experience. First, the group had to select a restaurant agreeable to everyone. This was done by reading the outdoor menu of several restaurants and, eventually, something would click for everyone. One evening, after completing this process, they selected a restaurant on rue Lombard near the Marais section of the city. They walked into what appeared to be a small restaurant. The waiter asked them if they would like to sit downstairs and, upon their agreement, were led down some old stone steps. A huge dining room practically full of patrons suddenly came into focus. From the base of the stairs, they looked up and saw a beautiful, vaulted ceiling. The waiter explained that this had once been a chapel built in the Middle Ages as a resting place for pilgrims on the route of St. James of Compostela, Spain.

They were taken to a table, seated, and given menus. The table was beautifully laid out, and the menu had many choices. As usual, Sam had a difficult time making a choice, but once everyone had decided, they began to notice more details, one being that all the waiters and chef were Chinese, but the menu was French. Pierre had a similar experience in San Francisco, and that had been one of the most memorable meals he had ever had. The exquisitely done orders came and immediately excited their gastric juices. Freddie and Jo Ann had salmon mousse, while Pierre had duck confit with potatoes cooked in the duck fat, one of his favorite dishes in France. Sam had a beef and potato dish and veggies. For dessert, Freddie and Jo Ann had chocolate mousse which was light as a feather and wonderful. Pierre and Sam had crème brulé, the best they had in Paris. What a gastronomical event in a most unlikely place. They got the check and again were pleasantly surprised—it was reasonable. They walked up the stairs to street level and then went underground again to take the metro back home. They felt like fat moles.

They enjoyed their little hotel and its excellent location near the Les Invalides. Each morning they came downstairs for breakfast (*le petit déjeuner*) and were greeted with strong coffee, fresh croissants, and fresh bread. The multilayered croissants, fused with butter, crispy on the outside and tender on the inside, were very satisfying. There were multiple varieties of preserves and butter to enhance the bread and croissants. To Pierre, not a ham and eggs person, this was the perfect breakfast.

Pierre and Freddie's room had a special bonus. When they opened the shutters, the window frame transformed into a picture frame for the gold dome over Napoleon's tomb at Les Invalides. The dome had been recently refreshed and gilded, and it appeared almost close enough to reach out and touch. An unforgettable view.

While visiting the left bank, they accidently discovered the Cluny Museum, a national museum of medieval arts and crafts. It was a wonderful accident. The Cluny is best known for its excellent collection of ancient tapestries. Pierre liked the way that tapestry provided him with another window into the past, and here they discovered some of the most famous ones, those most often pictured in art and history books. "The Lady and the Unicorn" tapestries were the most impressive to Pierre and Freddie. This set depicting the five senses were woven around the fifteenth century. The Cluny also had a collection of Roman antiquities, the remains of a Roman bath, and statues, carvings and relics of the Middle Ages. Truly a must see.

By the time they boarded the plane to return to Louisiana, they had seen and visited most of the major attractions in Paris. It had been a busy week of almost constant motion. They were thankful for the wonderful Paris Metro system that had made it all possible. Pierre was very happy to have introduced Freddie, Sam, and Jo Ann to his Paris. Now they would be able to share their memories of this unique experience for a lifetime.

Among all the glorious experiences Pierre had in the 90's, there was a very regrettable one. His close friendship of 36 years with Don came to an end in 1996. After they graduated from USL in 1965, they had remained close friends. Don had married his last year of college and Pierre was his best man. Don became a farmer and owner of grain elevators. He and his wife had five boys. When Pierre visited his family, he often spent more time with Don than with his own family. They would do a lot of hunting and fishing, playing pool for hours on end, and in the latter years, a lot of conversation. Then, they began to drift apart. There were no arguments or hard feelings, they just increasingly lacked commonality. Their lives were just so different. The last several visits were unrewarding and Pierre would leave with a hollow feeling. Finally, Pierre realized this relationship was over and he would not visit

Don again. Don never contacted him afterwards. Pierre was disappointed, and would always regret the ending of this long friendship. Without Don, Pierre almost definitely would not have gone to college—he cringed at the very thought of his life without college and Don.

He was now close to his retirement date. Thanks to an early start, he would still be a relatively young man at retirement. Additionally, he still had an abundance of energy and drive. He was still cycling 100 miles a week and completing three gym workouts a week; at work, he was as productive as ever. He had begun some time ago to plan what he would do after retirement. He and Freddie wanted to buy another home and do extensive traveling. He also wanted to continue working in some other capacity. He would not give up work at such an early age. He was not a "burnt-out" educator.

The last two years of his public school career were very busy. In addition to his regular responsibilities, he and Freddie were spending time looking for that new place they would call home for the foreseeable future. Their criteria were simple. Pierre wanted easy access to good safe roads for cycling. Freddie wanted a nice house in a nice neighborhood. After reviewing the whole New Orleans Metro area, they chose to concentrate on the North Shore of Lake Pontchartrain, which had a very good bike path. His friend Sal had moved there earlier, and Pierre knew the area quite well.

He also continued to prepare for the extensive traveling they were going to do. He had started this process several years before by reading his French magazines and newsletters and doing internet research. He had already learned where he wanted to go and how he was going to do it. His four trips to France were not enough; he now wanted more to live in France rather than to tour France. Freddie was very supportive of his plans.

In 1998, during the second semester of his last year, they had narrowed the search for their new home on the North Shore. After viewing dozens of houses, they found one which they both agreed on. It was a French provincial-style home (how appropriate) in a nice, quiet neighborhood with a bike path two blocks away. Freddie told their friends, "If left up to him, the house could have been a shack, but he still would have chosen it to be near the bike path."

He was also spending time looking for a new job, which after thirty-three years, was a strange experience. He wanted to teach high school students in a private school. He sent out many applications to various private schools in the metro area, but he got no suitable offers. By coincidence, Salvatore was just appointed principal of a private school and asked him if he would be his vice principal and counselor. The school was a fifty-minute drive from their new home—that was forty-five minutes more than he drove currently. They were such close friends that he could not just say "no." He agreed to take a look at the school. He saw that it would be a big job, but he told Sal he would try it for a year or so. He would spend sixteen years there. He still had not learned how to quit.

With the final school year over, there was still much to do. His last state convention was in New Orleans and one of his good friends, Bobby, the one who had asked him to do his first teacher training presentation, was now a book sales rep, and sponsored Pierre's retirement dinner at Tujaques in New Orleans' French Quarter. He was appreciative that many of his friends from throughout the state that he had worked with over the past twenty-five years were in attendance.

With the help of Bertha, Charles, and his nephew Daniel, they moved their belongings to the North Shore in August. They had only been there a few days when Pierre noticed something strange. Besides them, no one was moving about in the neighborhood. In their old neighborhood, there were always people moving out and about. Pierre told Freddie, "You know, this is eerie, we may be the only people living here. All these beautiful homes may be mere facades propped up by 2x4s in the rear."

She responded, "Could it be that it's August and people in their right minds stay inside?" They were kidding again. The people in this neighborhood were much more affluent than those around their previous home.

He started his job with the private school, Oak Forest Academy, which was fifty miles away from their home. It was a lot of work at the beginning because the previous administration had left the school in a less than well-functioning state, and also because of his lack of experience working in a private school. Once he got organized, and with the help of the office staff and Salvatore, he got on track with the job for which he was hired.

He really enjoyed working with the students, who for the most part, were very well-supported by their parents. Even the seventh and eighth graders were more manageable; they seemed less afflicted with the adolescent pox than he and his classmates had been. Certainly, students still had to bridge that obstacle between childhood and adolescence, but these students and their parents were so much better equipped to meet that challenge.

For an educator, it was an idyllic situation. At least eighty percent of the graduates were college-bound, and teachers never feared for their safety in that school. Pierre would have a world of fond memories from the sixteen years he worked there, and each summer, he and Freddie would carry out their plans to travel to France.

CHAPTER 14
LIVING IN FRANCE

"Every man has two countries: his own and France."

Thomas Jefferson

PIERRE and Freddie began to organize their plans for their summer vacation travels. Their goal was to live in France for three to four weeks each summer and eventually to experience every region of France. International travel is not inexpensive, but Pierre had learned techniques to minimize expenses. Food and lodging were the most expensive components of travel. Two concepts helped to reduce these costs. One was to rent a *gite*, which was a fully-equipped house, usually rurally located, but sometimes found in small towns and some cities. Depending on the area and the size of the gite, one could be rented for fifty to seventy dollars per day.

The other possibility for reducing lodging expenses is to do a home exchange with a family from the country to be visited. Often, cars are also exchanged. This arrangement provides free housing and free transportation—a tremendous saving over a three week period. Additionally, both the gite and the home exchange provide the possibility of doing breakfast and dinner at home at a greatly reduced cost. Exchangers should enjoy lunch at restaurants to experience the local cuisine—a must do.

The above would provide them with a true experience of living in France. They would have a home they returned to each evening, a car for daily excursions, neighbors with whom they might speak and socialize, and a place to just "be." Each summer, Pierre and Freddie would accumulate more and more unique experiences which would enrich their lives forever.

Summer, 1999, a Gite Near the Loire Valley

Thursday, June 17. While Pierre, Freddie, and the denizens of Selles, France were still in deep slumber, strange vehicles, alone and in caravans, were illuminating the roadways while en route to Selles and hundreds of other towns and cities throughout France. They crept into town practically unseen and unheard and arrived in the town center just as they had always done last week, last year, and decades ago. Their forebearers had been doing this since the Middle Ages.

Once on location, a flurry of silent activity began. The strange vehicles became even more bizarre as they transformed into shelters, display counters, and tents. Almost like magic, a town within a town popped up on the cobblestone streets and empty parking lots like mushrooms after a summer rain in Louisiana. From the vehicles, figures extracted practically anything anyone could want and placed it on display for the arrival of the still sleeping inhabitants of the town.

By 8:00, the awakened shoppers with bags and carts appeared by the hundreds or thousands to visit this overnight wonder. They were greeted with huge selections of fish, bread, cheeses, vegetables, wine, olives, fruits, rotisserie chicken, fresh paella, and practically anything edible. Choices were not limited to food, with clothing, shoes, hardware, house wares, mattresses, tools, and much more in evidence.

It was market day once more, just like any market day since the Middle Ages. Despite the onslaught of the huge chain supermarkets and fast foods, market day is alive and thriving in France. The market merchants offer, often at a better price, the freshest seafood, meats, cheeses, poultry, and produce available. As the same merchants come to town week after week, they and the shoppers have a personal relationship.

Shopping is not the only activity going on at market day as it is also a time for socialization. Friends and relatives often meet and exchange greetings and family news. Many have their usually unneutered dogs along for a walk. Invariably, there are tourists mixed in among the shoppers taking pictures and enjoying the ambiance of the market. Nearby restaurants and businesses also profit from the hordes of people the markets brings out.

The market lasts until around noon. The crowds go home with their purchases or linger with friends. Some tourists have lunch or go on to their next destinations. The merchants, with great efficiency, take down the tents, load up unsold merchandise and drive out of town. The street and parking lots now hold only a memory of what was a reality for a few hours, and, like an apparition, it just disappeared—until next week.

Pierre and Freddie loved their first market visit. He, because he loved to cook and imagined what he would do with the wonderful selection of meats, fish and produce, and she because of other unusual shopping opportunities. Pierre was excited when he saw the fresh seafood, farm grown chickens, ducks, rabbits, thinking how much he would enjoy cooking in France. He imagined buying something, running home, and cooking it right away. Unfortunately, that was not possible this time because the logistics were not right—they had already planned an outing for the afternoon. They did buy some paella, three types of cheeses, and olives to take back to the gite. The olive merchant had dozens of types of olives from France and the Mediterranean world. They saw black and green olives flavored with garlic, rosemary, onions, herbs and spices. The cheese merchant had an infinite variety of cheeses, some of which were in the form of huge, tire-like round disks weighing 40 or 50 pounds. Charles De Gaulle, often frustrated with the populace during his presidency, had asked, "How can you rule a country that has 246 varieties of cheese?" It seemed to Pierre that De Gaulle's estimate was too conservative as he felt there were more cheeses than that. He tasted many varieties before buying some. The secret of the great tasting cheeses was that they were made with non-pasteurized milk that allowed them to age, producing their distinctive flavors. The vendor usually provides a time frame in which to consume these unpasteurized cheeses—usually one to three days.

He especially regretted not being able to buy one of the chickens which were farm-grown and mature. It reminded him of the chickens his father bought from farmers and then corn fed for a couple of weeks before slaughter. These chickens were so flavorful. His father disliked supermarket fryers, calling them "little, embalmed chickens" because of their pale, white skin. However, perhaps the surviving fryers, as they paid their final respects to their loved ones, said, "They sure look good."

Summer, 2000, Provence

Already, Pierre had made several trips to France, including to Paris, the Loire Valley, Normandy, and Brittany. Then he read *A Year in Provence* (twice), in addition to everything else Peter Mayle had written, and also saw the movie. He saw Claude Berri's *Jean de Florette* (twice) and *Manon des Source* (twice) and quite naturally, a trip to Provence became obligatory. His mind was completely captivated with images of hilltop villages, purple fields of lavender, indigo and turquoise seas, and the beautiful light as painted by artists such as Van Gogh and Cézanne.

They got to Salon, close to Aix-en-Provence, around five o'clock and found their gite without too much trouble, considering they had to negotiate what felt like a thousand roundabouts. The owner, Madame Roussell, was waiting for them. She was sixtyish and very delightful. As her English was minimal, she was thrilled that Pierre could speak French so well. Then she showed them their gite. Their jaws dropped. It was nothing like they had expected —it was ten times better. The gite was one huge 78 by 36 foot room with vaulted ceilings—about 2,800 square feet—the size of an above average home. It was a former olive oil press built in the early 1700's. There was still an ancient olive press in the wall. It had a well-equipped kitchen, antique furniture, tiled floors, bathroom, TV, phone, bedroom area, living room area, and a dining room area. It was simply awesome, and all this for $46 per night. Additionally, there was a garage to park the car. What a deal!

In the front was a large yard filled with lavender, roses, fig trees, verbena, geraniums, passion flowers, trumpet vines, and large potted plants. Near the gite were huge, ancient olive jars containing large plants. There were gardens filled with different herbs such as thyme, rosemary, and basil, and other plants they could not identify. How lucky they were to find a place like this. It would be their home for two weeks.

A few days later when preparing for the excursion of the day, they were concerned about the threat of a *mistral*. Mistral winds can reach hurricane velocity. He asked Madame Roussell, who was in her garage, if she had seen the weather news, and if this wind was a mistral. She said that she had seen the weather and that this was not a mistral because when the mistral blows, the skies are always clear. She said the weather would be fine with no rain and that it would be safe to travel. Then she told Pierre she wanted to give him something because she and her husband had just sold the property —the house and the gites. She felt that the moving process would inconvenience them, and wanted to give them something to make up for this. He told her they were not inconvenienced and would continue with their original plans. She then led Pierre into her wine cellar and said, "You like Bordeaux wine, I have a bottle I want to give you." She picked out a bottle of 1987 St. Emilion (a great red wine) and gave it to him. A thick coating of dust covered the bottle from being cellared for so long. He wiped some dust off and read the label, seeing what a nice gift this was. He thanked her and again told her that she didn't have to do this, but she insisted. Pierre thought how coincidental it was that 19 years earlier in Belgium, a lady had given him a bottle of red wine—also a St. Emilion.

From this uniquely historical gite, they realized many of their travel dreams. There were the many hilltop villages which taxed their legs but provided vast panoramic views of this sunny region of France. They visited excavated Roman cities and monuments. Of course Pierre knew about the Roman presence in France, but he didn't realize how pervasive it was. There were several market days— all enjoyable. They got their first view of the Mediterranean Sea —how captivated they were by these waters of striking shades of blue. Then there was the food spiced with onions, garlic, Herbes de Provence, and tomatoes, which was quite amenable to Cajun taste.

Some of their best experiences were the many dinners Pierre prepared after a day of touring. He used his Cajun cooking techniques and Paul Prudhomme's seasonings along with the local ingredients to produce some memorable dishes. They enjoyed their dinners outdoors overlooking the fabulous gardens of lavender, rosemary, bougainvillea, sage, and a multitude of flowers unknown to them while they basked in the perfect Mediterranean evenings. They finished with bread, three kinds of cheeses, olives, and the fabulous red wines of Provence.

They would end up visiting Provence five times.

Summer, 2001, The Pigeon Drop

After having a dream-like experience in Provence the previous year, Pierre and Freddie wanted to return to continue the dream, so they planned a home exchange with a young couple whose home was near Aix-en-Provence, and back they went. Last year, they had run out of time and had not visited Arles, a major attraction in Provence, so this would be their first excursion.

They got an early start and arrived in Arles around ten o'clock. By coincidence, they almost literally ran into Arles' remarkable Roman amphitheater. They entered the theatre for a visit. As they walked around, they thought about all the drama which had taken place on the theater floor, all the lives lost in the bloody gladiatorial contests while the blood-thirsty crowds roared their approval. They could imagine the thousands of toga-clad spectators in the seats cheering their favorite thespians or gladiators. Human life was cheap at that time, especially if one was not Roman. From trying to imagine what it was like in Roman times, they realized how much they depended on movie depictions to form their mental images.

After the amphitheater visit, they moved on and were doing the obligatory shopping nearby when they realized it was getting close to lunchtime, and a search for a suitable restaurant was in order. They began their touristic amble (a slow, mindless, irregular walk with no particular destination in mind while searching for points of interest) up a street toward the city's center where they expected to select a restaurant from several choices. As they walked, they took in everything around them—the people, the shops, the narrow streets, and especially the wonderful architecture. The French-blue skies were typically impeccable, the sun was warm, they were about to eat and drink something good, and they were in Provence. What contentment—life was good!

Then it happened. As they stopped to look up to focus on some unusual architectural details, Pierre caught, through the corner of his eye, a blur of something falling and felt something warm hit him on his right shoulder. Almost simultaneously, he detected a very foul odor. Freddie, as she shrank away from him, shouted, "Look at you, it's awful, you are covered with pigeon doo-doo!" He looked at his right shoulder and saw that his new green and white awning-striped shirt and new travel vest were liberally covered with a generous portion of a multicolored, runny, horrible-smelling liquid. He was now less than hungry. Despite having lived in New Orleans Metro for many years where pigeons abound and visiting many of the great pigeon-infested cities of Europe, this was his first avian baptism. To compound matters, this was one sick pigeon. Freddie was just standing there saying, "Ooh, ooh, ooh." Not helpful!

After overcoming the initial shock, his first thought was that he needed to find a restroom where perhaps he could clean, to some degree, his shirt and vest as soon as possible. No longer in the touristic mode, they walked up the street in search of soap and water. Freddie, like a pre-World War II Japanese bride, walked behind him. The crowds on the street seemingly parted like the Red Sea to avoid him and the atmosphere surrounding him. He felt like a leper—abandoned, and shunned by all. He wondered if Van Gogh had suffered the same ignoble treatment in the streets of Arles.

Of course, a public restroom was not to be found. Has anyone ever found a public restroom while on vacation when they needed one? Feeling hapless, and helpless, they continued walking up the street. He was thinking, "Why me? Of all the people on the street, why me? Is it because my awning-striped shirt made me an inviting target?" If this happens at or near home, solutions are readily available; however, in a foreign country, the situation is more challenging.

Then, a miracle happened. As they neared a restaurant, a waitress, recognizing his plight, came out on the street and offered to help him. Her name was Sylvie. Sylvie got some paper towels and removed most of the droppings as she muttered, "*Ces pigeons sont détestables.*" He emphatically agreed with that statement as he had wishful images of pigeons going the way of the dodo bird. He felt somewhat better as she informed him that this happened to others quite often and that if the droppings were not washed out immediately, the acids could ruin clothing. If the acids were as powerful as the scent, he could believe that. She then brought him inside the restaurant where she got a towel and hot water to further clean the violated areas of his clothing. He had never been so grateful. As Sylvie worked on his clothing, she asked him if his wife minded her cleaning his shirt and vest. He assured her that Freddie did not mind at all. Who says the French are not nice?

Relatively clean and somewhat deodorized, they decided to eat at the waitress's restaurant. Still having some remnants of paranoia, they sat down at a table under an umbrella. Freddie had a quiche, and he got a pizza and salad. They washed everything down with a bottle of chilled rosé. As he finished with an espresso, he told Freddie that Sylvie recognized a handsome, young man in distress.

She responded, "Yeah, right!" All of this in the shade of plane trees and surrounded by an ambiance that only a long history can achieve. As they departed, he left the waitress an extra big tip and thanked her profusely again. Perhaps if all of the proverbially surly garçons were replaced by waitresses, waiters in France would have a different reputation. As she walked away, he was almost certain he saw angel wings on her back. "Thanks, and bless you, Sylvie," Pierre thought.

Summer, 2002, Brittany, La Soirée

This summer, Pierre and Freddie decided to try a home exchange near the city of Rennes, and this vacation would be filled with so many rich experiences. Their hosts, Jacques, and Rachelle, who were now in their home in Louisiana, prearranged a very memorable reception, a meeting with the mayor of their town, and many introductions to friends and family. Pierre and Freddie would visit with Jacques and Rachelle several times after the exchange.

They were invited to a block party a week after their arrival in Brittany by a local fireman, Emile, from down the street. The weather was cool and threatened to rain, so they drove a block down the street to the home of Emile and Regine, the couple who was hosting the welcome dinner in their honor. They were the first to arrive and got a tour of the interior of their house, which was about 150 years old, renovated, and beautifully decorated. The yard was also well done with a variety of flowers and gorgeous plants. As they were expecting rain, they showed them the large canopy where they would be having dinner. Ordinarily, these functions were held outdoors.

The hosts then led them to Alexandre's house to have an aperitif and to take a look at his old outdoor bread oven. Alexandre also owned the old unrenovated farmhouse and land across the street from Jacques's house. To say it was not restored was an understatement. The yard was filled with junk, old and new, and the interior of the house had a dirt floor and was filled with antiques, but no modern appliances. The fact that Alexandre was a 67-year-old divorced man explained the complete lack of housekeeping efforts. Despite the lack of order and cleanliness, there was a certain amount of charm to the house.

Alexandre was a story in and of himself. At 67, he had the appearance and vivaciousness of a 50-year-old man. He was well-educated, retired from a government job, and had a wonderful sense of humor. His farm contained a menagerie of ducks, geese, peacocks (which woke Pierre up before dawn each day with their shrill calls), chickens, dogs, cows, cats, horses, and God only knows what other animals. It was as if Noah's Ark had crashed on the rocky shores of Brittany and he had issued each survivor a GPS with coordinates to Alexandre's farm.

Inside Alexandre's house, aperitifs were served. Most had a Ricard, which is a *pastis*, a French liqueur flavored with anise which is most popular in Provence. Pierre was not particularly fond of pastis but took some to be sociable. Everyone sat around and talked and joked for about an hour. There was a pail of water on the floor in which a lady rinsed her glass just after a dog walked in and drank from it. So much for sanitation.

They then went outside to see the oven in which the chicken and potatoes would be roasted. It was an oven about 200 years old which the community had shared to bake bread. The thick-walled stone structure, about eight feet in diameter, looked like an igloo. The whole community would bring their bread for baking on designated days; this was much more efficient than each family firing up an oven to bake a few loaves of bread.

The oven had been fired up much earlier in the day by lighting sticks and logs inside. When a piece of paper placed in the oven ignited, it was time to bake. The hot stones provided heat which lasted for almost 24 hours. By now, the rain had started, but Pierre and Freddie had hooded windbreakers on as they watched the men place the chicken and potatoes in the oven for baking. The men, bareheaded, were oblivious to the drizzle and made Pierre feel like a sissy.

Next, they went to Emile's house for wine and snacks. They met some of the other people who would be sharing the evening with them. One woman was an English teacher, and Jacques had told them that she spoke English well. That was good news for Freddie. All sixteen adults, sat at the table, and a few children and a handful of dogs roamed around. The first course was a terrine of rabbit—a type of paté—and *rillette*, another type of paté. Of course, there was plenty of wine to accompany every bite. Pierre and Freddie, as guests, were always served first. Their hosts were so gracious. The hostess, Regine, saw to it that Freddie was comfortable and provided her with a warm sweater when she got chilly.

Pierre then realized that this event should be filmed and photographed, but he had not brought the cameras. He excused himself and walked back home in the rain to get them. When he returned, the main course, the oven-baked chicken and potatoes, was served. Again, they were served first. The chicken was cooked to perfection. They talked and laughed more than a class of eighth graders on the last day of school before the Christmas Holidays.

Then the people began to express their personalities. There was Clément and his wife Josiane, a witty couple. Clément had shown Pierre his house nearby, and it was exquisite and quite large. They invited them to dinner sometime before they would leave. Then, there was Auguste and Ninette, the in-laws of Jacques and Rachell. Auguste was profound, very intellectual, and had fantastic story-telling abilities. Auguste and Ninette sang and acted out an old and very humorous folksong that couples sang just before marriage.

Britannic Folk Song

Auguste: Do you know what we men say about the girls from your town? We say you cause us much embarrassment. Don't put on so many airs, and be less snobbish and less critical of us boys.

Ninette: We are not going to respond to your silly accusations. Our intent is to challenge you to win our affections, but you don't know enough to know that we are worth much to you.

Auguste: Everyone knows you girls talk too much and too loud. You are the worst because you chastise your husbands until they die from scorn.

Ninette: Who are you to say such things, you pile of vagabonds who often beat your women for no reason. Without her in your house, you are hopeless. Your lack of direction requires her to tell you off night and day.

Auguste: You know the girls we are talking about. Everything they do, we know it. We can do without women if we want to. Believe us, we would do it!

Ninette: It is impossible for you to do without women because you are too loose and feeble to take care of yourselves. Fondling the bottle is your greatest fault, and you often visit houses of ill repute.

Auguste: Often, my little girls, we hear you demeaning us boys in your beautiful language. So there, my little girls, as reprisal we declare a strike on marriage in Brittany!

Ninette: We are guilty? Why do you search for us? We are reproachable? Why do you make sweet eyes at us? For you to do without women would cause you superfluous regrets. Your brain is fuzzy from too much wine, don't talk about us women anymore!

The dinner continued and Auguste invited Freddie and Pierre to dinner the following night, and he assured them that it would be calmer than the present reception. Pierre felt better with that assurance because he didn't want to stay up extremely late two nights in a row. Then there was Emile, their host, and a fireman by profession, who had an endless supply of jokes and stories to tell. He was hilarious and a good actor. Pierre now knew what firemen in France do while waiting for fires. Colette was the charming woman who made the terrine and sang folk songs for the group. Annette, the English teacher, provided Freddie with much-needed English conversation. Her husband, Edouard, was soft-spoken but very likable. He had one of the best bottles of Bordeaux Pierre had ever tasted. There was Mathieu, Colette's husband, who laughed so hard that he cried. Luc, the sharp 84-year-old man who lived across the street from their house, participated fully in the food, conversation, song, jokes, and wine. He was the neighbor who had brought them a head of fresh lettuce from his garden several times.

After the chicken, they had salad, cheese, and, of course, more wine. Bottles of fantastic Bordeaux seemed to materialize on the table out of nowhere. These wines would have been extremely costly in the US and were not cheap in France either. More songs, jokes, and merry making! At this time, Pierre asked to speak to the group and expressed his and Freddie's profound appreciation for this reception. He went on to tell them that they were especially pleased because as tourists, they seldom got the opportunity to meet the real people. Even as a French speaking person, he normally didn't get to say more than "good day" or "how much does it cost," and "the bill, please." But here, he had extensive conversations and truly got to know a lot of people. He also gave them a little background on Cajun History, its language, and the differences from standard French. Finally, He thanked everyone profusely and assured them that they would never forget this wonderful experience as it was their most enjoyable trip to France ever. There was generous applause as he sat down.

For the first time, Pierre looked at his watch and was shocked. It was almost two in the morning and it was not over yet. Out came the dessert—three types of pie. They ate and talked some more. At 3:00 AM, the reception finally ended. They had been eating and drinking for eight hours. Auguste told them that these soirées sometimes last till seven o'clock in the morning, but for Freddie and Pierre, who usually finish dinner within less than one hour, eight hours of eating was enough. After getting home, they washed up and were in bed by 3:30. They had never stayed up that late before since they had been together. What a full and exciting day. The soirée imprinted their minds with images and feelings which would follow them home and live with them for a long time. Only their exhaustion allowed sleep to arrive. They did not tour much the next day.

About two weeks later, Pierre saw Luc, their 84-year-old neighbor, walking past the house pushing his wheelbarrow. They hadn't seen him since the soirée. He was dressed in his usual blue overalls and was still quite robust despite his years. He lived across the road, to the right of their house and kept a beautiful vegetable and flower garden. He also had goats, chickens, rabbits, and perhaps some other animals. What Pierre didn't know at first was that Luc also owned the house next door to them on the left. The house had belonged to his deceased sister, and he had inherited it after her death at the age of 93 a few years ago. He also maintained a large garden there. Auguste and Ninette had told Pierre that the interior of the house, a farmhouse, had been left in its original state along with its furnishings. Pierre's interest was highly piqued because, in the thousands of miles they had driven in France, they had seen a multitude of old picturesque farmhouses. They were usually 100 to 300 years old and usually included stables next to or nearby the house. These houses are often renovated or modernized, often by English citizens, and sometimes to the point where they have lost their history.

He walked to the old farmhouse to make conversation with Luc, hoping he would invite him inside the house. Luc was in the process of cutting grass for his rabbits. Pierre asked questions about the farmhouse which Luc willingly answered. Pierre was so happy that he spoke French well because there was no way he could have profited from this opportunity if he hadn't. After a little more conversation, Luc could see his keen interest, and asked him if he wanted to see the interior of the house. Excited, Pierre responded in the affirmative. Stepping into the house was tantamount to stepping back in time. The main room, which served as a kitchen and living room, was sparsely furnished with antiques. There was a wooden table in the center, and there were two mantles filled with family pictures, from ancient, faded, black and whites to relatively recent color photos. The two huge ancient, whitewashed support beams sagged due to their age, the weight of the centuries, and the brick floor above it in the attic.

Luc, in a reverent manner, proceeded to show Pierre around. He pointed out his military picture and explained that he had been a prisoner of war for seven years in Germany. There was also a military picture of his brother, Theophile, who was killed in action in WWII. He pointed to a picture of his third brother named Klébert, who had been a Catholic missionary bishop in Africa and had died of liver cancer at the age of 71. Luc proudly showed a large oval-framed picture of his parents on their wedding day. At this moment, Pierre asked Lucien if he could go get Freddie to share in this wonderful experience, and if they could take some pictures and videos. He readily agreed, and Pierre went and got Freddie and the cameras. Unfortunately, the video camera had no battery life left.

Back with Freddie and the camera, they continued the tour. He filled Freddie in on what he had learned thus far. Luc took them to the portion of the house that had been modernized for his sister while she was in the hospital with a broken leg during the last year of her life. She never returned to her house. He explained to them that part of the structure once had housed the cows which provided warmth during the cold, damp winters of Brittany. Next, they went to the bedroom whose ceiling had much smaller timbers which also had been whitewashed. There were two large old armoires next to the walls, and a fireplace with a mantel covered with family photos. The floor was of beaten earth, and Pierre had images in his mind of a modern housewife trying to keep it clean.

Luc then took them to a room in the back of the house which was a virtual museum. It contained items necessary for farm life and life in general from the past 100 years. There were tools such as a wheat flayer, scythes, wooden pitchforks, and a small barrel which was used to store salted pork, much like Pierre's family and ancestors had used crock jars for the same purpose. They also had a crock jar which was used after the barrels to store salted meats. There were two huge chestnut barrels which once stored apple cider. He saw an old rickety, wooden ladder going up to the attic and asked permission to go up for a look. With Luc's permission, he was quickly in the attic. His first impression was that it was enormous and constructed of rough-hewn timbers. He walked to the attic over the main room and saw the brick floor which provided insulation from the cold and a surface for processing the wheat. There were also manual machines used to process wheat. This large attic reminded Pierre of the early Acadian homes in Louisiana which also had large attics—he saw the connection.

After coming down from the attic, he asked Luc if the attic was ever used for living space. He responded by telling him that the attic was used only to store wheat. Next, he showed them his WWII military great coat and the blue jacket his brother used as a missionary. They took some pictures of Luc with the coats, which captured Luc's obvious pride and reverence. They walked outside and took some more pictures of the house, the outbuildings, some large cast iron pots, and Luc. It was a little past noon, and Luc told them that he had to go home for his lunch. They expressed their appreciation as he locked up the house, and they were soon on their way to their own lunch.

What a wonderful experience right next to their house. It was better than a museum as museums are often so contrived. This house was the history of a man, his family, and his culture. How unique it was to meet and know a person who could step into a house and see his and his family's long history preserved in all the tools, pictures, clothing, and furniture. One could understand his reverent demeanor as he walked into an abode frozen in time, an abode that contained memories of childhood, parents, ancestors, siblings, farm life, and indeed a way of life that has disappeared forever. How different from modern life where the evidence of existence is quickly discarded to town dumps which prompts many to compensate with endless searches at flea markets and antique stores to buy back their past.

The house was on the market, and undoubtedly someone would buy it. When these homes are sold, the contents are often sold with the house. He hoped that the new owner would understand and preserve the memory and the memorabilia of well-lived lives.

Summer, 2005, Provence, Veronique

The destination for the day was a town in Provence famous for its fountains. Reputedly, there were over 40 fountains dispersed throughout the town, and originally they were fed by natural springs and provided water for the townspeople. Until World War II, each fountain had a local employed to maintain it. As the village grew, there was not enough natural spring water to supply the people, so city water was piped to the fountains. As advertised, they did see a lot of fountains. Most were rather utilitarian, but a few were interesting. As they ambled, they saw three ancient medieval gates, remnants of a huge protective wall which once guarded the village. The town was less touristic than many others they had visited, but its authenticity, location, and flowers made it worthy of a visit.

Then, a bizarre event occurred. They were not far from city hall when a woman asked if they were touring the town. Pierre said that they were, and he complimented her on her dog, a pretty Shih Tzu. They had a few words of conversation. The woman was about their age, well-dressed, and well-made-up. Her dog evoked fond memories of the Shih Tzu they had had the year before. She introduced herself as Veronique and told them that she had a car parked nearby and would be happy to show them around town. Pierre thanked her for the offer but told her that they had just finished touring the town and were on their way to have lunch. Then she invited them to have coffee at two o'clock with her and a friend at her house, which, she let them know, was a big house on a large estate. Pierre began thinking that it was not a good idea to visit a stranger in a foreign country. She said her house was located just outside of town. Pierre made the excuse that he could never find her house. She then invited them to take a ride in her car to her house to show them the route. They were somewhat reticent to accept but did not want to refuse. She said that she was parked nearby and reluctantly, they accepted.

They got in her car, a new Peugeot, which she said she traded in every two years, and they took off for her house. Pierre still felt it was not a good idea to get into a car with a stranger even though he felt no threat from her at the moment; after all, he could easily overpower her if necessary. Within a few minutes, they reached her home which was a gated estate of about five acres. She opened the electric gate remotely and drove into a wooded estate. She drove them down the driveway to her house, a quaint two-story home built in the 1930's. She turned around in her driveway and started to head back. Pierre asked if she could stop for him to take a picture. She said, "We can do that when you come back at two o'clock." Still uneasy, Pierre told her he didn't believe they could find her home as she had taken so many narrow unmarked roads. She said that it would not be a problem. She would return them to where she had picked them up then go back for them at two o'clock to have coffee with her and her friend at her house.

After Veronique had dropped them off in town, they looked for a restaurant. It was already 12:15, and they were ready to eat. They found a restaurant that seemed to have something both could enjoy. They sat down, and Pierre ordered *Pied et Pacquet*, an exotic dish by American standards which consists of pig's feet and tripe cooked in a regional sauce. He convinced Freddie to get a stuffed tomato, and both of these turned out to be good choices. Freddie had the most excellent green beans and cooked vegetables with her meal. He had a salad and potatoes with his. As they ate, they talked about how unusual it was to be invited to a home by a total stranger, especially in France. The French usually do not invite someone into their homes unless they are family or very close friends. Veronique expressed that she enjoyed meeting new people, but there was still a little apprehension in the back of Pierre's mind. Each having eaten a large meal, they were now sleepy. They paid the bill and went back to their car. They set the seats back to snooze a little. Thirty-five minutes went by quickly, and it was almost two o'clock. They walked out in front of the city hall, and Veronique was soon there to pick them up. She took them to her car, and they reached her estate in a few minutes. The gardens around her house were almost park-like, as were the huge trees. She took them inside; their first observation was of artwork everywhere. She introduced them to her friend Claude, and to Pierre's relief, he was a very spry and alert 87-year-old with whom he immediately began to chat.

Of course, only French was spoken, and Pierre tried to keep Freddie apprised of what was being said. Naturally, Pierre spoke about who they were and a little about their backgrounds. Claude told them that he had been born on a boat in the Mediterranean Sea and first lived in Corsica. He did not have much formal education, but he had taught himself a great deal. He enjoyed geography and knew every state in the U.S. and its capital. He mentioned Baton Rouge as the capital of Louisiana, and Pierre explained to him how Baton Rouge got its name—from a pole rendered red by the Indians from skinning their game animals on it. His dialect was a bit unusual, probably due to his Corsican background, and Pierre had a little difficulty understanding him. He had made his living directing workers in the vineyards. He was the one who attended conventions on viticulture and passed on this information to the workers. He still rode a small motor scooter and was sharp mentally as he expressed and understood complex ideas.

Veronique's life was equally interesting. She had married an older man who had become her life. They had two children together and owned an art gallery in Avignon. She expressed how her husband had been everything to her. He gave her a comfortable living, introduced her to the art world, traveled all over the world, and of course, fathered her children. Then he left her for a younger woman which upset her world completely. He later died after a bout with cancer. She did see him before he died and he admitted sadly that he had made a mistake in leaving her. Pierre did not know why she would tell this story to strangers. As his wife of 20 years and mother of their two children, French law awarded her most of her late ex-husband's estate; therefore, the large property she lived on would be hers until she died, and then her children would inherit it.

They had coffee and spoke a great deal more about many topics. Then Veronique showed them part of her house. There were many valuable paintings from well-known artists. The antique furniture was also worth a fortune. She also had some of the most wonderful bronzes—some quite large. She also had some excellent watercolors which she had done herself. To protect her valuables, she had an alarm system which was connected to security people who would come if it went off.

Then she showed them the outdoors. They admired the trees, flowers, and shrubbery, and then, went in search of the deer. The property was five acres and wooded, so it took a little while to find it. When they found the deer, the dog, Jolie, chased it. It was a real comedy to see a fat little short-legged dog chase a deer. Of course, she didn't catch it, and what would she have done with it if she had? Veronique then showed them a small, eight by eight foot stone building which was a chapel. Nearby was a cherry tree loaded with cherries and they ate a few. She showed them where she kept her horse and saddle, commenting she had done some horseback riding a few years ago.

Pierre looked at his watch, and it after five o'clock already. He mentioned that they needed to get back home now. They went back into the house to get their cameras and use the bathroom. The bathroom was tiny for such a large home—one could barely close the door once in. They went back outside and took some pictures of themselves, the house, the couple, and the dog. They exchanged cards as they were on their way back to her car. When they got to town, Veronique kissed Freddie on both cheeks and said her goodbyes. She shook hands with Pierre as he expressed how much they enjoyed the afternoon. They got into their car and drove back to their gite which was a short distance away. What a unique experience despite his reticence! He had been apprehensive about the situation because of the many times he read about women leading victims to an accomplice for a robbery. Looking back, he may have been overly suspicious.

After so many visits and so much time spent in France, Pierre felt like he had achieved one of his dreams—living in France. He could never have imagined as a young man that it would happen this way. Certainly, he had been reasonably sure that he would succeed in getting there at least one time in his life, and like most tourists, visit Paris, take a few pictures, buy a few souvenirs and tell his family and friends he had seen France. Indeed, he enjoyed being a tourist and discovering the history, architecture, cuisine, wonderful climate, and wines of France, but he had needed a lot more than that.

He had needed to interact and communicate with the people. He especially enjoyed the extended conversations, discussions, and long dinners he had with them. Pierre believes the art of conversation is rapidly becoming a lost art. The French friends he spent time with usually had great conversational skills. Perhaps they had inherited some of the traditions from the French salons of the early fifteenth to the end of the eighteenth century. He found them to be often analytical with a penchant for seeking less than obvious causes, effects, answers, and solutions. Freddie often mentioned that he seemed happier when he spoke French. Perhaps. But perhaps just being on vacation makes one a little happier. Of one thing he was certain, he would not get to speak French again until the next summer vacation and felt driven to speak it as much as he could.

Ernest Hemingway famously stated that Paris was a moveable feast and that no matter where one went subsequently, Paris would follow. Pierre knew this to be true after his five visits to Paris many years ago; his psyche was indelibly etched with its images. Brittany, Provence, the Alps, Alsace, Normandy, Cote d'Azur, Picardy, Charente-Maritimes, Languedoc-Roussillon, and Aquitaine also followed him home. With a myriad of memories of these visits vividly populating his mind, the countless hours he spent in Louisiana planning these vacations, and one year of physical presence in France, he felt like he had truly lived there a long time in body and spirit. In addition to achieving his goals of mastering the English and French languages and assimilating into Cajun and American culture, Pierre received a very special bonus—he also assimilated in France!

Pierre, T-Boy, & Freddie

Freddie & Pierre in Provence

Epilogue

"The truth is that life is delicious, horrible, charming, frightful, sweet, bitter, and that is everything."

Anatole France

THEIR vacation plans for 2015 consisted of a Mediterranean cruise departing from Barcelona, Spain. They arrived in Barcelona a week before cruise departure to allow time to visit Yvette and her husband, David. Since Yvette had spent a summer with Pierre as a student in 1981, this would be their fourth reunion. They lived about four hours from Barcelona near Montaubon, France. There was no way Pierre would pass up an opportunity to visit in France being that close to the French border. Jet lagged, they picked up a rental car to begin the drive to Collioure, one of their favorite little towns in southwest France located in the region of Languedoc-Roussillon. They wanted to spend a day there to rest and recuperate before driving to Yvette and David's home.

After a two hour drive, they arrived at Collioure and found it as beautiful as ever, illuminated by some of the brightest sunshine they had ever seen in France. The little town was set on the coast of a small bay of the Mediterranean Sea and surrounded by hills covered with pastel-colored homes and businesses of pink, ochre, tan and yellow, all with red tiled roofs made famous by the artist, Matisse. Enhancing its allure were the ancient military fortifications constructed by Vauban, the foremost military engineer of the seventeenth century, a royal castle, and a lighthouse that had been converted into a church. Pierre and Freddie were not the only ones impressed with Collioure; famous writers and artists such as Henri Matisse and Pablo Picasso, in addition to hordes of tourists, had also visited there.

They checked in at their beachside hotel and went up to their second-story room. They had a balcony facing the castle and the historic town center, and beyond it, the beach and the sparkling turquoise sea. After a short rest, they walked out to tour and to have lunch. Pierre, forever nostalgic, often revisited sites and enjoyed them almost as much the second time as he had the first. Everything he loved was here—the bright clarity of light, the multicolored Mediterranean Sea, the historical setting, the perfect temperature, and last but certainly not least, his Freddie. They walked along the small beach which was well-populated with people of all types and ages fulfilling their obsessive desire for that perfect tan. Pierre, never a fan of lying on a beach for suntans, found it curious that so many loved it so much. To each his own. He did enjoy walking on the beach, beach combing, feeling the breeze, hearing the seagulls, and contemplating the power and infinity of the sea.

They continued their quarter-mile walk around the bay to the old town where the lighthouse that had been converted to a church was located. Here, not surprisingly, were many choices for restaurants.

They had not had anything but airline food during the past 24 hours and were ready to eradicate that memory with French food. They selected a little restaurant that had goat cheese salad on the menu, Freddie's link to life in France. As it was already well past noon, they each ordered a goat cheese salad and a half liter of rosé.

Sipping their rosés while waiting for their orders, they sat back and enjoyed the views of the beach, the town, and the hills in the background. Perched on top of one hill was a windmill that had probably not been operational for a hundred years or more, and on another hill were the remains of a fort that may have been there for centuries. Some might ask, "Why are these structures still there?" Pierre knew it was because France does not methodically destroy its cultural DNA. In every corner of France, rural or urban, are ruins from prehistoric times to the present which record France's history in stone. Even in the midst of a wheat or sunflower field, one often sees ancient rubble suggesting remnants of a tower or other structure. It was left there by design, not negligence, suggesting a reverence for the past. Since the nineteenth century, when Viollet-le-Duc began restoring cultural monuments, France has made concerted efforts to retain its architectural and historical treasures, which is one of the factors making France the top tourist destination in the world.

Their orders came, and the salads were large and beautifully done. While most goat cheese salads share similar ingredients, there are always differences in presentation and taste from one restaurant to another. The assortment of greens, tomatoes, olives, and ham were doused with a light, flavorful salad dressing and crowned with golden fried goat cheese rounds. Of course, as they ate, they enjoyed watching the legions of people walking up and down the street and the beach, all dressed with various degrees of exposure. They completed their lunch and did a little shopping in a nearby ceramics shop before walking back to the hotel for a much needed rest.

Though it would be a few days before they would be recovered from jet lag and fatigue, the nap was a good beginning. Afterwards, much refreshed, they went out for another walk to continue sightseeing. They found a little area they had not seen before that gave them a new perspective of this colorful little town of three thousand inhabitants, not counting tourists. They spent considerable time sitting on a bench under a tree just being there and observing life's flow in Collioure.

Around eight o'clock, they gave some thought to dinner. There was still two hours of daylight left, but they were not very hungry due to their copious late lunch. They thought about pizza and wine, a combination that never failed to please them. They began a search for a pizza shop. They found one, but wine was not served there. Who ever heard of pizza without red wine? They continued walking and searching, but could not find pizza and wine served in one place. Around nine o'clock, they settled for a little restaurant they had passed over several times while foraging. Pierre ordered steamed mussels and fries while Freddie ordered an assortment of grilled vegetables. Both were very satisfying served with the house rosé.

As they ate, they began to reminisce about the many great adventures they had experienced in France. Pierre had visited and lived in France on seventeen occasions, thirteen of those with Freddie. They had spent considerable time in most regions and had visited most major wine wine-producing areas. Despite all these visits, there was still so much they had not seen and done. Before, he had always thought they had all the time in the world to do it all. However, he had recently retired after working fifty years and was now approaching 72 years of age. He was still in excellent health, but airline travel had become such a hassle with comfort issues onboard and layovers of five or more hours having become rather common. A touch of melancholy began to creep over him as he thought this might be their last visit to France. They would just have to play it by ear.

As he thought about all the different factors and experiences that brought him to this point, he was very grateful. He felt like a pinball that had been shot into dozens of bumpers from which he had ricocheted into positive directions. He had certainly needed every bit of that help and owed so much to his friends and others who had influenced him throughout his life. One thing he knew for sure, he certainly could, but he never would, proclaim himself to be a self-made man.

Several of Pierre's longtime friends asked him how could he continue his strenuous workout routine as a "senior citizen." His response was always that, "I've done this so long that the only thing more difficult is not to do it." That's a convenient response and partially true, but he learned some time ago that his lifelong obsession with weight training was probably the result of insecurity. He felt that if he got physically bigger and stronger, he would gain more respect and confidence. He has no regrets for his lifetime of physical training—it provided him with excellent health and vitality. But whether it cured him of insecurity is another question. His theory was that insecurity is somewhat like alcoholism in that it can be controlled but not cured. His own insecurity occasionally revisited him as if it were a remnant computer cookie from a program installed and stored in his brain long ago. Insecurity may have also fueled his drives to perfect his English and French. If this is so, then he is grateful for this insecurity as it propelled him into a good education, a good living, complete bilingualism, a purposeful life, and, finally, multiple assimilations.

"Pierre!" Freddie said, "You have not talked to me for twenty minutes."

Slightly startled, he responded, "Oh, I'm sorry. I just got carried away with my thoughts."

"Thinking about your book again?" Freddie asked.

"Yeah, I guess so."

They enjoyed the last of their dinner. The mussels were fresh and well done, and so were Freddie's grilled veggies. They had an enjoyable conversation with the waiter who was very pleasant. He spoke English well, so Freddie could join in the conversation. They paid the waiter and began their short walk back to the hotel.

By now, it was well past 10:00 PM and darkness had finally conquered the brilliant sunshine. From the edge of the bay, they paused to observe the now-deserted beach. The breeze was gentle and the water, with a slight ripple, almost calm. The foot traffic was heavy as it seemed like the whole town, including tourists, was out visiting bars and restaurants. There must be a law in France that obligates all adults to eat out at least twice a week. A great atmosphere! Pierre and Freddie had such a sense of well-being.

A short walk of one hundred yards brought them to their hotel where they walked up the stairs to their room. They sat out on their balcony to enjoy the night views of Collioure. The still-darkening sky was now displaying a purplish tinge with stars well-defined due to the dry air. In the horizon over the castle was a pink, pearl-like glow that was probably caused by the lights of a nearby town. Between two palm trees to their right, they could see the castle, ramparts, and lighthouse church whose bases were illuminated by lights that reflected on the water. To their left, they saw the street lights emitting multiple orbs of golden light which reflected off the stucco walls of the historic edifices. Directly beneath them was the hotel's restaurant where a large portion of the street traffic ended up having dinner. The diners had no idea they were being observed from above. Pierre noticed the sheer pleasure they had enjoying their meal and each other. They were so animated. Certainly, most people enjoy a good meal at a restaurant with friends and family, but the French seem to enjoy it quite a bit more than most. Finally, the need for sleep caught up with them. Except for two short naps, their last good night's sleep was over thirty hours ago. They went inside and quickly prepared for bed.

They felt like they could have slept forever. Of course, Freddie nearly did. Pierre thought the sandman certainly would be waiting to sandblast him instantly into unconsciousness, but the sandman was late. Perhaps the mistral winds blew his sand away as he crossed Provence. Pierre was never guaranteed sleep. Though he usually got adequate sleep, he often got suspended somewhere between sleep and wakefulness. He was aware of his position on the bed but not aware of time. In this state, his mind would take flight and could end up anywhere as there were no external stimuli to impede it. Sometimes his thoughts were nonsense, but sometimes he came up with good ideas or recalled events long forgotten. The challenge was to remember them the next day.

In his semi-consciousness, his mind resumed the train of thought he had earlier at dinner. He often wondered if his life would have been easier and more successful if his parents had been English speakers, educated, and middle class. If success is analogous to climbing to the mountain top, then Pierre started that climb from the bottom of a mineshaft in the bottom of a valley. Some were more fortunate to begin their climb well up on the mountain with the tools and support to reach the peak.

Certainly, success is relative and difficult to define. In his fifty years as an educator, he had scores of students who were very intelligent and had educated, supportive parents, and who did not do as well as expected. He also had students with average abilities and little support who achieved far beyond expectations. Sometimes a student does not want to be a doctor or lawyer like his or her father or mother and is quite happy being a librarian or a lesser business person.

He thought of his little town on the bayou, Port Barre. It is not the same as when he knew it best. It had grown a great deal since then, and there were so many people he didn't know there. Even his beloved bayou was no longer the same. The thorn trees that once lined its banks have disappeared, as if an epidemic had eradicated them. Flood control measures and agricultural fertilizers and pesticides had emasculated his bayou and rendered it into a big, muddy ditch filled with turbid water where fish seldom jumped anymore. The old wild west saloon served its last ice-cold Jax beer long ago. Even snakes were rather scarce. Probably scarcer than the snakes were the small number of French speakers left. Only a few of the older citizens still remembered some French. The younger population's speech was rapidly morphing into a Southern accent resembling the rest of the southern states.

Like his hometown, Pierre was also not the same. He no longer aspired to be like someone else and had no remorse for his former aspirations. Shouldn't the non-assimilated strive to be like the population they live among? Do they really have a choice? He was quite content with who he was, a person fully assimilated into Cajun, American, and French culture and appreciating those gifts while retaining his parents' culture and language. It was a very late assimilation but appreciated all the more. He was happy that many of his relatives who came after him have also made that journey.

Of course, he thought of his parents and their profound influence on his life. Often, seemingly negative situations produce positive results. The fact that Pierre's parents did not speak English well led him to become bilingual, a gift he has treasured immensely and which empowered him to bridge his Cajun world with that of the French world and its people. His parents' impoverished background and lack of education enabled him to understand people from all walks of life and led him to choose a career that ultimately helped thousands of undereducated adults improve their literacy skills.

No, his parents could not help him with his homework or give the type of support regarded as necessary for educational success. However, through example, they did teach him three important habits—get up early, work hard, and be persistent. That and a lot of help from his friends served him very well. *Non, Il ne regrette rien.**

*No, he regrets nothing.

THE GENESIS OF THIS BOOK

DURING our vacation in France in 1999, Freddie, began doing an outline of our daily adventures. I thought this was a good idea, kidnapped it, and began writing more detailed notes. Freddie's mother, Helen, then 85 years old with a crystal-clear mind, loved reading our notes so much that I began writing more descriptively to give her more complete images of our vacations.

As the years went by, we ended up with a thousand typed pages of notes about our France experiences, and I began to entertain the idea that perhaps I could write a book based on our France vacations—something like a travelogue. I expressed my ideas to two of our very close friends, Dr. Sam Dauzat, PhD. and his wife, Dr. Jo Ann Dauzat PhD. Sam said, "Sidney, you can do much better than a travelogue. You have lived a very unusual life—you need to write about that." I knew that as a Cajun I was not like most Americans, but there are hundreds of thousands of Cajuns in Louisiana. I thought about it and decided to write a book about my memoirs and our travel experiences. Part I, memoirs, and Part II, travelogue.

In 2014, I began to do some serious writing, and by the time I finished my rough draft of Part I, the book was already 300 pages!

I knew Part II would be an additional 300 pages at least. Who would want to read a 600 page book about an unknown Cajun in Louisiana? After discussing my plight with Sam and Jo Ann, I decided to cut down on the France experiences and keep the ones most relevant to the Part I story lines.

So, I thought everything was set to get the book finished. Then, my editor, Mary Perrin, got hold of the book. She was much more than an editor as she was very helpful with suggestions to improve the flow and design of the book as well to navigate the bumpy road to publication.

Finally, the book took many different twists and turns during the writing as almost every memory would jog other memories. The book ended up nothing like what I had originally envisioned. Hopefully, it's better.

LAGNIAPPE

I hope you have enjoyed Pierre's book. As you know by now, he is quite fond of food and cooking. I have included some of his favorite recipes which I have developed or modified over the years.

Enjoy!

Sidney "Pierre" Bellard

Eggplant Dressing—One of Pierre's favorites, as a side or main dish. Great for the holidays.

2 large purple eggplants

1 lb. lean ground meat

2 cups cooked rice

8 slices crisp bacon

1 onion (chopped)

3 cloves garlic (thin sliced)

1/3 cup red wine (optional)

1 can drained garlic roasted tomatoes

1 can beef broth

1 tablespoon roux

1 teaspoon thyme

1/2 teaspoon red pepper

1 teaspoon black pepper

1 teaspoon garlic powder

1 teaspoon onion powder

1 cup plain or Italian bread crumbs

1 cup Romano cheese

salt—to taste

Peel the eggplant and slice lengthwise into ½ inch thick slices. Salt the slices heavily and let stand in a dish for about 2-3 hours. Rinse eggplant well and cut into ½ inch cubes. In a pot, mix the tomatoes, beef stock, and roux. Heat and stir this mixture until the roux is blended with the liquid. Then put in the eggplant, onions, garlic, red pepper, and black pepper. Cover pot and put on medium heat for about ½ hour. Stir occasionally for uniform cooking. While this is cooking, place the ground meat, wine, a pinch of salt and red pepper in a skillet and fry down meat until well-browned. Place bacon strips in micro-wave oven and cook until very crisp. Grind up the bacon strips and place in the ground meat and stir. Let cook a few more minutes while stirring constantly until the mixture is dry and well browned. By now the eggplant should be done. It should be reduced and tender. With a potato masher, mash the eggplant, but not completely. Add the meat/bacon mixture and rice to the eggplant and mix well. Add onion powder, garlic powder and stir. Let cook covered for another ten minutes. Then adjust seasonings to taste. Finally, pour the mixture into a flat tray or dish about 2 inches deep. Spread mixture about 1 ½" deep. Coat with cheese, bread crumbs, and then more cheese. Bake in the oven at 350 degrees for 25 minutes or until breadcrumbs and cheese are brown. (Makes about 10 - 12 servings) Freezes well.

EZ Jambalaya—This dish is easy, quick, and great tasting.

1 can onion soup (Campbell's, 10.5 oz)

½ can Rotel Tomatoes

½ can tomato sauce

1 cup large mushrooms cut in half

4 cloves garlic sliced fine

1 medium onion cut in half and sliced in 1/4 inch slices

½ bell pepper (chopped)

1 lb. deboned chicken cut into 1 inch cubes

½ lb lean sausage

1/4 lb tasso sliced in thin strips (optional)

2 cans long-grain parboiled rice (use the onion soup can to measure)

3 cans water (use onion soup can to measure)

2 teaspoons salt

4 tablespoons olive oil

4 tablespoons barbecue sauce (any brand)

2 tablespoons roux (heat water in one of the 3 cans and dissolve roux) optional

Place all ingredients in a rice cooker or 4 quart covered pot, stir well, and cook as you would cook regular rice.

For extra flavor, stir-fry the chicken (coated with salt, black pepper, and red pepper), mushrooms, and onions, and cook the rest of the ingredients separately as indicated. When the rice is done, spread rice in a flat tray and spread the stir fry over the rice. Makes 8 generous servings.

Cajun Bouillabaisse—A great, original, and healthful light meal for special occasions. In southern France, bouillabaisse is like gumbo in Louisiana—everyone has an opinion on how it should be made. Pierre's version is adapted to the seafood readily available in most areas and very different from the traditional French version.

4 medium catfish fillets (cut into one inch squares)

8 large shrimp (Peeled)

8 large bay scallops

½ cup white wine

2 small cans tomato sauce

½ cup olive oil

1 quart water

4 cloves diced garlic

½ medium chopped onion

1/4 cup chopped green bell peppers

1/4 cup chopped red bell peppers

1/4 cup chopped celery

1 cup fresh sliced mushrooms

2 tablespoons chopped green onions or shallots

2 tablespoons chopped parsley

salt—to taste

red pepper— to taste

black pepper—to taste

small pinch saffron, if available – if not – turmeric will work

1 teaspoon Herbs de Provence or Italian seasoning

Pour the olive oil in a 12 inch diameter pot and heat. Put in the onions, garlic, red and green bell peppers, mushrooms, celery, wine, and tomato sauce. Cook while stirring until vegetables are soft. Next, pour in the water and bring to a low boil and lower to a simmer. Add in Herbs de Provence or Italian seasoning, and salt, red pepper and black pepper to taste. Let simmer for about 10 minutes. Then put in shrimp, fish, and scallops, cover pot and cook gently for about 10 minutes or until seafood is done. (very important not to overcook the seafood) Add saffron, adjust seasoning, and swish sauce in pot to mix without breaking the catfish. If a thicker soup is desired, use a little cornstarch to thicken.

To serve, set out four plates and divide the seafood evenly in each plate. Stir the liquid well in pot and pour in each plate until the sea-food is almost covered. Sprinkle the parsley and chopped green onions over sea food and sauce. Serve with hot French bread. (It's OK to dip)

Get Rich Cabbage—Great for the traditional New Year's meal.

1 large head cabbage

½ pound smoked sausage or tasso or combination of both

1 can garlic roasted tomatoes and liquid

1 cans vegetable broth

1/4 cup olive oil

1 chopped medium onion

2 teaspoon yellow mustard

1 teaspoon salt – to taste

1 teaspoon red pepper

1 teaspoon black pepper

In a large pot mix the tomatoes, vegetable broth, olive oil, mustard, red pepper, salt, and black pepper. Next, cut cabbage into 1/8 pieces, cut out the core, separate the leaves and add to pot along with the sausage and/or tasso. (To reduce fat content of sausage, microwave in a paper towel covered plate for 3-4 minutes) Cover and cook over medium heat, stirring occasionally, until cabbage is tender and is consistency you prefer. Adjust seasoning. Cabbage can be a side dish or served over rice or with cornbread. Makes 8 - 10 servings. Freezes well.

Modified Omelet—Great breakfast for weekend guests.

4 large eggs

4 bacon strips (fried very crisp)

½ cup chopped mushrooms

½ cup chopped onions

1/4 cup chopped bell pepper

½ cup chopped tomatoes

½ cup milk

1 tablespoon butter or margarine

3/4 cup grated sharp cheddar cheese

1 teaspoon garlic powder

1 teaspoon onion powder

1 teaspoon salt

1 teaspoon black pepper

Place the four the eggs in a bowl along with salt, onion powder, garlic powder, black pepper and milk and beat well. In a skillet, place the onions, mushrooms, bell pepper, chopped up bacon strips and chopped tomatoes. Fry while stirring this mixture until vegetables are soft and cooked. In another skillet, melt butter or margarine and pour in ½ of the egg mixture. Heat over low heat until eggs are just about done. Next, spread the vegetables mixture evenly over the eggs. Then, pour the remainder of the eggs over the vegetable and place under the broiler in the oven until eggs are solidified (a few minutes). Finally, sprinkle the cheese evenly over eggs and return to oven to melt cheese. Cut like a pie to serve four. Serve with toast. Makes a good breakfast or a light lunch.

Crawfish or Shrimp Etouffée—A traditional Cajun dish sure to please everyone.

1 pound peeled shrimp or crawfish

1can of cream of celery soup

1/3 can tomato sauce

1 tablespoon roux (optional)

1 medium chopped onion

3 cloves of minced garlic

1/3 cup chopped celery

1/3 cup chopped green onions

1/3 cup chopped parsley

1 stick butter or margarine

1/3 cup chopped bell pepper

1 cup sliced fresh mushrooms

Salt—to taste

red pepper—to taste

black pepper—to taste

garlic powder—to taste

onion powder—to taste

Melt the butter or margarine in a 4 quart pot and add the onions, garlic, bell pepper, celery, and tomato sauce. Cook on low heat until the vegetables are soft. Stir often so vegetables don't stick. Then add the cream of celery soup and blend in with the vegetables by stirring often for about 6-8 minutes. Put in crawfish or shrimp, and mushrooms and stir until well blended. Cover pot and cook on low heat for about 20 -30 min or until seafood is done. Stir often the first few minutes until seafood releases water. If too much water is released and etouffee becomes too thin, thicken with one teaspoon cornstarch. When seafood is done, add salt, red pepper, garlic powder, onion powder, green onions, and parsley. Serve over rice or pasta. You can also stir in 12 oz. cooked pasta to make shrimp or crawfish pasta. Serves 6-8. Freezes well. Also makes a great topping for fried, baked, blackened or broiled fish. Note: The parsley and/or green onions can be added when served.

Potato and Egg Pie—Satisfying taste and easy to do.

4 medium red potatoes (peeled and diced into ¼ inch or smaller cubes

4 eggs

1 medium onion

½ medium chopped bell pepper

3 tbsp olive oil

½ cup grated sharp cheddar cheese

½ cup grated Swiss

Place oil in 10 inch cast iron skillet and heat. Add potatoes, onions, and bell pepper and cook over medium heat until potatoes are cooked. Be sure to scrape the bottom on skillet often while potatoes are cooking. Beat the 4 eggs and ½ cup milk in a bowl. Pour the egg mixture over the evenly spread, cooked potatoes and continue heating until the egg is mostly cooked. Place the skillet under the broiler to finish cooking the top of the eggs. Spread the two cheeses on top of the eggs and potatoes and return to broiler to melt the cheese. To serve, cut into wedges. Goes well with sour cream and/or salsa.

May be served as a breakfast dish, a light lunch, or quick dinner dish. Makes four servings. (Note: adding crisp, crumbled bacon to top of potatoes and eggs before adding cheese will give a different taste)

White Beans with Rice with Shrimp—this unlikely dish was in vogue in Louisiana several years ago. Pierre's version, which is very different from most is very easy to do, and delicious.

1 15.8 oz. can of Bush's Great Northern white beans

½ cup sliced onions

½ cup chopped red bell pepper

½ teaspoon liquid crab boil

1 lb. deveined medium shrimp or crawfish

3 cloves garlic

½ cup parsley

2 cups cooked rice (I use brown rice)

1 tablespoon olive oil

black pepper— to taste

½ teaspoon Paul Prudhomme's Blackened Redfish Magic

salt— to taste

½ teaspoon tumeric

Place drained white beans in a medium pot along with onions, red bell pepper and crab boil. Add chicken stock to cover beans and cook on medium heat until tender—usually about 20 to 30 minutes. Stir often. Add water if necessary to make beans soupy, but not watery.

For the shrimp: chop parsley and garlic separately and very fine. Then combine and thoroughly mix the parsley and garlic. Put olive oil in a 12" skillet and heat. Put the shrimp in the skillet and add salt, Redfish Magic and black pepper. Stir-fry the shrimp until partially cooked then add the garlic/parsley mixture and turmeric. The aroma will be fantastic! Continue stir-frying until done (don't overcook).

To serve, place portion of rice on plate and cover with white beans. Then place the shrimp over the beans and rice. Serve right away. Makes two, large servings.

It may be conspicuous that I did not include one of Pierre's gumbo recipes. The problem is that gumbo requires making a roux, and I find it impossible to properly explain how to make one. It is best to learn by watching someone do it. However, should you want to attempt a roux at home for the first time, I will give you the first and most important rule: First, you go to the bathroom. Once you start a roux, you cannot leave it.

Bon appétit!

ADDITIONAL PICTURES

Collioure

Market Day

Paella

Gordes, Hilltop Village

Lavender, Provence

Strasbourg, Alsace

Annecy, Haute Savoie

A Goat Cheese Salad

Pierre's HS Classmate's River Boat

Walt, Pierre, Freddie & Gail in Riverboat